D0592652

Adolescence

Transition from Childhood to Maturity

Adolescence

Transition from Childhood to Maturity

B. GERALDINE LAMBERT
University of Southwestern Louisiana

BARBARA F. ROTHSCHILD
Louisiana State University at Alexandria

RICHARD ALTLAND
Baptist College at Charleston

LAURENCE B. GREEN
University of North Florida

BROOKS/COLE PUBLISHING COMPANY
Monterey, California

A division of
Wadsworth Publishing Company, Inc.
Belmont, California

© 1972 by Wadsworth Publishing Company, Inc., Belmont, California 94002. All rights reserved. No part of this book may be reproduced, stored in a retrieval system, or transcribed, in any form or by any means—electronic, mechanical, photocopying, recording, or otherwise—without the prior written permission of the publisher: Brooks/Cole Publishing Company, Monterey, California, a division of Wadsworth Publishing Company, Inc.

ISBN: 0-8185-0040-9
L.C. Catalog Card No: 72-76432
Printed in the United States of America

1 2 3 4 5 6 7 8 9 10—76 75 74 73 72

This book was edited by Adrienne Harris and designed by Linda Marcetti. Cartoons were drawn by Don Sampson. Chapter-opening photographs and cover photo are by Lehman J. Pinckney, Jr.   The book was typeset by Continental Data Graphics, Culver City, California, and it was printed and bound by Colonial Press, Inc., Clinton, Massachusetts.

To
Chip
Debbie
David
Lance
Linda
Paul
and
Steve

Preface

Adolescence: Transition from Childhood to Maturity is directed to undergraduates in psychology, education, home economics, and sociology, as well as to their parents. It provides a forum on adolescent behavior that will help the reader better understand and accept the erratic, often unpredictable behavior of developing human beings in the complex and frequently confusing world of the late twentieth century.

The text deals with such current and pertinent subjects as the drug culture, alienation, and the difficulties in communication between generations, as well as the more traditional topics of physical, emotional, and social development. Part One defines adolescence in a nontraditional way. Part Two deals with environmental factors. Parts Three and Four cover the physical, sexual, and emotional development of adolescents. Finally, Part Five discusses the adolescent and the adult community in terms of learning, employment, and interpersonal communication. Also included is a comprehensive glossary of important terms that will facilitate understanding of the ideas presented.

The significant difference between this book and earlier ones is our thesis that adolescent behavior is not restricted to the "teen-agers." Certainly, the facts of pollution, crime, drugs, alcoholism, and death on the highway do not tend to reflect an "adult" society of mature human beings. Thus, it is probably more accurate to realize that at any age one's behavior can be "adolescent" in character. By refusing to limit our discussion of adolescence to chronological, physiological, or legal boundaries—by focusing on adolescence as a behavioral transition to maturity—we hope to encourage the reader, whatever his age, to learn to critically analyze his own behavior. It is our opinion that ignorance of self reduces man's ability to act maturely. If our perspective can lead the reader to self-examination, to an increased understanding of his own behavior, and thus to more effective personal functioning, then one of the goals of this book will have been reached.

Most of the source material cited in the text is based on the more traditional definition of adolescence as a physical or chronological period in an individual's development—few studies have been undertaken of those over 21 who tend to display adolescent behavior. Therefore, we hope that the reader will keep in mind our behavioral approach as he considers the information these sources provide and that from his own observations and experiences, he will come to feel, as we do, that adolescence is more than a physical or chronological period in life.

The references are taken from many fields outside psychology: education, history, sociology, medicine, and philosophy. Such an interdisciplinary approach encourages the reader to look many places for material that will help him gain an understanding of man's behavior. Also included are some newspaper and magazine articles, since we encourage the student to learn about life from all sources. However, we caution him to consider very carefully data that have not been subjected to scientific treatment and to weigh what has been said as he reaches his own conclusions.

Behind the scenes of every book there is usually a sizable group of people who have helped to make it possible. In our case these include the following individuals who kindly consented to serve as reviewers: Henry Angelino, Ohio State University, Frank Harper, University of Western Ontario, Richard Kalish, Scientific Analysis Corporation, Ruth Spangenberg, Cañada College, Jerome Seidman, Montclair State College, and Hershel Thornburg, University of Arizona.

In addition, there were several others without whose assistance we would surely have faltered. Among these were Nancy Beacham, Medical Librarian at Central Louisiana State Hospital, who so generously assisted in the compiling of our extensive bibliography; Joan Vater, who did the research on delinquency; Mrs. H. Lee Jones, Natchez, Mississippi, Perceptual Development Center, who served as a consultant on learning disability problems; George Tate of the

Veterans' Administration Hospital at Alexandria, Louisiana, and Frances G. Peters of the Oklahoma City Schools, who served as professional consultants; Morris Abrams of Louisiana State University at Alexandria and Clyde L. Rougeou of the University of Southwestern Louisiana, who made possible sabbatical leaves; Edna Hilton and Marcia McLaughlin, who so accurately typed the manuscript; Don Sampson, who did several humorous illustrations; and George H. Rothschild, Sr., who served as a lay reader and critic during the entire writing process.

Contents

I

Introduction to Adolescence

1

What Is Adolescence?

> It was the best of times, it was the worst of times. It was the age
> of wisdom, it was the age of foolishness. It was the season of light,
> it was the season of darkness. It was the spring of hope, it was
> the winter of despair . . .
>
> Charles Dickens
> *A Tale of Two Cities*

Dickens' description of France's adolescent period following the
French Revolution can easily be stretched to include the adolescent
in today's rapidly changing world. As apt as his description is, however, we must go a few steps further and attempt to provide a workable
definition as a foundation for our discussion of adolescence. How
can one define *adolescence* in a way that will enhance our understanding of this transitional period?

A DEFINITION OF ADOLESCENCE

We believe that adolescence can best be shown to be a behavior-
al/cultural concept if we reveal the inadequacies of the traditional
attempts to define it chronologically, physically, or legally. In the
past, the usual definition of adolescence has tied it to an age span,
with the starting age varying from 10 to 13 and the concluding age
varying from 19 to 21, according to the author one has read. It has
been quite natural, then, for studies on adolescence to be limited
to population groups in the second decade of life. Consequently,
the research and theory cited in this book inevitably reflect the limitations of this traditional definition.

3

It is our belief that a more realistic and meaningful definition of adolescence may be in order—a definition that relies on behavioral terms rather than chronological age as its reason for being. As the reader progresses through this book, he is invited to keep in mind our behavioral definition and to decide for himself whether he finds it more workable and meaningful than the traditional age-span definition.

Surrounding us today are many 35- or 40-year-old people who, in our opinion, manifest behavior typical of the "adolescent" period of life. And there also seems to be justification in noting that this behavior seems to predominate in many individuals' life styles. Thus, we are no longer able to accept the idea that adolescence is that period in life between the age of "childhood" and the age of "adulthood." We are seeking a definition that identifies adolescence in terms other than those of vague chronology.

The major thesis of this book is that adolescence is a behavioral phenomenon that occurs between childlike behavior and "mature" behavior. Accordingly, our task is to establish adolescence in terms of (1) an identifiable starting point, at which time childlike behavior should be fading, and (2) a general pattern of behavior signaling the end of adolescence and the attainment of "maturity."

A particular "starting point" that marks the beginning of the adolescent period can be identified with the onset of those physical changes that result in *puberty*. Therefore, we have the onset of a physiological phenomenon to guide us; for such onset is the precursor of some rather dramatic and sudden behavior changes.

Although we can approach the beginning of the adolescent period by focusing on physical changes, it is not adequate to consider the period as a whole from a physiological point of view. For example, although at a particular point in an individual's life the *pituitary* gland secretes the sex hormone in such amounts that the youngster develops certain sexual characteristics, of greater importance is the fact that significant sexual thought and behavior accompany this event. And, it is the emotional, social, and intellectual overtones of sex that are more deterministic of "maturity" or "immaturity" than just the physiological event alone. The research of Jones and Bayley (1950), Jones (1957), and Mussen and Jones (1957, 1958) has demonstrated the dynamic effects of early or late puberty on the behavior of boys and girls in the spheres of social, emotional, and intellectual development. Nor can we readily accept the ability to reproduce the human species as a criterion of adult "maturity"; parental irresponsibility, so evident about us, gives testimony to this lack of mature behavior.

If physiological occurrences alone cannot be used to define adolescence, can we perhaps resolve the issue by stating that adolescence encompasses those years between the onset of puberty and the magic age of 21? From a legal point of view, this might be true, but there is absolutely no evidence available that 21 is the automatic age at which an individual ceases to behave as an adolescent. It no longer seems adequate to consider adolescence as a phenomenon that can be defined in legalistic or chronological terms. Laws regarding the age of "adulthood" in each state of the United States and in Canada vary so greatly that any attempt to declare adolescence at an end when "adulthood" is reached is doomed to failure. The "adult" prerogatives of voting, drinking, marrying, going to war, and driving a car have no chronological denominator.

Having reached these dead ends, what can we state about adolescence that will help us understand this transitional period? Our approach is to seek a definition that will, as clearly as possible, establish those behavioral traits that characterize the nonadolescent. If one possesses these traits, it can be said that he is no longer adolescent, whether he is 18, 21, 30, or older. Our focus, then, is on the concept of "maturity."

Although most of us seem to recognize when a person is behaving maturely and when he is not, the concept of "maturity" is so great in scope that it defies precise definition. We are faced with a task similar to that of a physicist asked to define "electricity." Although he can tell us if electricity is present and what it can and cannot do, once he goes beyond "a flow of electrons," he is in trouble. Nonetheless, if our thesis of behavioral adolescence is to have any substance, an attempt at definition must be made.

As a first step, let us see what insight we can gain from a quick look at some personality theorists' views of "maturity." Alfred Adler (1935, 1939) believed that man reaches maturity as he learns to overcome his feelings of inferiority. One conquers these feelings by developing his potential for social functioning and his ability to create meaning in his life from heredity and experience. Harry Stack Sullivan (1953) describes maturity as the process of transforming one's "self-system" from that of an anxiety-ridden organism to that of a stabilized, secure human being. The essence of this process is developing satisfying interpersonal relationships. Henry Murray (1953) emphasized that maturity grows out of man's need to belong to and be accepted by a functioning group, which he achieves by compromising between his own impulses and the demands, interests, and impulses of other people.

To Abraham Maslow (1954), maturity is dependent on self-actualization—that is, the process of fulfilling one's genetic potential, as opposed to depending on external forces to shape one's personality. If we look at Gordon Allport's personality theory (1955), we see that maturity results when an individual has shifted his loyalties from self, to possessions and loved objects, and then to abstract moral and/or religious ideas. For Erich Fromm (1955), however, man moves toward maturity because of his desire to create, or his "productive orientation." This orientation helps the individual to relate to himself, his fellow man, and nature, eventually in a mature way.

And, finally, Carl Rogers (1955) believes that an individual cannot be considered mature until he can accept himself ". . . as a decidedly imperfect person, who by no means functions at all times in the way he would like to function" (p. 17). Once a person reaches this conclusion, he can work toward changing himself to become more personally effective with other people, and thus more mature in his functioning.

This brief look at personality theorists should point up the general level of thought and behavior that must be present before an individual can be described as "mature." However, there is one additional thought that should be considered before we attempt a definition of maturity. The usual definition of maturity sets it as a state of adulthood; however, because such a definition can imply that behavior development or change ceases at the onset of maturity, it is not accurate for our purposes. Rather we would like to point out that during middle age and old age (which traditionally and perhaps erroneously have also been considered chronological periods of life) any previously acquired behavioral pattern can change to a more effective pattern.

It is clear from our look at the numerous approaches to maturity chosen by personality theorists that it is nearly impossible to arrive at a comprehensive definition of "maturity." However, we believe that it is possible to arrive at a general description of this period, which we propose as follows:

> The state of life which occurs when one's biological and psychological potential develop through favorable growth and experience and interact with the social and physical world to the extent that self-controlled, productive, and stable behavior clearly dominates[1] the personal and societal spheres of life; although inappropriate and ineffective behavior does not disappear, it is uncommon; and there are always possibilities for later change in the behavior structure.

And it is with the attainment of this general level of behavior that adolescence ends. That maturity is not likely to occur automatically at 21 should be evident, for maturity connotes a healthy personality capable of functioning effectively in the intellectual, emotional, and social spheres of existence. English and English (1964) have provided us with short descriptions of what marks mature functioning in each sphere: intellectual maturity reflects the acquisition of "practical wisdom"; emotional maturity is characterized by "steady and socially acceptable emotional behavior"; and social maturity is "mastery of effective social techniques." From these criteria and from our review of personality theories, it should be clear that the behavioral state of "maturity" probably cannot be approached before 25 or 30 years of living.

It should also become evident that it is not merely living through the adolescent period that is of most importance; it is the nature of the adolescent's existence—physically, intellectually, socially, and emotionally—that will provide a weak or strong foundation for a mature adulthood. It would appear that the experiences of adolescence are as important to the final character of the adult as are the experiences of childhood. Although an individual comes to adolescence from childhood with a fundamental structure of personality, it is during adolescence that many rapid and dynamic changes in behavior take place.

---

[1]Quantification of "clearly dominates" is difficult; 51 percent of the time would not be appropriate, whereas 99 percent of the time would be overly optimistic. It would tend to imply, however, that in most instances effective mature behavior would be evident.

What, then, is adolescence and what should characterize an individual during this part of life? An admittedly too-brief definition follows:

> Adolescence is a dynamic, developmental *process*—roughly spanning the years from the onset of the pubertal process to "maturity"—during which an individual comes to terms with himself and with his unique place in the environment; he transits from childhood to maturity (as we have defined it).

The phrase "comes to terms with himself" is not meant to imply that an individual should adopt a passive acceptance of the status quo or believe that he is a pawn in the hands of fate. Rather the phrase describes the dynamic, unique growth potential of each individual and his ability to exercise some control over his development. This growth concept, as noted by Allport (1955), Rogers (1961), and Nixon (1962), involves a constant striving toward the final goal of becoming one's self. Whether one ever reaches his final goal is debatable; it is the striving that really matters—the continual striving that will sustain behavior in the inevitable moments of defeat and despair. To endeavor to come to terms with one's self includes the physical self, the intellectual self, the social self, and the emotional self. Actually, no one comes to terms with all aspects of his self at any given period. Generally he will tackle one aspect at a time as the occasion arises.

Susan, 15, is a vivacious girl with a pretty face. However, she constantly complains about her appearance. She feels that because of her 5'9" height she is much too tall for the boys to ask her for dates. As a consequence, she slouches in an attempt to disguise her height, which only makes her appear to be taller and more gawky than she actually is. Susan has not yet accepted her physical self.

John, 19, is a college sophomore from a working-class family. His father has a limited education and is employed as a custodian in a hospital. His older brother, the first in his family ever to attend college, is in law school. John also wants to be an attorney. However, he has rather low reading comprehension and actually dislikes to read; he is therefore not well suited to enter the field of law. On the other hand, he has a strong interest in and an aptitude for mathematics. John has not yet demonstrated the phenomenon of coming to terms with his intellectual self.

Sixteen-year-old Frank, outwardly somewhat arrogant and cocky, has difficulty in gaining the acceptance of his *peers*. He wants to assert his leadership skills but doesn't recognize that his plans and ideas cannot always be carried out; he is not willing to listen to those of others in the group and refuses to do things their way rather than his. He has not come to terms with his social self.

Nancy, an only child of 18, wishes to attend college out of town but her parents do not want her to leave home. Although she really would like to go away to school, and her family is well able to afford it, she timidly accedes to their demands. In counseling sessions she expressed considerable hostility toward her parents because of their refusal to permit her to leave. In addition, she showed guilt resulting from her suppressed anger at them, although she attempted to deny that such feelings existed. For a considerable period of time, the combination of hostility and guilt adversely affected her performance at college. Nancy had not yet learned to come to terms with her emotional self.

When we speak of coming to terms with one's "unique place in the environment," we are referring to both the physical and the interpersonal aspects of living in a real world of things and of people. One must not only find his place in a physical world, he must also find his place in an interpersonal world; and, he must do so as an individual, uniquely separate from, yet with, society. For example, poverty is a physical condition, and we have generally treated it in a physical manner by providing welfare money, food, and clothing. However, in such treatment we have tended to overlook the emotional and social effects of poverty. Although we have come to terms with the physical world of a man on welfare, we have failed to recognize his unique interpersonal or *intrapersonal* world.

The words "transits from childhood to maturity" connote a phase in an individual's life through which he must pass. It is not a question of passing through successfully or unsuccessfully, but rather a question of either passing through or not passing through. Additionally, in the dynamic striving toward maturity an individual may reach a certain point and then experience a traumatic episode, such as the violent death of a parent, and *fixate*, or begin a drastic *regression*. Although it might not appear normal to regress drastically, it is indeed an aspect of the process which requires recognition and consideration. One should note that a normal passage through adolescence is not characterized by a smooth arithmetical progression that correlates with the passing of the chronological years. The period is more erratic in nature, characterized by peaks of success and valleys of defeat, but nonetheless progressing forward in a total process toward maturity.

THE ADOLESCENT TRANSITIONAL PERIOD

Rereading Dickens' quotation can give us a clue to the nature of the adolescent period. "Best"–"worst," "wisdom"–"foolishness," "light"–"darkness," and "hope"–"despair" set up the typical polarities that are said to make up adolescence. Indeed, an examination of the literature on adolescence brings to light two basic positions which themselves create a kind of polarity.

One position characterizes adolescence as a period of inevitable "storm and stress." The other position maintains that if too many emotional or traumatizing events occur, the personality will become distorted for life. Consequently, a somewhat smooth, relatively non-traumatic transitional period is advocated.

An examination of the literature of the past six or seven decades reveals that an interesting sequence of thought has taken place. About the turn of the century, G. Stanley Hall (1904) wrote a two-volume treatise on adolescence, *Adolescence: Its Psychology and Its Relation to Physiology, Anthropology, Sociology, Sex, Crime, Religion, and Education,* in which he introduced the notion that the adolescent period is one of storm and stress, or as was so fashionable in those days, the German *Sturm und Drang.* Hall reflected his thoughts about adolescence in such statements as "The 'teens' are emotionally unstable" (Vol. 2, p. 74) and "We here see the instability and fluctuation now so characteristic" (Vol. 2, p. 75). It is evident from these quotes that Hall considered turmoil to be an unavoidable fact of life for the adolescent. He left no room for environmental influence.

In evaluating Hall's statement, one must admit that the "instability and fluctuation" are readily apparent in adolescent behavior. Young people can be seen exhibiting dynamic energy one hour, extreme lethargy the next. They can demonstrate a great degree of *euphoria* one day and almost complete *depresssion* the next. They can show vain conceit one moment and ultramodesty the next. Furthermore, their egocentric selfishness of wanting to do their own "thing" can be later replaced with great *altruism* toward the conditions of those less fortunate than themselves. (This idea will be treated in more detail in Chapter 6.)

Hall's attempts to place adolescence in a historical context ("now so characteristic") tend to reflect his acceptance of Haeckel's classic concept that *ontogeny is a brief but rapid recapitulation of phylogeny:* a theory which stated that the development of the individual parallels the historical evolutionary development of the human species. Hall attempted to relate Haeckel's concept to man's life by comparing the child of ages 8 through 12 with the savage era of man's history, ages 12 through 22 or 25 with the stage of man's development called barbarism, and from 25 into adulthood with that part of man's development called civilization. One might describe Hall's position as being a *biogenetic* one in that he appears to be saying that adolescence is built into us—that it's hereditary, and therefore not very vulnerable to modification.

About a quarter of a century later, anthropologist Margaret Mead reported on her studies of primitive cultures in Samoa (1928a) and New Guinea (1928b) that she had observed that adolescence didn't seem to be a stormy, stressful experience for these youngsters. They were initiated into the adult world when they were ready. As young girls became capable of reproduction, they were married, had children, and took care of their households. When young boys were physically able to hunt and became sexually mature, they married and took their places in society as hunters and as workers. Mead concluded that the stormy nature of adolescence was a "cultural invention" rather than the inevitable aspect of development that Hall had suggested.

Thus, although she has not explicitly stated so in her early writing, Mead seems to imply that the adolescent in our culture need not experience *Sturm und Drang.* Her writings seem to suggest that adults should endeavor to smooth out this transitional period and that our young people would probably be emotionally healthier if they did not have to experience great stress.

Another quarter of a century later Havighurst (1953) introduced the idea of developmental tasks. He proposed that at certain ages in life each of us is confronted with certain tasks that must be accomplished at least somewhat successfully if we are to be adequately prepared to go on to the next stage. If one has not sufficiently mastered a physical, intellectual, social, or emotional task at any given level or age, then the task at the next higher level will be less easy to accomplish, and the probability of successfully completing later tasks will be reduced.

According to Havighurst (1953), learning and accepting a socially approved adult masculine or feminine role is a developmental task that needs to be mastered during the adolescent period. To cite an example, Charles, a 16-year-old of lower socioeconomic status, ultimately failed in the acquisition of this important developmental task. An illegitimate child of a mother who had never married, he was reared in a home with two sisters and no father. Nor were there any close male relatives with whom Charles could identify. He was taught solely by women teachers, and although he joined a Boy Scout troop, it dissolved shortly after he became a member. As a consequence, he sought the friendship of a gang of neighborhood youths, with whom he began to identify. Gradually, he began to adopt many of their pseudomasculine traits. On one occasion he joined the gang in robbing a railroad refrigerator car, apparently believing such behavior reflected courage and daring. Placed on probation as the result of this delinquent act, he soon got into further difficulties at school and was finally sent to the state reformatory. After a six-month term, he was released and returned to the custody of his mother and thus to the same matriarchal environment. Once again he resumed his relationship with those he mistakenly regarded as truly masculine. A few months later he was involved in a fight with one of the gang members and was fatally wounded. Of course, one can only speculate that if Charles had had a strong favorable masculine figure with whom to identify, he might have been able to master the task of learning and accepting a truly masculine role and avoided the companionship of the gang possessing such pseudomasculine traits. Nonetheless, the evidence is sufficient to indicate that he had never resolved the task of learning and accepting a socially approved masculine role.

Thus, one can infer from Havighurst's writings that if there are developmental tasks that must be performed successfully at certain stages in life, then adults have the responsibility of seeing that adolescents are confronted with these tasks at the appropriate age. Like Mead, Havighurst seems to indicate that by learning the appropriate tasks successfully at a certain chronological age, young people can avoid the "hard knocks" of adolescence and be better off for it.

More recently, Friedenberg (1959) took a different position. He stated that many problems of today's youth are the consequence of adults' having taken over the tasks that adolescents should have been permitted to undertake themselves. He proposed that adults have not allowed young people to experience the conflicts that can prepare them for adulthood and maturity.

A few years ago, in a small southern city, a group of high school students took the initiative in organizing a teen-age center to provide recreation and a meeting place for adolescents during their free time. They enlisted the aid of several interested adults, who, in turn, secured from the city an old building, which they proceeded to remodel and paint without asking the youths to assist in the alterations. Although the young people at first shared in formulating rules and regulations, they soon found themselves being pushed into the background as adults took over most of the policy making. The center quickly came to reflect adult standards and values rather than those of the adolescents. According to one of the adults who worked in the program, the students' loss of interest seemed to be directly related to increased adult domination. Within a few years the center closed its doors.

Like Friedenberg, Erikson (1950, 1968) also proposes that the primary task of adolescence is to acquire an identity. And he also states that an individual cannot find a lasting identity if there is no personal conflict during adolescence. Although a young person will inevitably make mistakes along the way and undergo repeated failure, Erikson maintains that he must be permitted to experience the conflict in decision making so vital to mature development.

In examining Friedenberg's concept, it seems appropriate to describe it as a *dialectic*[2] pathway to maturity; by experiencing conflicts and confrontations, and resolving them as much on his own as possible, the individual grows in psychological stature and progresses toward maturity.

Although Hall (1904) maintained that conflict is a natural *biogenetic* phenomenon and Friedenberg (1959) maintained that conflict derives from a social dialectic involving interpersonal and intrapersonal confrontations, it seems that both men would agree that "from the crucible of conflict comes the steel of character." Implicit in

[2]A *dialectic* is a process by which one idea, a thesis, is confronted with the opposite idea, an antithesis; the amalgamation of these opposing forces, a synthesis, results in a higher truth.

their thinking (with which we agree) is the idea that all human beings, when they reach the point of adolescence, must be permitted by adults to experience conflicts and battles, from which they will emerge more mature individuals. Friedenberg (1959) summarized the importance of adolescent conflict in the following statement: "Adolescent conflict is the instrument by which an individual learns the complex, subtle, and precious differences between himself and his environment. In a society in which there is no difference or in which no difference is permitted, the word 'adolescence' has no meaning" (p. 13).

We would like to hypothesize that the violent, militant young people on college campuses in the late sixties, while searching for identity, actually forced themselves into conflict, which had been denied them earlier by an affluent, permissive adult society that wanted for its children an easier life than it experienced during the depression of the 1930s. The irony of the recent unrest is that during the years from ages 14 through 17 confrontation and conflict with the world of adults is much safer than confrontation with the law and society at ages 20 to 25.

There are many arenas into which the young person must enter, do battle, and from which he must emerge somewhat successful in order for him to attain maturity. Of course, the critical issue facing any adult who deals with adolescents is the extent and nature of the conflicts and the limits to which one can permit the youngster to proceed. How deeply should an adult let an adolescent suffer defeat and failure? There is no single answer. Each individual adolescent will have his own tolerance limit, beyond which it may be dangerous to allow him to go. And the question of "how far is safe and productive and when does the conflict become destructive" is the dilemma that makes rearing children so difficult and so demanding of adult knowledge, patience, and wisdom.

GOALS OF THE ADOLESCENT PERIOD

What goals should the adolescent move toward during this transitional period? Hopefully, during the unfolding of this book, all of the goals of maturity will come into focus at various times. However, at this point, let us look at four general problem areas, which the adolescent will encounter in passing through this transitional period:

(1) acceptance of his physical self, (2) attainment of emotional control, (3) achievement of social maturity, and (4) development of intellectual sophistication and sensitivity.

Accepting One's Physical Self

First, everyone must come to terms with his body, or physical self, for the body can be described as a symbol of the self or body image. On the one hand, moderate care of the physical body, including proper diet, exercise, and good body hygiene, can enhance the attributes with which each individual is endowed, and can therefore enhance his self-confidence. On the other hand, man can readily destroy his self-image, as well as his physical self, by abuse, disuse, and neglect. Coming to terms with one's body does not demand surrender to one's imperfections, nor does it demand an unrealistic attempt to conform to the ideal physical image of a Miss America or an All-American football hero. On the contrary, physical acceptance involves making the most of one's imperfections and learning to accept the physical changes of growing up and aging.

For example, consider our example of 5'9" Susan. Once she can accept her height as an asset rather than a liability, she will improve her posture and will appear less ungainly and awkward. Her new poise and self-confidence will be a sign that she has come to terms with her height.

Attaining Emotional Control

One sign of emotional maturity is the ability to avoid two extremes; adherence to either would prove to be damaging to the individual's adjustment. Thus, one must attain a balance between a childish free expression of emotions without inhibition and a complete suppression of all emotion. Somewhere between the completely uninhibited expression of emotion of the child and the Victorian suppression of all emotions, each human being must come to accept his emotions as real and valid, as well as his responsibility for channeling those emotions into constructive outlets. In addition, each adolescent faces the task of learning to expect and accept the inevitable frustration of failure without degrading himself or disintegrating into uncontrolled rage or immobilized fear of future failures.

A secretary once remarked, "I always know when my boss has had a fight with his wife or has been bawled out by the Vice-President; he yells and insults me." Apparently, this young lady's boss had not acquired the emotional maturity that precludes attacking a blameless bystander every time he himself is threatened or attacked.

Achieving Social Maturity

Social maturity centers around the ability to establish good interpersonal relationships. The adolescent comes to recognize that his very existence has no meaning other than that meaning given to it by himself and by his fellow man. Without friends and family to reflect one's wishes, attitudes, and feelings an individual will remain a stranger unto himself.

Allport (1955) and Toynbee (1956) have theorized that man has two great innate conflicting forces within him: (1) a striving for individuality, and (2) a striving to belong to a society. And, of course, one cannot acquire either without doing a disservice to the other; a *synthesis* is demanded. The individual who is completely self-centered, striving only for his own welfare, is eventually cast out of society. And the person who places "belonging" above all else sacrifices his individuality and thereby loses his identity. When one recalls Friedenberg's (1959) and Erikson's (1950, 1968) position that the primary task of adolescence is to develop an identity, it becomes evident that complete subservience to society prevents the acquisition of maturity. The adolescent's goal is to acquire a unique identity and still function *within* the limits set by society, for one characteristic of maturity is relative success in resolving this conflict.

Developing Intellectual Sophistication and Sensitivity

An individual of intellectual sophistication and sensitivity relentlessly questions what he hears or reads, and he has an urgent need for his questions to be answered (Nixon, 1962). Intellectual sophistication demands a balance between gullibility, or a belief in everything, at one extreme and an agnostic position, or skepticism of everything, at the other extreme. Neither position alone can insure effective intellectual functioning.

In acquiring intellectual sensitivity, one must develop an ability to face reality. One of the most basic realities is failure. In a demonstration of intellectual sensitivity, one is able to come to grips with failure by intellectually picking up the pieces and putting them back together, gaining knowledge from the experience, and going on from there.

Let us look again at the case of John, who thought he wanted to become an attorney. When he began recognizing his weaknesses in English and his lack of aptitude in reading, he sought vocational counseling. Test results and an understanding counselor revealed to John his strong mathematical ability and increased his interest in math. Consequently, he decided to change his major field from pre-law to accounting, from which he ultimately graduated with success. John was learning to face failure realistically and constructively—he was gaining intellectual sensitivity.

Every adolescent also finds it necessary to come to terms with the idea that freedom is no guarantee of success. He learns that if success is guaranteed, he will not be able to decide for himself what success is or how to attain it; the definition of success and the means of reaching it are determined by the guarantor. Thus, intellectual sensitivity involves understanding that "freedom" means freedom to fail as well as freedom to succeed. For adults, this understanding implies that allowing adolescents to make decisions should not have built-in guarantees of success. In being given gradual freedom to arrive at his own decisions, the adolescent should gradually become more proficient at making them.

PROBLEMS OF ADOLESCENTS

There are certain problems that typically confront the adolescent and demand difficult answers of him. Although it is impossible to present all of these issues, the following appear to be representative of the complexity of growing up.

First is the need for achieving *heterosexual* compatibility—that is, emotional, intellectual, and social compatibility free of distorting sexual overtones. Observation of contemporary adolescent and pseudo-adult behavior suggests that many heterosexual relationships are marred by the discomfort that comes from viewing each other as

sex symbols rather than as complementary individuals who can enhance the meaning and significance of each other's existence. Because of this orientation, many adolescents equate rejection by the
opposite sex with failure as a human being. The result is often the
trying out of certain social selves because of a fear of risking rejection
by acting naturally or being "real." For heterosexual relationships
to be handled maturely, men and women must be able to relate
to each other for reasons other than self-aggrandizement, sensual
pleasure, or reproduction alone.

A second problem confronting the adolescent is the acquisition
of an ability to tolerate "aloneness." In essence, aloneness is an ability
to separate from others and not feel lost, as distinct from "alienation,"
which persistently isolates one from meaningful interactions with
one's fellow man. Some people are so dependent on others that
effective functioning constantly demands the physical presence of
other people, even if it's only on television or on the radio. In fact,
the modern media extol us to attain happiness by surrounding our-
selves with beautiful Coke-drinking people; the implication is that
aloneness is equivalent to rejection.

Although it is doubtful that anyone ever comes to the point of
being completely independent of other people, a compulsive need
always to be in the company of others seems to reflect an immature
fear of being abandoned or of being alone with one's thoughts. A
person who can be alone with himself and his thoughts, be it alone
in a room, walking in the city, or driving in the country, is approaching a mature understanding of himself and his place in society.

A third problem, which is becoming increasingly important in
our society, is how to use one's leisure time. The transitional period
of adolescence spans those years in which an individual can establish
a behavioral pattern in his use of leisure time that will persist
throughout his life.

The combination of increased longevity, a constantly lower age
of retirement, and shorter working hours demands adequate planning
and the development of the wise use of leisure-time activities. Failure
to come to grips with this problem in the formative years of life
may result in premature physical and mental deterioration through
illness, boredom, and psychological atrophy. Berg (1965), in his pres-
idential address to the Southwestern Psychological Association,
pointed out that behavioral scientists had better involve themselves

in this problem, that unless people begin to learn how to re-create their psychological, physical, and spiritual selves through leisure-time activities, the need for the treatment of emotional disorders will increase tremendously.

The adolescent is faced with what to do with his present as well as his future leisure time. He knows some of the activities in which he would like to participate, but he often lacks the finances to pursue these activities. It is necessary for him to learn to spend his leisure time in activities that are not too expensive for his economic level but that provide educational, social, and possibly even spiritual benefits. During these years the adolescent is also preparing for his future retirement because he is forming leisure-time habits that he will probably carry throughout his lifetime. He must come to realize that his ability to socialize, to be accepted, to be employed, to be alone, and to be satisfied or happy is in part determined by his use of leisure time.

A fourth problem that must be resolved by the adolescent before he can be considered mature is the acquisition of a relatively stable value system on which to base his behavior. Without a value system to guide his thoughts and actions, an individual will find himself at a loss to know how to behave from one situation to the next. This problem is intensified by the fact that our society presents to the adolescent so many different values from which to choose. And choosing involves frustration, pressure, conflict, and time—time to try, time to sift, time to try again, and to sift again—and again and again. This reasoning has been behind many behavioral scientists' conclusions that it requires approximately 25 years of living before one really begins to achieve maturity. It may well be that many, if not most, people, never achieve complete "maturity" in all aspects of their lives. Nonetheless, no matter how many years it takes, the problems of adolescence must be confronted and reckoned with if "maturity" is ever to be attained. Adolescence should be marked by a continual striving to achieve those behaviors that mark the mature human being.

ADOLESCENCE IN HISTORICAL PERSPECTIVE

"The more things change, the more they remain the same." This statement by Alphonse Karr (1849) seems to be true of the adolescent experience throughout history. It is nearly impossible to find a period in history during which the younger and older generations have not been at odds with each other over values, standards, morals, and the exercise of judgment and restraint (Fredenburgh, 1968). In order to give today's reader a sense of this continuity, we will present a brief description of what it meant to be an adolescent in each of the decades of the twentieth century. The reader will note that each decade is marked by ambivalent strivings. On the one hand is a need to hold on to the security of childlike dependence; on the other is the need to establish one's independence and autonomy.

Many adolescents in the first decade of this century had returned from the Spanish-American War and the Boxer Rebellion of the 1890s. Consequently, their experience was broader than many of their parents' and they were awakened to the desirability of attaining more education. Nonetheless, of 21.5 million persons between the ages of 5 and 18 in the United States between 1900 and 1920, only 15 million were enrolled in public schools, only 10.5 million of whom (approximately 50 percent) were in average daily attendance (*Statistical Abstracts of the United States*, 1931). Because of economic necessity, many adolescents had to leave school in order to help support their families. Of the 1910 population, 16 percent of the boys and 8 percent of the girls between the ages of 10 and 13 were gainfully employed, while 41 percent of the males and 20 percent of the females of 14 and 15 years old, and 79 percent of the males and 40 percent of the females between 16 and 20 were gainfully employed. Thus, young people of the first decade essentially held the roles of economically contributing adults in society, and consequently adult status.

Most adolescents knew of the electric light and the telephone but few experienced these inventions as parts of their daily lives. They viewed nickelodeon scenes and occasionally saw an automobile, but seldom drove one. Their interest in pioneering and flight was sparked by the Wright Brothers' flight in 1903. Consequently, when World War I loomed on the horizon, many young men were preparing to volunteer, often dreaming of flying airplanes themselves. Many adolescents were beginning to become aware of civic and national problems through sensational newspaper stories of murder and scandal, as well as through stories of crusades against poverty, trusts, white slavery (Dulles, 1965), and Carrie Nation's demonstrations for prohibition. There were even occasional campaigns against the corrupting influence of comic strips.

By the "Roaring Twenties," World War I, "the war to end all wars," was only a memory for the adolescent and his parents. However, its influence could be seen in the job market as returning veterans competed for jobs. Recently passed child labor laws began to have an effect on school attendance since young adolescents could no longer find employment in the sweat shops which had exploited them during earlier decades. Among those 14 and 15 years old, only 23 percent of the males and 12 percent of the females were reported to be employed—a decline of almost 50 percent. And, for the first time in the nation's history, more than half of those between 5 and 18 (55 percent) were in daily attendance in the public schools.

In the political arena of the twenties, young women participated in suffrage demonstrations, which resulted in the passage of the Nineteenth Amendment. And other young people were upset by such government scandals as the Teapot Dome and the questionable private lives of some public officials, especially President Harding.

The social sphere was dominated by the effects of Prohibition. Young people engaged in illegal drinking, had petting parties (it was rumored that many girls carried contraceptives in their vanity cases), and girls wore short skirts that sparked a national campaign by the YWCA against this scandalous dress of the "flappers." Charles Lindbergh became the dashing hero of the decade for many young people when he made his solo flight in 1927.

The stock market crash in 1929 brought the "Roaring Twenties" to a close and began a much less exuberant decade. Young people were hit by the decrease in the availability of material things and the lack of job opportunities. Consequently, school attendance again rose; by 1930, more than 66 percent of the individuals between 5 and 18 were attending school.

Interestingly, the thirties saw a large number of young people participating in radical political activities, such as demonstrating, picketing, organizing the unemployed, signing the Oxford Pledge against bearing arms for their country, and holding Army Day antiwar rallies and strikes. According to Lipset (1966), more than 100,000 students were members of the American Student Union, an amalgamation of most of the radical groups of that time. Other estimates put participation in antiwar parades as high as 200,000.

Since economic hardship made it difficult for young people to marry, there was an extended increase in premarital sex (Allen, 1939). One survey of a group of young business-class males revealed that

70 percent experienced sexual intercourse prior to marriage (Lynd & Lynd, 1937). And sales of contraceptives to single as well as to married people totaled in the millions of dollars. Those young people who did marry found it extremely difficult to establish economic independence and often lived with their parents.

The repeal of Prohibition in 1933 seemed to cut down on adolescent consumption of alcohol, possibly because the thrill of defying the law was absent.

The hardship of the depression years was disappearing in 1940, but a second world war appeared to be imminent. Although most young men accepted their draft calls, it appeared that many were skeptical about their country's entering another war. To Morale Officers in the Army, it appeared that the chief aim of the servicemen in the forties was to get back home (Allen, 1952). Young women, as well as young men, bore much responsibility during World War II. Many joined the WACS, the WAVES, the Red Cross, volunteered to work in the United Services Organizations, or made up for the shortage of men in factories or civil service jobs.

Thus, the war gave many young people new ways of asserting their independence and new experiences through travel and news of other countries. These new factors showed up most strikingly in the number of GIs who went back to school (with the important help of the GI Bill of Rights) when they returned from the war. Education began to be viewed as a mass phenomenon. (The new availability of married students' housing greatly helped this increase.)

The focus on war and peace in the forties shifted to a focus on rapid scientific and technological advances in the fifties. The most influential of these advances was television, which made it possible for young people to see world events as they happened and opened their eyes to available material goods through advertising.

The affluence brought on by technological advances also made "have nots" more visible. The 1954 Supreme Court decision to abolish segregation in public schools had a major influence on young people. Civil rights demonstrations, sit-ins, and rallies set the stage for the turmoil of the sixties. Ghettos and "Blackboard Jungles" (violence-ridden inner-city schools) also became more visible. Changing neighborhoods began to result in rising juvenile delinquency rates and interracial gang wars and rumbles.

The reader has probably noticed many parallels between the adolescent of the sixties and seventies and his counterparts in preceding decades. In the sixties, the trend toward increasing school attendance continued and youth employment opportunities continued to decrease with the advance of technological progress. The astronauts became the pioneers of the sixties. The distaste for war evidenced in the thirties and forties came back even more vehemently in the sixties as young people saw the grime of war on their television screens and failed to find meaningful reasons for our presence in Vietnam. Racial hostilities broke into riots, and protest spread to campus demands. Radical organizations such as the Students for a Democratic Society and the Black Panthers drew some disillusioned adolescents into their membership.

What's the matter with kids today...?

NEW YORK, N.Y. (AP) — A cry "strike against war" resounded on many campuses today, summoning students to drop their books at 11 a.m. and demonstrate for peace. Even before the movement got officially under way it resulted in bruises for about 20 persons.

In a riot-launched peace drive on Brooklyn last night, about 500 students of an evening high school joined 2,000 other persons in trying to persuade 1,500 remaining students to join their ranks.

There was a melee in which police swung night sticks and demonstrators swung fists and feet. After the wild turmoil was over, two policemen were treated for sprains and bruises and a citizen for scalp wounds. Many others limped away before the ambulance surgeon could get to them. Eight persons were arrested.

Detectives said known reds led some of the groups of rioters.

CAMBRIDGE, Mass. (AP) — Flying grapefruit and onions today turned an anti-war meeting of Harvard students into a burlesque battle.

There seemed to be a division of thought on the subject of war versus peace.

More than 2,000 students gathered in the Harvard Yard for an anti-war conclave called by the National Student League and the Student League for Industrial Democracy.

BALTIMORE (AP) — An anti-war demonstration by liberal students from the Johns Hopkins University today turned out to be anything but peaceful.

Five minutes after the demonstration opened in a Hopkins assembly hall, the air was filled with oratory cat calls, overripe tomatoes and eggs of undetermined age.

(The Cambridge story noted that the National Student League distributed circulars demanding that ROTC be abolished and criticizing the Civilian Conservation Corps (CCC) as too military.)

Sound familiar?
These reports went out over the Associated Press wire more than 35 years ago and were carried by The Washington (D. C.) Evening Star on April 13, 1934.

FIGURE 1-1.

The emancipation of women which had begun with the Nine-teenth Amendment and continued through female participation in the war effort of the forties also came back in the form of the Women's Lib movement.

On the other side of shouting protest were many private expressions of altruism, for many adolescents volunteered their services for tutoring and other community programs.

Drug use began to replace drinking as a form of adolescent rebellion, and sexual permissiveness again became evident. More and more students went to college and stayed to acquire advanced degrees, prolonging their economic dependence longer than their predecessors had. (It has been hypothesized that this sacrifice of economic independence may partially explain the need for today's young people to assert themselves through political activity.)

In any case, we can see that, from the era of the Wright Brothers to the era of moon exploration, the adolescent has tended to react against adult authority and power (see Figure 1-1). He has protested against schools, government, wars, social injustices; in short, he has considered the older generation to have failed and has looked toward his assertion of independence as the beginning of new solutions.

SUMMARY AND CONCLUSIONS

We have introduced the hypothesis that the period of adolescence is not determined solely by chronological age nor by physiological factors; rather we have suggested that it is a transitional process involving a dynamic interaction of interpersonal and intrapersonal behavior in a real and physical world. This definition raises the question of what the nature of this transitional period should be. We have hypothesized that a certain amount of conflict is beneficial in that it develops the individual's decision-making ability, which is a prerequisite for mature functioning.

We suggest that the goals of the adolescent period should be acceptance of the physical self, emotional control, social maturity, and intellectual sophistication and sensitivity. The individual adolescent must achieve these goals with at least some degree of success if he is to become a mature adult.

Traveling through adolescence to maturity is certainly a traumatic phenomenon involving numerous problems with which a youth must learn to cope if he is to attain a satisfying maturity. He will be confronted with social situations requiring the achievement of heterosexual compatibility. He will be faced with the need to tolerate being alone and to find satisfaction in solitary pursuits. He will be encountering more and more leisure time, a modern trend which may prove a blessing or a curse, depending upon the wisdom with which he learns to use it. And he will find it necessary to develop a value system that will prove to be both personally satisfying yet socially acceptable. Surely, no other period of life presents more complex problems than this transitional period of adolescence.

Nor do the problems of adolescence seem to have changed much throughout history. In our survey of the past century, we have attempted to point out the common denominators of adolescence. Some common factors we have pointed out are resistance to adult authority through political activity, liquor or drugs, and school protests. We have also noted the increase in school attendance throughout the twentieth century, and the simultaneous decrease in youth job opportunities. Common to adolescents of all eras are ambivalent strivings toward both childlike dependence and adult independence.

REFERENCES

Adler, A. The fundamental views of individual psychology. *International Journal of Individual Psychology*, 1935, **1**, 5–8.

Adler, A. *Social interest.* New York: Putnam, 1939.

Allen, F. L. *Since yesterday.* New York: Harper & Row, 1939.

Allen, F. L. *The big change.* New York: Harper & Row, 1952.

Allport, G. W. *Becoming.* New Haven: Yale University Press, 1955.

Berg, I. A. Cultural trends and the task of psychology. *American Psychologist*, 1965, **20**, 203–207.

Dulles, F. R. *A history of reaction—Americans learn to play* (2nd ed.). New York: Appleton-Century-Crofts, 1965.

English, H. B., & English, A. V. *A comprehensive dictionary of psychological and psychoanalytical terms.* New York: David McKay, 1964.

Erikson, E. H. *Childhood and society.* New York: W. W. Norton, 1950.

Erikson, E. H. *Identity: Youth and crisis.* New York: W. W. Norton, 1968.

Fredenburgh, F. A. An apologia for the hippie generation. *Mental Hygiene*, 1968, **52**(3), 341–348.

Friedenberg, E. Z. *The vanishing adolescent.* Boston: Beacon Press, 1959.

Fromm, E. *The sane society.* New York: Holt, Rinehart & Winston, 1955.

Hall, G. S. *Adolescence: Its psychology and its relation to physiology, anthropology, sociology, sex, crime, religion, and education.* New York: Appleton-Century-Crofts, 1904.

Havighurst, R. J. *Human development and education.* New York: David McKay, 1953.

Jones, M. C. The later careers of boys who were early or late maturing. *Child Development*, 1957, **28**, 113–128.

Jones, M. C., & Bayley, N. Physical maturing among boys as related to behavior. *Journal of Educational Psychology*, 1950, **41**, 129–148.

Lipset, S. M. Student opposition in the United States. *Government and Opposition*, 1966, **1**, 351–374.

Lynd, R. S., & Lynd, H. M. *Middletown in transition.* New York: Harcourt Brace & Jovanovich, 1937.

Maslow, A. H. *Motivation and personality.* New York: Harper & Row, 1954.

Mead, M. *Coming of age in Samoa.* New York: William Morrow, 1928. (a)

Mead, M. *Growing up in New Guinea.* New York: William Morrow, 1928. (b)

Murray, H. A., & Kluckhohn, C. Outline of a conception of personality. In C. Kluckhohn, H. A. Murray, & D. Schneider (Eds.), *Personality in nature, society and culture* (2nd ed.). New York: Alfred A. Knopf, 1953. Pp. 3–49.

Mussen, P. H., & Jones, M. C. Self-conceptions, motivations, and interpersonal attitudes of late- and early-maturing boys. *Child Development*, 1957, **28**, 243–255.

Mussen, P. H., & Jones, M. C. The behavior-inferred motivations of late- and early-maturing boys. *Child Development*, 1958, **29**, 61–66.

Nixon, R. E. *The art of growing.* New York: Random House, 1962.

Rogers, C. *On becoming a person.* Cambridge, Mass.: Riverside Press, 1961.

Statistical Abstracts of the United States, Department of Commerce, Bureau of Foreign and Domestic Commerce, Superintendent of Documents, Washington, D.C., 1931.

Sullivan, H. S. *The interpersonal theory of psychiatry.* New York: W. W. Norton, 1953.

Toynbee, A. *An historian's approach to religion.* New York: Oxford University Press, 1956.

II

Environmental Factors in Adolescent Development

2

The Family's Influence on Adolescent Development

> As are families, so is society. If well ordered, well instructed, and well governed, they are the springs from which go forth the streams of national greatness and prosperity—of civil order and public happiness.
>
> William Makepeace Thayer (1820-1898)

As they reach adolescence, many young people may begin to feel that they have become young adults and therefore no longer require parental guidance. They assume that their families will now have little influence over them and their behavior. Although this is indeed a period of increased independence, family attitudes and practices do continue to play important roles in the adolescent's development, as do family environment and socioeconomic factors.

With the beginning of the adolescent period, the family continues to be a primary socializing agent, although its authority must yield at times to competing socializing forces such as the peer group, as well as to the adolescent's growing need for independence. Family members are also called upon to cope with the problems and perils of the adolescent's increasing sexual maturity and his troublesome, often disturbing, ambivalence about his changing role in the family. Thus, the central problem facing the parents of adolescents is how to help their children gradually acquire *autonomy* and independence yet still continue to provide certain restraints and limitations necessitated by immature behaviors. As Douvan and Adelson (1966) have succinctly stated, "The problem the parent faces is in adjusting his loosening of control to the child's capacity to regulate himself, letting the reins slacken at the right time and in the right way, neither holding them so tightly that the child resists nor releasing them so suddenly as to endanger him." (p. 163). Achieving a satisfactory balance between these two factors depends to a considerable extent on the parental practices and attitudes that have been followed during early childhood, as well as during the adolescent period. Even the types of conflict and the degree of conflict between the two generations will be affected by the parental practices and attitudes pursued throughout the child's life.

VARIATIONS IN FAMILY STRUCTURE

Parental Power Structure

To a considerable extent, parental behavior will be determined by the type of power structure that characterizes the family. Elder (1962) has classified child-rearing practices into seven categories: (1) autocratic, in which the child is not allowed to express his views or participate in any decisions affecting him; (2) authoritarian, in which the adolescent may contribute to the solution of a problem but must always yield to his parents' final decision and judgment; (3) democratic, in which the youth is encouraged to actively participate in family decision making, although final approval rests with the parents; (4) equalitarian, in which there are minimal role differences between parents and offspring, with both generations having equal say in family matters; (5) permissive, in which the young person is given greater responsibility than his parents for making decisions affecting him; (6) *laissez faire*, in which the adolescent has the choice of following or disregarding parental wishes in his decision making; and, finally, (7) ignoring, in which the parents divorce themselves from the adolescent's behavior and allow him to go his own way without question.

According to a study conducted by Elder (1962), about one third of all American adolescents reported that their families possess a democratic structure. However, they often perceived their fathers as more autocratic or authoritarian than their mothers, whom they more frequently described as permissive or equalitarian.

Despite Elder's conclusions regarding the widespread existence of the democratic or equalitarian family pattern, a more recent study (Kandel & Lesser, 1969) comparing the parental power structure of American adolescents with that of Denmark, noted that authoritarian patterns are still the most prevalent in the United States yet very infrequent in Denmark, where the typical family structure is democratic. It was also observed that American parents establish more rules and provide fewer explanations for them than do Danish parents. The authors concluded that the prevalence of authoritarian attitudes among many American parents reflects the tendency of our culture to treat adolescents as children longer than do parents in Denmark. They believe this situation is an outgrowth of the fact that American youths remain in school longer than do Danish children and are therefore not expected to make adult decisions as soon. It is possible that this delay in American adolescents' acquisition of autonomy may reflect a lack of parental discipline, or perhaps inconsistent parental control when they were very young children. The more firm but democratic discipline of younger children in Denmark may very well contribute to the adolescent's development of self-discipline which in turn encourages Danish parents to allow their children greater freedom.

Regardless of one's conclusions about the prevalence of one structure or another, it is evident that there are numerous factors affecting what kind of family structure emerges. For example, the individual appears to have some impact on family attitudes, for both parents are more likely to treat older adolescents more permissively than those still in the early adolescent period. The sex of the child also influences parental practices, for boys tend to be given more freedom and independence earlier than girls (Bowerman & Kinch, 1959). And family size is another variable affecting the family structure. Parents of large families have been noted to be more authoritarian and less equalitarian than those of small families. Other factors influencing family structure include socioeconomic class and level of education reached by the parents. Parents from the lower social classes often have less education and a more limited knowledge of the developmental needs of adolescents than do those from other social levels. As a consequence, they are more likely to adopt autocratic or authoritarian attitudes and practices (Elder, 1962).

Within the framework of the family power structure there are also other factors that have an impact on the adolescent. For instance, the consistency or inconsistency of parental discipline plays a role in determining the child's behavior (Bath & Lewis, 1962). There may also be discrepancies in parental power. The father may be more dominant than the mother, creating a *patriarchal* family structure, or the mother may be more dominant than the father, creating a *matriarchal* pattern, or conceivably the parents' individual influence may be equal, and they may follow equalitarian child-rearing practices (Bowerman & Elder, 1964). However, it should be mentioned that dominance is not synonymous with autocratic or authoritarian control. It should also be pointed out that adolescents report that their parent of the same sex tends to be much more active and firm with them than their parent of the opposite sex.

The type of parental power structure determines, to a considerable extent, the kinds of sanctions or punishment generally used by the parents although no parent is likely to rely solely on one kind of punishment. Douvan and Adelson (1966) divide sanctions into three categories: physical punishment, a deprivation of privileges, or psychological punishment. Parents who resort to physical punishment can usually be described as authoritarian or autocratic in their approach to child rearing. The form of punishment they choose may be partly motivated by their need to vent their own turmoil or anger and their focus on immediate results rather than on the long-range goals of encouraging the development of self-discipline in their children. Those who resort to a deprivation of privileges tend to stress the need for the child to pay for his misdeeds. On the other hand, parents who rely on psychological sanctions, such as statements that they are disappointed in some of their offspring's behavior, are usually attempting to encourage the child's development of his own inner controls and conscience. Parents employing this means of discipline would generally be termed equalitarian or democratic. However, it should be pointed out that not all parents who resort to physical punishment are being autocratic or excessively punitive. Some children actually respond more favorably to fairly administered physical methods, which may bring about a release of tension and anxiety and produce a feeling in the misdoers that they have paid for their errant ways. Conversely, some types of psychological punishment may actually be more vindictive and cruel than certain physical methods. For example, a parent who tells his child he doesn't love him because of a certain behavior can cause the child to feel, if only temporarily, that he is not an individual of worth and value.

The Effects of Parental Practices and Attitudes

Adolescent behavior is strongly influenced by the kinds of practices and attitudes that grow out of the family power structure. For example, in another study conducted by Elder (1963), more than 70 percent of the adolescents with parents classified as democratic and permissive reported that their parents frequently provided explanations for their rules and actions, while less than 40 percent of the adolescents with autocratic parents made the same statement. Further, it has been observed that young people having democratic parents are more likely to model their behavior on that of their parents and to associate with peers approved by their parents than are those from autocratic homes. In addition, it was noted that democratic parents are also more likely to be consistent in their attitudes and practices and encourage the acquisition of independence and autonomy in their youngsters than are autocratic parents (Elder, 1963).

Where inconsistencies in parental practices do prevail, greater conflict between the two generations is likely to occur. Bath and Lewis (1962) conducted a study of 103 college women, who were given a questionnaire covering 37 problem or conflict situations involving parental control. The young women reported that the more inconsistent and severe their parents' practices had been, the more conflict they recalled arising between them and their parents. Another investigator (Peck, 1958), in an eight-year *longitudinal study* of adolescent character development, noted that the acquisition of emotional maturity was positively correlated with a stable, consistent family pattern along with the existence of warm, mutual trust and approval between parents and children.

As one might expect, adolescents subject to coercive parental rules rather than to democratic practices are much less likely to adhere to these rules when their parents are absent than are other young people (Raven & French, 1958). On the other hand, children of democratic parents who explain the reasoning behind their restraints and restrictions tend to maintain conformity toward these rules. Apparently, frequent explanations indicate the presence of considerable parental warmth (Elder, 1963). In any case, when young people participate at least to some extent in decision making affecting them, two results become apparent: (1) participation tends to facilitate communication between the two generations, and (2) it enables the adolescent to feel that he has had a role and consequently responsibility in establishing rules pertaining to him. Such guidance is more likely to be perceived as just by a child than the handing down of rules by parents in an arbitrary manner. Such arbitrary parental behavior is likely to result in delayed self-reliance for the adolescent, strained affectional relationships, and a widening of the communication gap between the two generations (Elder, 1962; Douvan & Adelson, 1966).

It has been noted that parents are able to govern their families in a democratic manner if they feel comfortable in their own roles and feel fairly confident in their abilities as parents. Such feelings are subtly conveyed to their offspring, who in turn develop their own inner controls and self-direction, as well as gradual confidence in their ability to make their own decisions (Douvan & Adelson, 1966).

Parental practices and attitudes also appear to have an impact on adolescent motivation and achievement, although the reports on this topic have been extremely contradictory (Straus, 1962; Bowerman & Elder, 1964). One investigator did suggest that an adolescent in a mother-dominated family may be more achievement oriented since the parent (mother) demanding excellence in the performance of her sons is also the *nurturant* parent—the one holding the greatest emotional power over her male progeny. There has also been some evidence to indicate that achievement-oriented people tend to recall their childhood and their relationships with their parents as characterized by emotional rejection (Straus, 1962). On the other hand, Bowerman and Elder (1964) noted in a study of 19,200 white high school students from unbroken homes in Ohio and North Carolina that academic motivation appeared to be highest among boys who perceived their fathers as the heads of their families, as well as democratic in their relationships with their sons. In any case, it is quite possible that autocratic family structure results in creating a greater dependency on others in decision making—a result that can carry over to low educational goals and low levels of aspiration. A study by Elder (1963) of Ohio and North Carolina white public school adolescents from unbroken homes disclosed that approximately 50 percent of the boys and girls in grades seven through nine with autocratic parents felt doubtful about completing high school, a trend of considerable significance to those involved with the dropout problem. Such parental dominance was especially noted among parents of the lower socioeconomic class, parents of the Catholic religion, and parents who headed large families (Elder, 1962). (This topic will be discussed in more detail in Chapter 9.) Apparently a youngster's autonomy in making decisions and his level of motivation are strongly dependent on the nature of the parent-child relationship. "Moderate or low parental power appears to be essential in fostering ambitions and effectiveness outside of the family" (Elder, 1963, p. 64).

Sex-Role Identification

As you may recall, Havighurst (1953) has described the acquisition and acceptance of a masculine or feminine role as one of the most important developmental tasks of the adolescent period. Among the major factors contributing to the accomplishment of this task are how sex roles are interpreted by the parents, the extent to which the parents serve as appropriate models to their youngsters, and parental responses to their offspring, especially to those of the opposite sex.

Acquiring a suitable sex role involves the process of *sex-role identification*. According to Lynn (1966), "Sex-role identification . . . refers to the *internalization* of the role typical of a given sex in a particular culture and to the unconscious reactions characteristic of that role" (p. 466). It is possible for an individual to identify completely with a role typical of the same sex and yet be poorly identified with the same-sex parent. Conversely, the opposite situation can occur; the parent with whom the youngster closely identifies may himself be poorly identified with the characteristic sex role of his culture, and thus the youth fails to identify with an appropriate sex role.

There is considerable controversy over how parents influence the development of a suitable sex-role in their children. Some studies indicate that females acquire a strong feminine identity through close identification with their mothers and males a sturdy masculine identity through strong identification with their fathers (Mosby, 1966; Lynn, 1966). Others suggest that identification will depend on which parent is perceived as having the greatest control of desirable privileges, such as the use of the family car or telephone. Such parents are viewed as holding more parental control and consequently higher status, and their youngsters are more likely to identify with their interests, attitudes, and behavior than with those of the parents perceived as having less command in the family power structure (Grinder & Spector, 1965). Still other investigators maintain that the father, through his responses to his daughter, may influence her acquisition of femininity more strongly than her mother (Johnson, 1963; Heilbrun, 1965).

According to the *reciprocal-role* explanation of sex-role learning (Johnson, 1963) a father's behavior and the nature of his relationship with his sons and his daughters are likely to be quite different. That is, he may assume an *instrumental role* toward his sons, characterized by an emphasis on disciplined responsibility and the encouragement of goal acquisition. In other words, the father serves, according to this explanation, as an interpreter and a teacher of the world beyond the family. The son's instrumental orientation is said to be facilitated by his fear of overt punishment and his desire for paternal respect.

The father maintains a more *expressive,* nurturant role toward his daughter to encourage the development of her femininity. He is a giver of love and a source of pleasurable, affective responses. Thus, this position sees the father as filling the role of male admirer to his daughter. He serves as a prototype of her future husband.

The mother's role in the family is essentially an expressive one. She is loving, affectionate, and supportive and makes no distinctions in her attitudes toward both sexes. Her children learn most of their expressive behavior from her, a learning that begins with their earliest attachment to her.

Included in this analysis of the reciprocal roles of mothers and fathers are the concepts of identification and modeling. Children identify with certain sex-typed behavior in their parents. Consequently, a son's strong identification with an active, strong father will help him develop the same masculine traits in his adulthood. Similarly, a mother will serve as a model for her daughter.

There are psychologists who would argue with this explanation of sex-role identification. They would say that fathers and mothers need not necessarily fill set instrumental and expressive roles, respectively, in order for their sons and daughters to grow up well adjusted. That is, they would attribute a father's different treatment of his sons and daughters to *his* socialization and learned attitude that boys should be active and aggressive and girls should be passive and home oriented. Studies have been conducted which point out that boys and girls are treated differently according to preconceived notions of what is masculine or feminine and that these children eventually conform to the expectations implicit in the differential treatment (Johnson, 1963; Lynn, 1966). It has been suggested, therefore, that there is reason to examine the traditional patterns of child rearing as social developments rather than as built-in, "natural" roles.

Nonetheless, the father's impact on the sex-role development of his offspring is considerable. This fact raises the question of how sex-role development is affected when the father plays a very passive role in the family power structure or is absent frequently or permanently from the home. In a study conducted by Rohrer and Edmonson (1960) it was found that girls reared in a matriarchal home—characterized by a strong dominant mother and a submissive father or an absent father—are likely to establish this same matriarchal pattern in homes of their own, as well as choose to live with or near their mothers. In the case of boys, Barclay and Cusumano (1967) state that "The absence of an adequate male model within the family forces the male child to identify with available male models in the external environment" (p. 249). Boys from such homes, who come under the influence of older boys who are members of gangs, often demonstrate the presence of considerable sex-role conflict, which is reflected in their compulsive rejection of anything they consider feminine and in their adoption of many pseudomasculine traits (Rohrer & Edmonson, 1960). It has also been noted that young people with fathers absent from the home often show low academic achievement. In fact, a recent study indicated that a positive correlation exists between underachievement and a lack of sex-role identification in males (Granlund & Knowles, 1969).

Martin, the youngest of five children, lost his father when he was two years old. The other siblings, who were all girls, tended to baby and spoil their young brother. Martin developed into a poor student at school, although it was noted by his teachers that he consistently underachieved in his academic performance both in public school and later on at college. During his adolescence he acquired many pseudomasculine traits including considerable boasting, cockiness, and deceit, as well as a general lack of perseverance. As an adult he began to drift from one job to another, from one business to another, constantly depending upon his older sisters to "bail him out" of his difficulties. Ultimately his wife had to take over the support of the family, while Martin continued to rationalize his failures and shortcomings, blaming everything in his environment but himself. Many psychologists would say that Martin would have turned out differently if his father had lived to provide him with a masculine model of responsibility.

THE INFLUENCES OF SIBLINGS, FAMILY SIZE, AND BIRTH ORDER

In addition to parental practices and attitudes, the adolescent's behavior is also affected by other familial factors including his siblings and their sex, the size of the family, and his *ordinal position*, or birth order, within the family constellation.

The Roles of Siblings

It has been said that the relationships between and among brothers and sisters in most homes are second only to the parent-child relationship (Irish, 1964). Such *sibling* associations may have a lasting influence upon an individual's ultimate adult roles (Sutton-Smith, Roberts, & Rosenberg, 1964)

Much emphasis has been placed on the effects of sibling rivalry in human development, but there has been little empirical research into the effects of other kinds of interactions between brothers and sisters. Irish (1964) has suggested eight functions served by sibling relationships: (1) They provide a means of socialization in that young people can try out different behaviors with their brothers and sisters before attempting them with the world beyond the family. (2) Siblings, especially the older ones, can act as *surrogate,* or substitute, parents to the younger members of the family. (3) Further, siblings can serve as teachers. For example, in the acquisition of such skills as learning to ride a bicycle, older siblings might prove more able teachers than their parents. (4) Since they are closer in age and experience, siblings may understand certain problems and situations of their brothers and sisters better than adult members of the family. (5) Brothers and sisters can often contribute to sibling emotional security by serving as safer targets for the release of emotional tension than their parents. (6) Siblings may act as *role models* for one another.

For instance, the feminine role established by an older sister may serve as a model for a younger sister to follow. (7) Siblings can be sources of motivation through challenge and stimulation. Younger siblings may often accept challenges from older brothers and sisters that they might not accept from parents. (8) Finally, they contribute to a feeling of belongingness, which provides a sense of security within the family structure.

Of course, certain negative aspects are possible in sibling associations. Parental and sibling relationships may create so much security within the family constellation that its young members become reluctant to leave even for short visits, feeling insecure or "homesick" when they are away from home. In a family with many children there may be added difficulties engendered by the presence of so many children with varying needs. In the clamor for the satisfaction of these needs, the less vocal, less outgoing members of the family may often be overlooked, or the talents of some may be sacrificed to satisfy the needs of others. Rivalry and jealousy, sometimes accompanied by the bullying of younger family members by the older, can also disrupt satisfying, cordial interpersonal relationships and impede the attainment of personal and social adjustment, both within the family and outside of it (Irish, 1964).

However, it should be noted that only children are often in an even more unfavorable position, for at home they have only their parents to whom they can turn and from whom they can learn (Toman, 1961). They may also be denied the opportunity of developing the early socialization patterns—such as sharing—that commonly exist in larger families and that are so necessary for later development of satisfying relationships with their peers.

Age and Sex Differences of Siblings

The age differences between siblings will usually affect the relationships between them. For example, if siblings are six or more years apart, they will tend to grow up like single children. If there is less than six years difference between them, however, they are often a threat to each other's power and command over their parents. Generally, the closer in age they are, the more severe will be the conflicts between them but the greater their tendency to hold on to one another later in life (Toman, 1961).

The sex of siblings also appears to have considerable influence, particularly on the sex-role behavior of each youngster. Sutton-Smith and his colleagues (1964) noted that in a family consisting of two boys, the male twosome leads to masculine qualities, such as dominance and independence, and a strong interest in economic and financial activities. In the case of a female twosome, these authors observed that the girls tend to exhibit feminine traits, such as submissiveness and dependency, and interest in the more feminine vocations, such as nursing and teaching. If two siblings are of opposite sexes they tend to show more expressive creativity than do either of the other two sibling patterns. The investigators further observed that the sex of siblings appears to have a stronger impact upon adjustment, anxiety, and interest patterns, whereas birth order, which is to be discussed shortly, seems to have greater influence on mental abilities. They also noted that brothers appear to have greater affect on their sisters than do sisters on their brothers.

Another study by Brittain (1966) disclosed that girls with brothers near their own age exhibit more conformity toward parental expectations, while girls with sisters seem to be more conforming toward their peers. He suggested that these trends may be due to the existence of greater sibling rivalry in families with two daughters and that this competitive situation may contribute to hostility toward the parents and hence conformity away from them; or possibly a peer-group orientation may reflect the modeling of female sibling behavior and early awareness of the need for peer conformity.

Other research (Douvan & Adelson, 1966) has noted that firstborn girls with younger brothers may be likely to experience problems in their development of a suitable and satisfying feminine role, reflected in hostile, competitive feelings toward their brothers. These investigators also found, however, that a second-born daughter in a two-girl family may experience even greater difficulties with her sex role, as her parents may consciously or unconsciously convey to her their disappointment in not having a son. Thus, the second-born girl, like the firstborn with a younger brother, is likely to wish she were a boy and to reject the idea of marriage. Witness the case of Laura.

Laura, the second and last-born child in a college-educated family of two daughters, became the focal point of her father's regrets about not having a son. Although a mediocre student, she was a likable individual and a leader in school. Through her father's urging, she became president of her junior-college student body, and at his insistence she went on to the large state university that he had attended, although she previously had voiced a desire to attend a smaller school. Upon graduation, at his prompting she entered law school, where she had difficulty in meeting the stringent demands placed upon her by the curriculum and almost failed. Ultimately she did obtain her law degree, but at considerable cost. Laura became an extremely tense, anxiety-ridden young woman, who found it necessary to take tranquilizing drugs in order to maintain the pace established for her by her father because of his disappointment that she had no male sibling.

Family Size

The number of siblings within a family constellation appears to have an impact on the development of the children. According to Douvan and Adelson (1966), adolescents from small families appear to possess greater poise and self-confidence in their relationships with adults than do those from larger families. They seem to be more social-minded, and they tend to date earlier, engage in more leisure-time activities, and belong to more organized social groups than adolescents raised in large families. They are oriented toward long-range goals, are more concerned with future educational plans, and are more interested in bettering themselves and in achieving a higher status than their parents. In other words, they are more active, energetic, motivated, and future oriented than their counterparts with larger families. Adolescents from small families also appear to be closer to their parents and in some ways identify more intimately with them, sharing more recreational activities, relying more often on their advice, and confiding in them and in other adults more frequently than do youths from larger families.

In keeping with the findings of Douvan and Adelson, Holtzman and Moore (1965) have found that adolescents from larger families report that a greater distance exists between their interests and those of their parents. Such young people from large families tend to be more peer oriented, relying on the advice of their contemporaries more often than on that of their parents. They are more likely to choose a model from among young adults, older brothers or sisters, and other young acquaintances. Those from large families also tend to be less independent of their parents and other adult authority, while at the same time manifesting ambivalence and resentment about this dependency, as well as a lack of well-developed autonomy and internal controls.

These variations between large and small families seem to be independent of the factor of social class, for they exist among both middle-class and lower-class youths (Douvan & Adelson, 1966). However, distinctions in the patterns of family power and authority between large and small units do seem to play a role. For example, parents of large families with several children seem to be more traditional, strict, and punitive in expressing their authority compared with those from small families. They are more likely to be autocratic or authoritarian—relying on physical punishment, permitting their children little opportunity to participate in rule making, and generally expecting unquestioning obedience and respect. On the other hand, parents of small families (usually two children) more often appear to be democratic or equalitarian, encouraging personal responsibility, high achievement, and early independence in their offspring. A further difference in socialization stems from the fact that individuals from sizable families are frequently expected to assume responsibility for their younger siblings, a practice that allows them less time for membership in social groups and for participation in leisure-time activities.

Birth Order

Although the influence of birth order is affected by other factors such as family size and the sex of other siblings, research has come to indicate that the role of any individual in the family group is at least partly determined by his ordinal rank within the family structure—that is, whether he was the firstborn, second-born, or last-born child to arrive on the family scene.

Interest in the effects of birth order on the individual's development was first manifested in the past century. Sir Francis Galton reported on the first-known data in 1874, when he published the book *English Men of Science.* Through his examination of the biographical data of these outstanding men of science, he discovered that only sons and firstborn sons were more prevalent among this group of renowned men than might have been possible through chance alone. He concluded that because of the law of *primogeniture*, under which the eldest sons inherited the bulk of the family estate, they were able to become financially independent and follow their own inclinations. Galton also suggested that parents tended to treat an only child and a firstborn (who actually is an only child until a later sibling arrives) as a companion and to give him greater responsibility than later-born children.

Among the best-known modern research on the effects of ordinal position is that of Bossard and Boll (1955). In a six-year study of 100 families of at least six children, with a total of 879 living children (458 males and 421 females), they observed that each child selected and filled a specific role in the family structure, with the role selected being largely determined by the youngster's ordinal position, by the roles already preempted by the older children, and by the parental and sibling attitudes and behavior toward them. Eight distinct role patterns emerged from this investigation:

(1) Every family identified at least one child as filling a responsible role, in which he assumed the direction or supervision of other siblings or provided them with some type of service. Usually, but not always, this was the oldest child in the family. A male, often the older son, would assist his parents and serve as a father surrogate in the absence of the father. With a daughter, it was most frequently the eldest, and she often served as a second mother.

(2) A second child was most likely to be described as a popular, sociable, likable youngster, who, upon finding the responsible role filled, sought to gain recognition and self-esteem through the use of personal charm rather than through the use of personal power.

(3) Another child was apt to be a socially ambitious individual with the term "social butterfly" serving as the most suitable description of his behavior. Usually this was a girl ranking third, fourth, or fifth in birth order, and it was noted that she tended to turn from the family to the community for recognition.

(4) Fourth in the order of frequency was the role described as a studious one, wherein the youngster apparently searched for and found recognition through his academic achievement. This role seemed to be equally divided between male and female offspring, who were characterized as being quiet, hard working, and preoccupied with their books.

(5) A fifth role was distinguished as being that of the self-centered isolate, who demonstrated a reluctance to participate in family activities and a general withdrawal from the family and family life. Three situations seemed to contribute to the development of the isolate: (a) sometimes it was observed that he was the odd number in a family in which the other siblings tended to pair off; (b) in other instances, it was noted this child tended to possess a unique interest or hobby not shared by other family members; (c) and in other cases, it was reported that in families characterized by early parent-child conflict, the youngster's early rebellion against his parents spread to a larger behavioral pattern of rebellion, marked by self-imposed isolation.

(6) A sixth role was described as that of the irresponsible child, who commonly withdrew from responsibilities. He was the one most likely to lose his possessions, "forget" to do his homework, or neglect his household chores.

(7) Another role was assumed by a child possessing poor health or generally described as being unwell. This child might have a physical defect that created special problems, or he might suffer from a chronic illness, or he could be feigning illness as a means of gaining recognition or justifying his failures.

(8) And in almost every family, there seemed to be a spoiled sibling, usually the last-born child or one who had held that position for several years. It has been suggested that the discipline for the last-born member of a family may be less severe and less rigid; he may also be given fewer responsibilities, while at the same time enjoying more opportunities and privileges.

According to Bossard & Boll (1955), ". . . in a large family each child's drive for recognition is expressed in a specialized role related to the roles already pre-empted" (p. 77). In addition, each family member is confronted with different patterns of expectations. The eldest child faces only the expectations of his parents, while the second-born is confronted with the expectations of both his parents and his older sibling, and so on. And with the passing of time, it has been suggested by these investigators, sibling expectations based on their own roles and experiences may accumulate and ultimately outweigh the expectations of parents.

Other investigators (Parsons & Bales, 1955) have noted that balance in the family structure demands that *all* roles must be filled in the *microsocial* family system, meaning that one child may fill several roles. For example, in smaller families of two or three children it seems plausible that one might observe one child possessing the

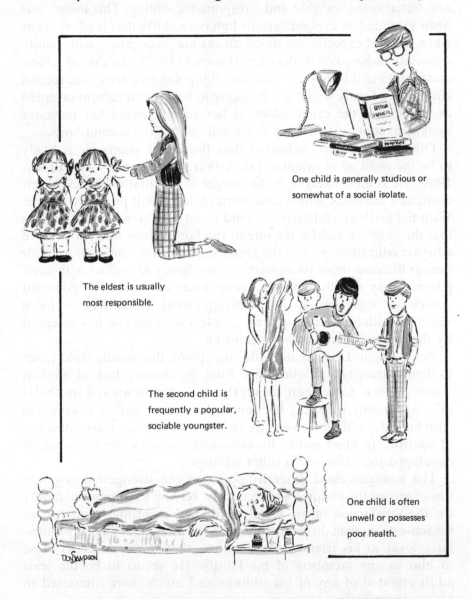

One child is generally studious or somewhat of a social isolate.

The eldest is usually most responsible.

The second child is frequently a popular, sociable youngster.

One child is often unwell or possesses poor health.

As each child arrives on the family scene, he selects and fills a specific role in the family structure.

traits of several roles. The eldest of two might be not only the responsible child but also the studious one, as well as the *social isolate*, while the younger child could conceivably be not only the spoiled one but also the sociable and irresponsible sibling. This theory has been extended to explain certain behavior shifts that tend to occur when cultural expectations based on sex are incongruent with family expectations based on birth order (Hancock, 1967). The case of Laura, cited earlier in this chapter, illustrates this point. Ordinarily the second child in the family would not be likely to be as achievement oriented as Laura, but the expectations of her father caused her behavior to shift to some extent from the usual role of the second-born.

Other studies have indicated that the oldest youngster is likely to be the most adult oriented (McArthur, 1956; Altus, 1966; Brody, 1968). He is most likely to be the target of parental pressures, ambitions, and anxieties, which later-born children will probably escape. With the firstborn child parents tend to set high standards. It follows that the firstborn child is the one in the family most likely to receive a higher education, possess the greatest motivation, and achieve eminence. Because these youngsters are so closely identified with their parents, they usually develop strong inner controls or a powerful conscience, sometimes to an inhibiting extent. Often they are more sensitive, withdrawn, high-strung, and less sociable and less accepted by their peers than later-born children.

According to Douvan and Adelson (1966), the middle child tends to demonstrate two unique traits. First, he shows a lack of motivation—which has been described as "downward mobility"—apparently reflecting his demoralization at having to compete with his older sibling. Second, he seems to show a low internalization of controls. In other words, his conscience is apt to be less strongly developed than that of his other siblings.

The youngest child generally possesses the strongest peer-group ties of any of the children in the family, relying less upon the family for the satisfaction of his social needs and as primary sources for his self-esteem than do older siblings (McArthur, 1956). He is particularly loyal to his friends, often feeling that they can be as close to him as any members of his family. He seems to be the least adult oriented of any of his siblings and much more interested in his contemporaries.

The only child also occupies a unique position. Bossard and Boll (1960) suggest that certain common hazards or handicaps tend to characterize only children. They observe that the only child has no other children with whom to engage in play and competition within the intimacy of the family. In addition, he fails to receive important lessons in living with others that brothers and sisters would provide, for siblings offer a chance to obtain intimate knowledge about those of a similar age, ability, and type. They can reflect each other's thoughts and behavior and provide assistance in self-correction and self-discipline. The parents of only children also tend to be oversolicitous, possibly because their attention is focused on one child rather than on two or three. Perhaps fear of losing an only child is also greater.

Warren (1966) reported on one study in which he observed that only children tended to be more like the youngest child in the family constellation than like any other. On the other hand, Altus (1966) suggested that the only child is more like the oldest child; both have an opportunity for interaction with their parents, which they do not have to share with their brothers and sisters. From these contradictory points of view, it is apparent that at the present time more research is necessary before we can come to any positive conclusions and point to either hypothesis as correct.

Schachter (1963) observed that the percentage of only children among graduate students at the University of Minnesota was considerably higher than their percentage in the general population. He thought it possible that the only child is more able and thus demonstrates greater persistence in remaining in school than children from larger families. However, such a tendency may also reflect the more favorable economic position possessed by only children.

More recent studies of ordinal position (Miller & Zimbardo, 1966; Radloff & Helmreich, 1968; Toman, 1970) have also revealed interesting data of possible significance in the selection of job applicants for positions of responsibility and in one's choice of a marriage partner. Miller and Zimbardo reported a study of three groups of subjects, who were classified according to their birth order: (1) first-born, (2) last born and at least five years younger than the next oldest sibling, and (3) last born and not more than three years younger than the next oldest brother or sister. The investigators observed that the eldest and youngest children in the family who were at least five years younger than any other sibling (or in reality almost like an only child) showed a stronger need to affiliate or to lean on others in times of stress than did other brothers and sisters. Such a need to affiliate may reflect the greater feelings of insecurity which are typical of firstborns. Often parents feel very insecure with their first child, and their insecurity is reflected in the later behavior of this eldest child.

In 1968 Radloff and Helmreich noted in their studies of United States Navy Aquanauts engaged in underwater research that firstborn and only children demonstrated greater fear and a lower level of performance than later-born children. This fear may also have reflected greater feelings of insecurity characteristic of the first child.

Toman (1970) suggested that birth order may also affect how one selects a spouse, a friend, or a business partner. He observed that the pattern of a new relationship tends to duplicate the pattern of an old one and that the greater the similarity between the two, the more likely the new relationship will be a lasting one, as well as a happy one. He pointed out that brothers and sisters constitute a child's first peers and are usually present during one's crucial formative years. Thus, the eldest child who tended to dominate his younger siblings would probably be happiest as the dominant partner in marriage; and, conversely, younger brothers and sisters will be accustomed to being followers and being dominated and will be likely to select friends and occupations that will allow them to remain followers and dependent on others to lead them. Despite these interesting findings, however, one must remain cautious in his interpretation of the impact of birth order on personality development, for there are other relevant factors which may be equally responsible.

ENVIRONMENTAL FACTORS AND THE FAMILY

Not only is adolescent development influenced by parental practices and attitudes, the family power structure, the size of the family, the sex of the children, and the ordinal position of the individual, but adolescent behavior is also affected by such environmental factors as the family's socioeconomic status, its mobility, the absence of a parent from the home, and the employment of the mother.

Socioeconomic Status

In contrast to Western European countries, where until recently heredity was the chief determinant of social class, social status in the United States and Canada has been based mainly upon economic level. Several measurements of American social class have been devised; perhaps one of these most frequently used has been the *Index of Social Position* (Hollingshead, 1949; Hollingshead & Redlich, 1958). According to this index, socioeconomic class can be determined by three primary factors: (1) the family's residential address, (2) the occupation of the household head, and (3) the years of formal education completed by the head of the household. Through an assessment of these three factors, five social classes have been established. In brief, Class I members may be described as belonging to the upper class. They are usually the community's professional and business leaders, they are college educated, and they possess high incomes, often due to inherited wealth. Those in Class II would be defined as upper-middle class. They have had some formal education beyond high school graduation; their household heads occupy managerial positions and engage in the lesser-ranking professions; and they are usually described as "well-to-do," but unlike Class I members, they have only rarely inherited their wealth. Members of Class III are typically referred to as middle class. They are high school graduates, and the heads of their families are usually employed in salaried and clerical pursuits, own small businesses, are semiprofessionals or technicians, or serve as plant supervisors. Class IV, described as the lower-middle or working class, is frequently composed of second- or third-generation members of an ethnic group, such as Italian or Polish. They are less educated than those of Class III, with many household heads not having graduated from high school, and most of their males are engaged in skilled or semiskilled manual employment. Class V or the lower class, if employed, is mainly composed of semiskilled and unskilled factory hands and laborers. Generally, most adults in this group have failed to complete elementary school. They typically live in the urban slums, and their households are characterized by brittle family ties and many broken homes.

Hollingshead's categories are now considered somewhat dated by some psychologists. For example, Packard (1959) also breaks down the social structure into five categories, but he takes a somewhat different approach from that of Hollingshead and Redlich. He suggests that there are two major divisions in our present class system: (1) the college-diploma elite consisting of the real upper class and the semi-upper class who are at the helm of society; and (2) the supporting classes composed of the limited-success class, the working class, and the real lower class. Thus, Packard considers the main class divisions to have changed since a generation ago when the primary division fell between the white-collar class and the blue-collar class. He points out that this change may reflect the growing demand for a college diploma as a prerequisite for most upper and semi-upper class occupations. And at the same time clerical jobs, which were once considered white-collar, have frequently been downgraded, while factory work has become cleaner and has offered greater remuneration than white-collar occupations.

Why is it necessary in a study of parental practices and attitudes to delineate socioeconomic classes in a democratic society such as that existing in the United States today? The answer lies in the fact that each socioeconomic class is characterized by a unique pattern of norms, values, and concerns which generate different types of parental responses to problems created by adolescent development, problems which occur uniformly within all social class groups (Kobrin, 1962). For example, the middle class tends to encourage impulse control, the planning of future goals, and raising one's status in society, aims which demand the acceptance by youth of adult authority. Achievement orientation—that is, motivation toward attaining worthwhile goals, is significantly higher among Class I, II, and III boys than among those from Class IV and V, although other factors such as family size and ordinal position may also play a role in the acquisition of motivation (Rosen, 1961). The lower classes, because they are not governed by a positive program in child training, foster impulsiveness, aggressive behavior, and independence from adult authority, while placing less stress on achievement. Among such groups there is often a general lack of knowledge about child care, especially the psychological aspects. In addition, parents from these lower socioeconomic levels tend to be limited in the time and energy they have available to devote to rearing their children.

Socioeconomic cultural factors can also affect how young people respond to the demands of the adult world, especially during the period of late adolescence. Middle-class norms, which emphasize supervised training and socializing institutions prepare young people to accept a certain amount of adult authority. In contrast, adolescents of the lower socioeconomic classes are often given unlimited freedom and are thus unlikely to accept adult authority as valid. Although they may not overtly manifest more rebellious behavior than do middle-class youths, lower-class young people frequently find it difficult to assimilate certain elements of adult authority and consequently tend to come into scrapes with the law (Kobrin, 1962).

Another area of difference between middle- and lower-class adolescents is how they resolve the conflict between their dependency needs and their need to become independent and acquire autonomy. Middle-class parents, who are likely to be protective and controlling with their children, more readily accept the dependency needs of their adolescents' development and sometimes prolong them through their encouragement. Lower-class parents, however, being less protective and controlling, may facilitate the acquisition of early independence among their youth, especially among their sons (Kobrin, 1962; Straus, 1967).

Lack of parental interest and involvement in their youngsters' problems is also noted to be more common among lower-class parents, although sometimes this pattern exists among middle-class parents as well (Douvan & Adelson, 1966). Such a lack of parental concern, however, may merely reflect the family's struggle and preoccupation in supplying its children with the basic needs of food, shelter, and clothing rather than its indifference toward the other needs of their young people. The reader should keep in mind the fact that all kinds of child-rearing patterns appear in every socioeconomic class. The trends we have been discussing are common ones that can be generally attributed to socioeconomic factors.

Family Mobility

At the turn of the century, a vast majority of Americans were born and reared in a community and stayed to marry, raise their children, and die in that same community, often in the same home as well. In recent years, however, it has been estimated that one out of five families move every year, many of them from one city or town to another (Birren, 1970). This trend toward increased mobility, which has considerable impact on family life, reflects the tendency of business, industry, and the armed forces to transfer their personnel with relative frequency, as well as reflecting the desire of many Americans to seek "greener pastures." Such mobility can be difficult for all members of the family but no more so than for adolescent members, who develop extremely close ties with their peers at this stage (see Chapter 3). In such instances, youthful family members may feel as if they are leaving part of their families behind when they move. And if the moves are too frequent, they will begin to refrain from establishing any new close interpersonal relationships as they move into another strange community. In addition, gaps in their learning often occur, as they transfer from one school to another, where the material may be presented in a different sequence from the school they have just left. Hence, they begin to feel more and more inadequate and insecure, as they find themselves constantly uprooted from their comfortably familiar surroundings.

In one community visited by one of the authors, the members of the local mental health unit reported a common behavior pattern, which they termed "Air Base Syndrome." Among the common symptoms were excessive anxiety, usually noted in the mother but sometimes observed in the children as well. In addition, many parents engaged in sexual promiscuity, the use and abuse of hard drugs, and excessive drinking, while their youngsters tended to display unruly behavior, were difficult to discipline, and were beset with numerous academic problems. Transferred frequently from one military post to another, with the fathers absent from the homes for extended periods of time, the mothers often had to serve as both fathers and mothers to their children, making many parental decisions alone. At the same time, their youngsters were confronted with the problems of adjusting to new schools and to new communities. The impact of such moves, especially during the high school period of adolescence, was noted to be quite traumatic for many young people, sometimes resulting in youths' dropping out of school.

At the same time, it should be pointed out that some adolescents of military families have reported that such mobility has caused their families to become especially close knit, for the families prove to be a major source of stability and security in an otherwise swiftly changing environment.

In certain respects, military service people, who move from one military installation to another, may have an advantage over others who move from one city or town to another. There are usually certain similarities among different military posts, such as similarities in the social structure, that do not necessarily prevail from one community to another in the world at large. Therefore children and adolescents whose fathers are employed in business or industry may experience greater emotional *trauma* if their families are subject to frequent transfer than the offspring of service personnel.

The Broken Home

"The broken home may be defined as one in which one or both parents are not living in the child's family unit; it may be caused by death of one or both parents, divorce, separation or continued absence of one parent whose job demands it" (Horrocks, 1969, p. 217). It may even be a home in which the parents are "living together" but in reality are psychologically separated. However, whether a home is broken by death, divorce, or psychological estrangement, it appears to influence the adolescent's development and behavior. Douvan & Adelson (1966) have noted that the effects of paternal deaths seem to differ from the effects of divorce. According to these investigators, the results of premature loss of the father through death appear to be largely situational. For example, such early losses often create a financial crisis, forcing the adolescent to take on heavy responsibility and to develop precocious seriousness. In other respects, they differ little from youngsters of intact families, however.

On the other hand, Bartlett and Horrocks (1958) have noted that in homes in which one parent is deceased, there tends to be less affection and less recognition both from adults and from peers. It is common for adolescents to try to compensate for this lack by seeking attention from the opposite sex. Individuals from such homes also seem to have fewer friends; apparently the formation of friendships is impeded by the need for these young people to work after school or to care for younger siblings in the home while their mothers work (Douvan & Adelson, 1966).

Among youths from homes broken by divorce, who are reared by their mothers, even more noticeable differences are evident between them and children of intact families, especially among boys (Douvan & Adelson, 1966). Sons from divorced families commonly develop traits of cockiness and overassertiveness, pseudomasculine traits that become almost a caricature of masculinity. At the same time, they find it difficult to internalize controls and to accept authority. They are likely to be "loners," rarely belonging to organized groups and having few close friends. Girls, on the other hand, seem to suffer less visibly from divorce and show problems in fewer areas, although they seldom belong to clubs or engage in leisure-time activities, which may reflect their greater home responsibilities more than psychological difficulties in accepting divorce.

Throughout the United States and Canada it has been customary for mothers to obtain custody unless fathers have been able to substantiate that such placement would result in an environment injurious to the health or morals of the child. Goode (1956) reported on one study of 425 children, in which the mothers were given complete custody in 94.8 percent of the cases, although the fathers were generally granted visitation privileges. Nonetheless visits from the father usually became less frequent with the passing of time, often reflecting limited time and energy, emotional stress, and financial complexities.

Blaine (1966) has suggested that children over 12 years of age should live with the parent of the same sex whenever possible. In view of the impact of the father on the sex-role identification of both sons and daughters, the courts' practice of giving custody of the children of both sexes to the mother in almost all divorce cases perhaps should be questioned.

It has further been suggested that schools make special efforts to place children from broken homes in classes taught by male teachers and that boys be provided with male "tutors" (older high school boys or college students) when they demonstrate a need for extra academic help or masculine emotional support.

Working Mothers

Since World War II, as more and more mothers with children under the age of 18 have gone into the labor force, numerous questions have been raised about the effects of mothers working outside the home on the behavior and development of their children. According to various investigators, the consequences of maternal employment on adolescents have come to depend mainly on four factors: (1) the sex of the adolescent, (2) whether the mother is employed part-time or full-time, (3) the socioeconomic status of the family, and (4) the stability of the family constellation (McCord, McCord, & Thurber, 1963; Douvan & Adelson, 1966).

The employment of the mother, either on a part-time or full-time basis, seems to have a much greater effect on adolescent girls than on adolescent boys (Douvan & Adelson, 1966). Apparently a larger proportion of daughters of working mothers carry heavier household responsibilities than do daughters in homes in which the mothers are not employed.

Generally it appears that daughters of part-time working mothers lead more balanced lives than those of mothers employed full-time. Girls with mothers who work full-time tend to carry a heavy load of responsibility, and as a consequence they report that they participate very little or not at all in clubs or organized groups, engage in few leisure-time activities, and do little reading. In addition, their mothers often have little time to promote and supervise any extracurricular activities for their offspring. In fact, Douvan & Adelson (1966) have suggested that full-time maternal employment may cause a premature separation of adolescent daughters from their parents, as reflected in their tendency to date and go steady early and the minimal amount of time they spend with their families. Conceivably, such behavior may be indicative of the fact that the emotional needs of these young women are not being met at home and must therefore be satisfied elsewhere.

A difference in motivation also appears to distinguish part-time working mothers from those employed full-time. Women working on a part-time basis appear to be less motivated by economic necessity and more inspired by a need for self-fulfillment than do women employed full-time (Douvan & Adelson, 1966). The results of this motivational pattern among mothers employed part-time can be observed in the behavior of their daughters. In addition to a high energy level, which is also quite apparent in the behavior of their mothers, daughters of part-time working mothers tend to show early development of autonomy, independent thinking, and early self-reliance, all behavior traits which their parents seem to encourage. Apparently these daughters rather closely model the behavior of their mothers. In constrast to daughters of mothers employed full-time, these girls also seem to have a closer and happier relationship with their parents. But it is of interest to note that they are not as oriented toward "feminine" interests as girls of mothers working full-time, for they tend to choose more "masculine" vocational goals and more often aspire to upward social mobility.

A third factor in maternal employment, which appears to have some effect on female adolescent behavior, is socioeconomic class. Among the middle class, the development of daughters of mothers employed full-time seems to be quite similar to that of daughters with mothers employed part-time. Girls from both groups exhibit a higher degree of participation in leisure activities and in organized groups and an earlier acquisition of autonomy and self-reliance than do girls of working lower-class mothers or even middle-class girls whose mothers are unemployed (Douvan & Adelson, 1966). In the lower class, however, daughters of mothers working full-time are unlike girls of other working women, for they are more emotionally dependent upon their mothers and less encouraged by their parents to become self-reliant. The daughters may feel neglected and tend to experience deprivation in their family life, probably not as a result of intentional behavior on the part of their mothers but because of the fact that these mothers are often harrassed and overextended in their commitments.

Among lower-class families in which maternal employment is a matter of economic necessity and may therefore reflect unfavorably on the father's role as a family provider, boys are likely to experience certain difficulties, particularly in regard to sex-role identification. Mothers who are employed tend to decrease the status of the fathers, who consequently serve less often as role models, thereby increasing the sexual anxiety of their male offspring (McCord, McCord, & Thurber, 1963). It has also been observed that sons from such backgrounds are more apt to exhibit greater rebellious behavior against adult authority and are likely to show evidence of poorer conscience development than do boys from other environments. They also possess a short time perspective and a low level of energy, hold part-time jobs less frequently than boys from other groups, belong to fewer organized activities, and engage in fewer leisure pastimes (Douvan & Adelson, 1966).

On the other hand, McCord and his colleagues (1963), in a longitudinal study of 140 boys from lower-class families, have suggested that it is not the lower-class background and the working mother that so much determines the effects of maternal employment on the son as the stability of the home. Working mothers from unstable homes tend to increase the dependency of their male offspring and increase their chances of engaging in delinquent behavior. Although all of the youngsters of the study were from a lower socioeconomic class neighborhood, few of the boys reared in stable homes, regardless of the mothers working, had become criminals. Certainly the quality of the relationship between mother and child rather than the quantity of time spent together would partly determine the impact of the mother's working. Perhaps it would be most logical to conclude that if a family is unstable, and if the mother is cold and distant, then maternal employment may increase the possibilities that youths will become delinquents and criminals.

COMMUNITY FACILITIES TO ASSIST PARENTS IN COPING WITH ADOLESCENT PROBLEMS

It has often been said that the peer group serves adolescents as a *reference set* and as a support for common youthful dilemmas or predicaments. On the other hand, parents have generally had no group toward whom they could turn for guidance and reassurance at this period in their children's lives. Often suffering from what might be described as an "adjustment reaction of parenthood," when earlier applied principles of child rearing no longer seem applicable, these parents commonly begin to experience grave doubts about their youngsters and about themselves (Helfat, 1967).

Even though child-guidance material and the mass media may temporarily reassure them that they share numerous problems in common with other parents of adolescents, these aids still fail to provide many parents with support sufficient to withstand the emotional trauma of this period in the lives of their children. To combat this dilemma, a program entitled "The Parents Exchange on Problems of Youth" was set up in Silver Springs, Maryland (Cooper, 1967). Meeting once a week with a professional worker and volunteer mental health aides (all having adolescent youngsters of their own), this group was established to identify areas of concern to parents of youths, elicit information, provide support and reassurance, offer suggestions, and exchange ideas on adolescent and parent mental health issues. In other words, the function of this group was primarily group education, rather than group therapy, for its emphasis was the healthy factors in the personality rather than the deviant, and the parents met to share common problems and experiences.

Helfat (1967), reporting on a discussion group of parents whose children were attending an adolescent outpatient clinic on Long Island, New York, noted that most of the mothers possessed little insight into the nature of the adolescent period. Though they were theoretically aware of the fact that the adolescent period is a time of "growing up," they were not cognizant of the intensity of the conflict experienced by the typical youth in giving up the security of his home and parental support. Gradually, however, as they began to perceive the adolescent's plight with greater sympathy and objectivity, these parents also began to accept their own feelings about no longer being indispensable to their offspring and began to seek other means of self-fulfillment. As they started to acquire insight into the turmoil and stresses of adolescents, they were able to gain support and reassurance from one another. They were also able to recognize that parents are humans and bound to become impatient and intolerant at times no matter how well-meaning they may be and that such reactions do not necessarily indicate a lack of love or concern for their children.

It has also been suggested that exchanges for adolescents be formed (Cooper, 1967). Such groups might appeal to young people and provide them with the opportunity to discuss their problems with their parents and to acquire from professionals and mental health aides (themselves parents of adolescents) another point of view. Hopefully, such groups might ultimately help to narrow the gulf existing today between many young people and their parents.

SUMMARY AND CONCLUSIONS

Despite the denial of many adolescents, parental practices and attitudes continue to assume significant roles throughout the period of adolescence. Numerous factors influence the various child-rearing practices pursued by parents, including the family power structure, the numbers and sex of the children, and the ordinal position, or birth order, of each. Environmental elements, such as socioeconomic class, residential mobility, the broken home, maternal employment, and family stability, also have an impact on parental-adolescent interaction. Siblings, too, contribute to the behavior and development of each individual within the family constellation.

Just as the adolescent needs the support and reassurance of his peer group during this often trying period, it is becoming more evident that parents, too, need the support of others in order to share some of the problems pertaining to their young people and to maintain their confidence in themselves as parents. It has been suggested that discussion groups might be one form of assistance that could be made available to parents of adolescents.

REFERENCES

Altus, W. D. Birth order and its sequelae. *Science*, 1966, **151**, 44-48.

Barclay, A., & Cusumano, D. R. Father absence, cross-sex identity, and field-dependent behavior in male adolescents. *Child Development*, 1967, **38**(1), 243–250.

Bartlett, C. J., & Horrocks, J. E. A study of the needs status of adolescents from broken homes. *The Journal of Genetic Psychology*, 1958, **93**, 153–159.

Bath, J. A., & Lewis, E. C. Attitudes of young female adults toward some areas of parent-adolescent conflict. *The Journal of Genetic Psychology*, 1962, **100**(2), 241–253.

Birren, J. E. The abuse of the urban aged. *Psychology Today*, 1970, **3**(10), 37–38, 76.

Blaine, G. B., Jr. *Youth and the hazards of affluence.* New York: Harper & Row, 1966.

Bossard, J. H. S., & Boll, E. S. Personality roles in the large family. *Child Development*, 1955, **26**(1), 71–78.

Bossard, J. H. S., & Boll, E. S. *The sociology of child development.* New York: Harper & Row, 1960.

Bowerman, C. E., & Elder, G. H., Jr. Variations in adolescent perception of family power structure. *American Sociological Review*, 1964, **29**(4), 551–567.

Bowerman, C. E., & Kinch, J. W. Changes in family and peer orientation of children between the fourth and tenth grades. *Social Forces*, 1959, **37**, 206–211.

Brittain, C. V. Age and sex of siblings and conformity toward parents versus peers in adolescence. *Child Development*, 1966, **37**(3), 709–714.

Brody, J. E. It can be tough to be first-born. *The New York Times*, Sunday, February 18, 1968.

Cooper, M. The parents exchange on problems of youth. *Community Mental Health*, 1967, **3**(4), 355–357.

Douvan, E., & Adelson, J. *The adolescent experience.* New York: John Wiley & Sons, 1966.

Elder, G. H., Jr. Structural variations in the child rearing relationship. *Sociometry*, 1962, **25**(3), 241–262.

Elder, G. H., Jr. Parental power legitimation and its effect on the adolescent. *Sociometry*, 1963, **26**(1), 50–65.

Goode, W. J. *After divorce.* New York: Free Press, 1956.

Granlund, E., & Knowles, L. Child-parent identification and academic underachievement. *Journal of Consulting and Clinical Psychology*, 1969, **33**(4), 495–496.

Grinder, R. E., & Spector, J. C. Sex differences in adolescents' perception of parental resource control. *The Journal of Genetic Psychology*, 1965, **106**(2), 337–344.

Hancock, F. T. An empirical investigation of the relationship of ordinal position, sex, and sex of sibling to socialization, personality, and choice behavior among adolescents in one- and two-child families. *Dissertation Abstracts*, 1967, **28**(2-A), 781–782.

Havighurst, R. J. *Human development and education.* New York: David McKay, 1953.

Heilbrun, A. B., Jr. An empirical test of the modeling theory of sex-role learning. *Child Development*, 1965, **36**, 789–799.

Helfat, L. Parents of adolescents need help too. *New York State Journal of Medicine*, 1967, **67**(20), 2764–2768.

Hollingshead, A. B. *Elmstown youth.* New York: John Wiley & Sons, 1949.

Hollingshead, A. B., & Redlich, F. C. *Social class and mental illness: A community study.* New York: John Wiley & Sons, 1958.

Holtzman, W. H., & Moore, B. M. Family structures and youth attitudes. In M. Sherif & C. W. Sherif (Eds.), *Problems of youth: Transition to adulthood in a changing world.* Chicago: Aldine Publishing, 1965. Pp. 46–61.

Horrocks, J. E. *The psychology of adolescence* (3rd ed.). Boston: Houghton Mifflin, 1969.

Irish, D. P. Sibling interaction: A neglected aspect in family life research. *Social Forces*, 1964, **42**(3), 279–288.

Johnson, M. M. Sex-role learning in the nuclear family. *Child Development*, 1963, **34**, 319–333.

Kandel, D., & Lesser, G. S. Parent-adolescent relationships and adolescent independence in the United States and Denmark. *Journal of Marriage and the Family*, 1969, **31**(2), 348–358.

Kobrin, S. The impact of cultural factors on selected problems of adolescent development in the middle and lower class. *American Journal of Orthopsychiatry*, 1962, **32**, 387–390.

Lynn, D. B. The process of learning parental and sex-role identification. *Journal of Marriage and the Family*, 1966, **28**(4), 466–470.

McArthur, C. Personalities of first and second children. *Psychiatry*, 1956, **19**, 47–54.

McCord, J., McCord, W., & Thurber, E. Effects of maternal employment on lower-class boys. *Journal of Abnormal and Social Psychology*, 1963, **67**(2), 177–182.

Miller, N., & Zimbardo, P. G. Motives for fear-induced affiliation: Emotional comparison or interpersonal similarity? *Journal of Personality*, 1966, **34**(4), 481–503.

Mosby, D. V. P. Maternal "identification" and perceived similarity to parents in adolescents as a function of grade placement. *Dissertation Abstracts*, 1966, **26**(11), 6841.

Packard, V. *The status seekers.* New York: David McKay, 1959.

Parsons, T., & Bales, R. F. *Family, socialization and interaction process.* Glencoe, Ill.: Free Press, 1955.

Peck, R. F. Family patterns correlated with adolescent personality structure. *Journal of Abnormal and Social Psychology*, 1958, **57**, 347–350.

Radloff, R., & Helmreich, R. *Groups under stress: Psychological research in SEALAB II.* New York: Appleton-Century-Crofts, 1968.

Raven, B. H., & French, J. R. P., Jr. Legitimate power, coercive power, and observability in social influence. *Sociometry*, 1958, **21**, 83–97.

Rohrer, J. H., & Edmonson, M. S. *The eighth generation.* New York: Harper & Row, 1960.

Rosen, B. C. Family structure and achievement orientation. *American Sociological Review*, 1961, **26**, 574–585.

Schachter, S. Birth order, eminence and higher education. *American Sociological Review*, 1963, **28**, 757–768.

Sears, R. R., Maccoby, E. E., & Levin, H. *Patterns of child rearing.* New York: Row, Peterson, 1957.

Straus, M. A. Conjugal power structure and adolescent personality. *Marriage and Family Living*, 1962, **24**, 17–25.

Straus, M. A. The influence of sex of child and social class on instrumental and expressive family roles in a laboratory setting. *Sociology and Social Research*, 1967, **52**(1), 7–21.

Sutton-Smith, B., Roberts, J. M., & Rosenberg, B. G. Sibling association and role involvement. *Merrill-Palmer Quarterly of Behavior and Development*, 1964, **10**, 25–38.

Toman, W. *Family constellation.* New York: Springer, 1961.

Toman, W. Birth order rules all. *Psychology Today*, 1970, **4**(7), 45–49.

Warren, J. R. Birth order and social behavior. *Psychological Bulletin*, 1966, **65**(1), 38–49.

3

Adolescent Social Development: Peer Groups and Dating Patterns

The most powerful and the most lasting friendships are usually those of the early season of our lives, when we are most susceptible of warm and affectionate impressions.

William Melmoth (1710–1799)

The socialization process during adolescence assumes an importance second only to that which takes place during infancy. At this time, the last stage of intensive socialization in the approach to maturity takes place. Once adulthood is reached, personality traits are somewhat fixed, and modifications in social behavior become relatively difficult (McGovern, 1967). With adolescence, social development demands that the young person start to free himself from what one psychologist calls the "social incubator" of the family (Nixon, 1962). But like the butterfly emerging from his cocoon, the adolescent is at first unsure of himself and lacks sufficient experience and the perspective of experience to make the leap from the security and warmth of his family to the outside world. In his need to establish independence from his family, to resolve the conflict of who he is and what his roles in life will be, and to establish autonomy, he turns to his peer group.

In brief, the peer group has been defined as ". . . a peripheral subculture of his [the adolescent's] own making, which cherishes values and establishes criteria of status distinct from those of the

63

adult community" (Ausubel, 1954, p. 343). Some psychologists also describe peer groups as reference groups that enable the young person to assess his own problems, drives, and goals (Sherif & Sherif, 1965).

MAJOR FUNCTIONS OF PEER GROUPS

The peer group serves many functions, but probably none is more important than its provision of the kind of environment for growth and acquisition of knowledge about the self that the family is generally unable to offer and that few individuals are capable of finding alone. The peer group also presents opportunities for its members to learn new roles and to revise old ones, thereby enabling them to discover more effective means of functioning in society. When an individual becomes capable in a given role, he may frequently transfer his newly discovered knowledge from one group to another (Horrocks & Benimoff, 1966; McGovern, 1967). For example, a youth who becomes a leader in his own crowd may acquire skills that will enable him to become a leader in other groups, such as his high school student council.

Through his membership in a peer group, the young person also acquires a certain status. All peer groups become distinctive in their dress, their language, their loyalty and dependability, and in their participation in extracurricular activities at school, as well as in other pursuits. In turn, individuals are generally classified according to the group in which they are members (Hollingshead, 1949). It is through the adoption of such symbols of peer-group status that adolescents begin to acquire their own identity separate from that of "child" in the family.

The peer group further facilitates the adolescent's emancipation from his family by helping him to balance his ambivalent needs for independence and dependency. In a group of his contemporaries, where he is more likely to be treated as an equal, he can begin to move out of the subordinate position he is likely to hold in his relationships with adults (McGovern, 1967). Thus, the peer group can provide young people with an instrument for bargaining with adults. Through the support of their friends they can often gain privileges already held by other members of the group. When an adolescent daughter tells her mother that all of the girls in her crowd can stay out with their dates until midnight, it puts considerable pressure on her parent to reconsider her restrictions. However, Blos (1967) points out that if peer-group relationships merely replace childhood dependencies and fail to provide for growth and development, then they are not fulfilling their proper functions.

The development of a social, personal, and sexual identity, known as the process of *individuation,* is facilitated by membership in a peer group (Blos, 1967). Friends can help a young person acquire a clear, stable identity in several ways: (1) they assist the adolescent in resolving his conflicts within himself and with others; (2) they teach him respect for competence, (presumably social competence) which is necessary for the acquisition of maturity and autonomy; and (3) they are a source of feedback to the individual about his personality and behavior, thereby enabling him to assess his own development and modify his actions when necessary (McGovern, 1967).

Doris, who was somewhat shy, rather tall, and relatively attractive, was a "loner" in the ninth and tenth grades. In her junior year, she entered a new high school, where she was accepted by a small group of girls. In their company she became more careful about her appearance and her grooming. Formerly heavy in her stride, she started to walk more gracefully. With her new friends, her latent vivaciousness and love of fun began to emerge. She also learned to play a guitar with considerable skill and soon found herself in frequent demand to perform at various social functions. Before long, the boys who had almost ignored her until this time, began to show an interest in her, and she started dating fairly regularly. Undoubtedly, her new friends played a major role in Doris' development of poise and social skills, thereby assisting her in the process of individuation.

The peer group is also one of the primary sources of sex education, for peers can often provide information on topics likely to be avoided by adults (McGovern, 1967). His contemporaries can also help an adolescent prepare to make decisions about premarital sexual activities and about marriage itself; the peer group provides a setting in which young people can try out various *psychosexual* and sociosexual roles. In addition, the peer group develops its own norms of sexual behavior, which generally serve as guidelines for individual behavior.

Participation in many group recreational activities is facilitated for the adolescent if he belongs to a peer group. Such activities are usually informal, relatively inexpensive, and unsupervised by adults (Horrocks & Benimoff, 1966). Adolescent pursuits can range from endless discussions and just "fooling around" to attending spectator sports, dances, movies, and rock concerts or participating in peace marches, "rap" sessions, and other political efforts. These activities are important to the adolescent's social development, because they offer opportunities to develop leadership and autonomy, to test oneself socially, and to establish one's own set of values.

Peer-Group Communication

Without a doubt, one of the most common and most time-consuming activities of adolescence is just plain talk, otherwise known as a "gab fest" or "bull session." Such "rap sessions" first take place in the context of *unisexual* peer groups—those made up of all girls or all boys.

Sometimes a peer relationship may serve no other purpose than that of a sounding board, wherein one member serves primarily as a listener (Douvan & Adelson, 1966). At other times, it provides a two-way street for the exchange of ideas, thoughts, and feelings. In reality, the never-ending conversations of young people are actually practice sessions in the skills needed for successful social interaction among well-adjusted adults. The results of failure to engage in frequent conversations can often be seen in orphanages and corrective institutions and among low socioeconomic groups (Staton, 1963). One of the authors recently observed several classes of students in a high school located in a slum area. Quite evident among a majority of the students was a lack of verbal facility, possibly reflecting limited conversation in the home and a fear of ridicule and rejection for verbal ineptitude. Such lack of practice in conversational skills often results in retarded intellectual and social development.

The peer group seems to have a language all of its own, a language which tends to change to some extent with each succeeding generation. Such verbalization not only enables members of the group to communicate with one another, but it also provides a barrier that excludes outsiders. Thus, the common language creates a feeling of group identity, a sense of belonging, and a degree of status (McGovern, 1967).

Perhaps the adolescent idioms of today are more descriptive and more earthy than those of past generations. Some of the current terms used openly in the presence of adults would have caused more than raised eyebrows two or three decades ago. Undoubtedly, much of this idiomatic language reflects the impact of our mass media, recent news, and technological advances. In addition, the former tendency to protect women has lost much of its force, and many frank terms for drinking, lovemaking, and other activities are expressed just as readily by girls as by boys in our present society. But in any case, adolescent language is a natural outgrowth of the world in which young people live and is possibly a vital factor in helping to keep the English language alive. The White House Conference in 1950 concluded that not only are social skills developed by lengthy adolescent conversations but also greater insight into how others think and feel, thereby enabling young people to develop a more complete sense of self-identity (Midcentury White House Conference on Children and Youth, 1951).

Since the invention of the telephone, adolescents have been known to tie up the lines for several hours at a time. Although few parents are enthusiastic about the practice, it is likely that telephone conversations serve many of the same purposes as face-to-face talk sessions. The adolescent is learning to express his ideas, determine their effect on others, gauge the meaning of what his peers are saying, and evaluate the significance of ideas left unsaid or incomplete.

PEER-GROUP STRUCTURES

There are basically two major types of peer groups—cliques and crowds—with the main determining factor being the size of the group.

Cliques

Cliques are generally smaller than crowds, ranging anywhere from two to nine members, with the mode of such groups being five. Hollingshead (1949) offers the following definition: "A clique comes into existence when two or more persons are related one to another in an intimate fellowship that involves 'going places and doing things' together, a mutual exchange of ideas, and the acceptance of each personality by the others" (p. 205).

Cliques tend to be of a "closed" nature—that is, they have an "elite" membership and generally forbid entrance by "outsiders." Usually, cliques can be defined as one of three types: (1) school cliques, (2) recreational cliques, or (3) institutional cliques, such as church youth groups (Hollingshead, 1949). During early adolescence they are always unisexual in nature, but according to Dunphy (1963), a transformation in structure may take place with the middle-adolescent period, at which time many cliques tend to become heterosexual.

An interesting study of school cliques conducted in Sydney, Australia, between 1958 and 1960 uncovered 44 cliques among a total of 303 predominantly middle-class boys and girls, who were about equally divided in number and ranged in age from 13 to 21. The small size of these cliques—they had an average of 6.2 members—reflected the intimate relationships of the group, which was also characterized by a strong cohesiveness (Dunphy, 1963). Perhaps it is no coincidence that the clique tends to compare in size with the average family, a fact that may help to explain the ready transfer of adolescent allegiance from family to peer group.

Such cliques are generally composed of members of the same socioeconomic class or of adjacent classes and tend to be limited to those in the same grade level at school. Membership is voluntary but dependent upon the acceptance of other group members and terminated by the mutual consent of these same group participants. Members usually have a common set of values, interests, tastes, and moral standards, which tends to allow for considerable intolerance and contempt for those who are different. However, a moderate amount of difference can add to the dynamics of the group, as Douvan and Adelson (1966) suggest: "Qualities of personality must vary between friends enough to give the relation the zest, tension, and enrichment that comes out of differences" (p. 184). Should such conflict become too severe and become the group's *raison d'être*, the clique may then evolve into a gang (Hollingshead, 1949).

However, it should be noted that there are several major differences between a clique and a gang: (1) While a clique is relatively small, a gang may number into the hundreds through an interlocking membership. (2) A clique is less formal and less organized than a gang, which usually has a formal leadership, stated functions and goals, and regular times or places for assembling. (3) A clique is likely to be a middle-class group that reflects middle-class values, whereas a gang is apt to reflect the lower-class culture, especially the delinquent subculture. (See Chapter 7.) (4) A clique prefers social and recreational activities, whereas a gang tends to engage in antisocial or deviant behavior. (5) Both groups demand certain standards of behavior from their members and place certain sanctions on them, but a clique uses manipulation and control, avoidance or rejection, and constructive criticism, whereas the gang tends to resort to physical coercion (McGovern, 1967).

Crowds

The average crowd is considerably larger than the average clique. In his study of the Australian students cited earlier, Dunphy (1963) noted that there were 12 crowds among the 303 subjects, with the size varying from 15 to 30 members and average membership being 20.2. He concluded that a crowd is basically "an association of cliques," with the average crowd being composed of 3.1 cliques but ranging in number from no more than 4 cliques to no less than 2. At the same time, he observed that not all cliques were associated with crowds. However, clique membership appeared to be a necessary prerequisite for membership in the crowd; in no case did a person belong to a crowd without concurrently being a member of a clique.

The large size of the crowd prevents the formation of intimate relationships, and members tend to regard each other as "acceptable associates" rather than as "real buddies." The functions of the crowd also tend to differ from those of the clique. Whereas a clique tends to be preoccupied with conversation and communication, a crowd is more concerned with organized social activities like parties and dances, which tend to take place on weekends in contrast to clique functions, which are most likely to occur during the week (Dunphy, 1963).

Membership in a crowd does offer one very important benefit not generally available from membership in a clique. It provides a means of transition from puberty to courtship, permitting progress from unisexual to heterosexual relationships through inter-clique activities that allow group members to practice new roles in a heterosexual setting (McGovern, 1967).

FACTORS AFFECTING PEER-GROUP MEMBERSHIP

It is generally agreed that adolescents must develop an increasing ability to get along with their peers if their personal and social adjustment is to be adequate (Bowerman & Kinch, 1959). According to McGovern (1967), getting along requires that adolescents conform to a certain extent to the social values of the group, that they possess a sufficient number of common interests, and that they come from similar socioeconomic backgrounds. Of course, the emphasis on compliance can become so strong that group members almost seem to be prisoners of group norms, depending on them for advice in how to dress, how to talk and what to do, and even what to think and believe (Douvan & Adelson, 1966). Staton (1963) suggests that this kind of conformity reflects the tremendous insecurity of youths who are trying to adjust to a strange and fearsome, yet often delightful, social structure, a structure which is easily subject to change. But such conformity is by no means limited to young people; many adults also exhibit a high degree of conformity, reflecting their own uneasiness and anxiety about the rapid changes with which they must also contend in today's world.

Among girls in middle adolescence, those who possess such personality traits as sensitivity, warmth, tact, and sympathy are the ones most likely to prove acceptable as friends to other girls. During this period girls seek like-sexed peers who will provide understanding and emotional support during their inevitable trials, discoveries, and despairs. At this time, the investment in unisexual friendships is so great that to lose a friend through disloyalty or through mobility is almost like losing a part of the self and can indeed be a painful experience (Douvan & Adelson, 1966).

In his study of ten Midwestern high schools in the United States, Coleman (1961) notes that athletic accomplishments appear to be important in adolescent boys' attainment of status and acceptance. He suggests that athletes visibly lead their teams to victory for their schools and for their communities. This visibility is not true of outstanding scholars, who have few means of bringing glory to their schools since their achievements are basically personal and sometimes attained through competition at the expense of their peers. Those who acquire the greatest status and acceptance appear to be students who are actively engaged in visible activities which they are able to call their own. In addition to athletics, visible functions would include active participation on school newspapers, in drama clubs, and in social affairs. Scholars who are not engaged in any of these activities generally fill rather passive roles.

A study by Horowitz (1967) supports Coleman's findings but produces the additional finding that a combination of athlete and scholar is the most popular selection of all. The results of three studies reported by Friesen (1968) dispute those cited above. Approximately 15,000 students from 19 public high schools in an eastern Canadian city, a large western Canadian city, and a central Canadian urban and rural area participated in the research. The 10,019 subjects who participated in one study reported that the traits that would gain acceptance by the most elite group were friendliness (51.3 percent), good looks (25.4 percent), money (13.8 percent), athletic ability (7.0 percent), and academic excellence (2.5 percent). These same 10,019 subjects felt that popularity was determined by the following criteria: membership in the leading crowd (64.3 percent), athletic stardom (18.7 percent), possession of a nice car (12.7 percent), and academic excellence (4.2 percent). Interestingly, however, in all three studies students wanted most to be known as outstanding scholars, a choice far ahead of their desire for athletic recognition. Apparently, those selecting athletic success as most important recognize that it can provide immediate gratification, especially among the peer group, but that it has little value for the future. From the results of these three studies, it appears that the enduring respected values for boys are (1) academic achievement, (2) athletic prowess, and (3) popularity, and for girls (1) academic achievement, (2) popularity, and (3) athletic ability.

In summary, Friesen makes three important observations: (1) Young people fail to give adequate support to academic excellence and give most visible recognition to star athletes. (2) Athletic achievement is actually only attained by a very small group. (3) Though popularity is desired by most students, only about 25 percent claimed to be in the elite crowd, only 22.6 percent had been elected to any type of leadership during their junior or senior years of high school, 28 percent expressed concern about being accepted and liked, and 28 percent never socialized with their peers.

The results of these various studies suggest that there is room for greater recognition of academic excellence. Some have suggested that letters be given for scholastic achievement as well as for athletic performance. Rallies, in which outstanding students participate in teams against scholarly teams from other schools, might be another means of extending recognition to outstanding academic performance, which could also enable scholars to bring glory to their schools.

In every school there are some students who may be described as popular and toward whom classmates just seem to gravitate. At the other end of the continuum are those to whom no one seems to pay much attention, youths who might be called "loners" or social isolates. Most young people tend to fall somewhere between these two extremes. Of course, the factors contributing to social acceptance in one school might not be the same as those of another school. Nonetheless, there are certain personality traits, such as friendliness, enthusiasm, and cheerfulness, which seem to be partly responsible for the acquisition of popularity at least among youths of middle-class society.

At one time or another, many adolescents experience social rejection by their peer group. Dunphy (1963) found that an adolescent could be rejected if he ignored the authority of the group or if he failed to keep up with his peers in dating. Horrocks and Benimoff (1966) also found that some adolescents are never accepted by their peers. On two occasions one year apart they administered a *sociometric* questionnaire to the entire population of students enrolled in junior high school and high school in a midwestern community of about 10,000. The students were asked to list the names of their best friends. On the first occasion, about one seventh, or 102 of 749 students, were chosen by no one. On the second sociometric questionnaire, this figure rose to about one fourth, or 157 of 549 students. In comparing the responses to both questionnaires, it was noted that 24 adolescents were not selected at either rating period.

Ausubel (1954) has classified adolescents who experience social rejection into three main groups: (1) those who are socially unacceptable to their peers because they possess personality traits, physical characteristics, or interests that are unacceptable to the group; (2) young people who themselves reject the peer group because they find it emotionally disturbing, or unrewarding, possibly because they lack certain necessary social skills or have deviant personality traits; and (3) youths who are neither accepted nor rejected by the group but who demonstrate a strong interest in other activities, which they prefer to pursue, even at the risk of peer-group rejection. For example, a young person interested in a career as a pianist might be willing to forego social contacts in order to devote his free time to practicing the piano. Conceivably, all three situations might apply to the same individual. A young person might be rejected by the group because of undesirable personality traits, such as excessive bragging about his family's social status, as a result withdraw from engaging in any social interaction with the group because of his failure to acquire the necessary social skills, and then turn to the piano in an effort to compensate for his status as a social reject.

As the study of Horrocks and Benimoff (1966) pointed out, however, a youth accepted by his peers at one time might later find himself rejected, or conversely, one rejected during an early stage of social development may later be accepted. The group norms may change as the group gets older, and behavior once accepted may no longer be approved. For instance, the boy who becomes popular through his clowning during the early teen years may later find himself rejected for the same behavior. Or the girl who does not start to date when many of her friends do may have little in common with them and consequently face rejection, yet later be reaccepted into the group when she begins dating.

Although some adolescents prefer to go their own way, many young people become quite unhappy when they are not accepted by their peers. Social rejection can impair their ability to learn, as well as their emotional adjustment. Consequently, there is a strong argument for schools to provide counseling services that can help the adolescent come to terms with some of the problems that make it difficult for him to relate to his peers. Such counseling can enable him to modify such personality traits as lack of concern for others, tactlessness, or excessive timidity. Encouragement from an empathetic counselor can also give some adolescents the boost they need to participate in extracurricular activities that can help them become more visible and more accessible to their classmates.

Peer-Group Leadership

Dunphy (1963), in his field study of adolescent peer groups, noted that although they usually deny the presence of a group leader, group members implicitly accept one member in a leadership role. A clique leader usually represents his group to those outside it, he cooperates with other cliques, and he plays a larger role in decision making than do other group members. He generally becomes better known to the members of other groups than his followers, and the group is often identified by his name as his group. The clique leader occupies a position in which he can impart the wishes and ideas of his followers to those of other cliques (who may be in the same crowd) which gives him a degree of power and status.

Crowd leaders, on the other hand, appear to occupy a coordinating, integrating position, are inevitably males, and generally serve also as leaders of the largest, most heterosexually advanced clique in the crowd. Holding a role superior to that of other clique leaders, a leader of the crowd can exercise considerable influence over other clique leaders (Dunphy, 1963).

Certain traits seem to be deemed necessary for skillful leadership by group members. Certainly the leader of a crowd must possess sufficient organizational skill to coordinate the activities of different cliques. Dunphy (1963) also observed that crowd leaders are generally more advanced in their heterosexual social development; they date more frequently, go steady more often, and go steady earlier than other crowd members. In addition, they tend to serve as confidants and counselors in matters of heterosexual problems and exert considerable pressure in encouraging their followers to attain more mature development in their heterosexual relationships.

Popularity and leadership are not necessarily synonymous. An adolescent may be very popular and well liked, but this fact does not inevitably insure that he will be accepted as a leader. At the same time, it is unlikely that a leader could remain unpopular and disliked for any period of time and still retain his position of leadership (Ausubel, 1954).

Leadership among youth is often rather tenuous and easily subject to the whims and desires of group members (Staton, 1963). Sometimes the needs and goals of the group change and demand new leadership. At other times, although a leader may occasionally be less conforming to group norms than his followers, he may do something that seriously displeases his peers and interferes with the attainment of certain group aims and thereby find himself replaced by another member as group leader (Wiggins, Dill, & Schwartz, 1965).

DOES A PEER-GROUP CULTURE REALLY EXIST?

In recent years one of the most controversial issues in the area of adolescent social development has been the question of whether or not there is a genuine peer-group culture. As early as 1942, Parsons (1954) claimed that there was a youth culture unique to the United States. He described its characteristics as irresponsible behavior with heavy emphasis on "having a good time," much heterosexual socializing, and reluctance to comply with adult norms and demands. Elkin and Westley (1955), however, maintained that the youth culture was subject to control by parents and that it was marked by acceptance of parental values. They felt that unique interests, language, and customs among adolescents do exist but that the stereotype of a youth culture is erroneous, at least in terms of middle-class society. They disagreed with the idea that adolescent needs for independence and security inevitably lead to the development of an adolescent culture.

In a study of adolescents and their parents from a suburban, well-to-do, upper-middle-class Montreal, Quebec, community Elkin and Westley (1955) observed that one dominant pattern emerged. Most adolescent activities appeared to be directed and approved by adults and generally to take place within the community in view of adults. In other words, the young people had little unstructured, unsupervised time, and much of their recreation and entertaining was in many respects similar to that of the older generation. The authors also pointed out that many youths in this community learn to forego immediate gratification of their desires for future goals—a pattern of behavior which they felt was contradictory to the views of the youth-culture advocates. Consequently, they concluded that the adolescent peer culture was a myth. However, it should be noted that this study, which dates back to the mid-1950s, dealt primarily with a select segment of society, and it may no longer be characteristic even of this group.

More recently, Coleman (1961), Smith (1962), and McGovern (1967) have observed that a distinct youth culture does exist, which is relatively independent of parental control and generally in conflict rather than in harmony with adult society. Coleman states that the ". . . setting-apart of our children in schools—which take on ever more functions, ever more 'extracurricular activities'—for an ever longer period of training has a singular impact on the child of high school age. He is 'cut off' from the rest of society, forced inward toward his own age group, made to carry out his whole social life with others his own age. With his fellows, he comes to constitute a small society, one that has most of its important interactions *within* itself, and maintains only a few threads of connection with the outside adult society" (p. 3). And Smith points out that "The autonomy of youth culture has been verified by the setting up of norms, which, although they change from institution to institution, in all cases dominate and pattern youth behavior" (p. 218).

There is a more middle-of-the-road approach expressed by several social scientists (Bealer, Willits, & Maida, 1964; Epperson, 1964; Snyder, 1966; Brittain, 1967). They suggest that adolescents possess multiple loyalties, which vary according to the situation. The fact that young people physically withdraw from many family functions in preference for peer-group activities does not necessarily imply a rejection of parental norms. They also note that society tends to concentrate on the "idiosyncratic aspects of adolescent behavior" (Bealer et al., 1964) and thereby overlooks the similarity in values that does exist between the two generations. Too often, investigators have assumed that conflict occurs between parents and their children in all areas because of differences in some.

Various studies by Brittain (1963; 1967) indicate that young individuals are inclined to turn to those whom they believe will provide them with the most competent advice, and they perceive their peers and their parents as being competent in different areas. They appear to adhere to peer-oriented counsel in social values which are subject to rapid change and where they can anticipate immediate consequences rather than long-range effects. For example, they would probably rely on their friends in regard to matters of taste in dress, while they would be likely to consult their parents on such issues as whether or not to work part-time while attending school or on matters involving important, difficult decisions, such as what college to attend.

DATING AND COURTSHIP

People tend to regard dating and courtship as different terms for the same process. Actually, the practice of courtship dates back many centuries and is an adult-oriented pattern of behavior whose ultimate goal is marriage, whereas dating, which is a relatively recent American phenomenon, is geared to present needs and desires and has no long-range aims. Although it is true that dating tends to go along with courtship as well as chronologically precede it, the date is basically an end in itself; it fills in the period of prolonged adolescence with heterosexual relationships (Smith, 1962; Rogers, 1969).

Dating is actually an American institution, which was first introduced in our cities among college students in the 1920s. It reflected the new female emancipation, the increase in the amount of leisure time, the greater freedom available to young people, higher standards of living, greatly expanded commercial recreation, and the widespread development of coeducational institutions. With the late 1930s and early 1940s, dating activities emerged at the high school level (Burchinal, 1969), and today we see junior high school youths emulating the dating patterns of their older brothers and sisters. Dating is still relatively unique to the United States and Canada, for most contemporary nations and cultures offer no comparable phenomenon (Smith, 1962).

Adolescent Dating Patterns

Of all of the adolescent institutions, dating tends to vary the most from adult norms, as Smith (1962) points out: "Romantic love is least relevant during dating, although it simulates romantic love by using its language devoid of 'meaning' " (pp. 147–148). Surprisingly, it is often the parents who unknowingly perpetuate the idealization of romance by their belief in the myth that romance will "change all" (Cervantes, 1965). They tend to regard dating as a romantic pastime, whereas their adolescent offspring, although they may describe their dating in romantic terms, tend to view it primarily as engaging in fun and having a good time. Until the early sixties, sex taboos were rather rigorously enforced during adolescent dating and were relaxed only as youth approached marriage or in cases of exploitative dating by upper- and middle-class boys with lower-class girls.

Two different dating patterns can usually be distinguished among today's American youth: competitive dating and noncommitment steady dating. The first pattern involves a frequent change of dating partners with no emotional involvement, while the second involves dating only one person at a time (Smith, 1962).

Young people from the middle and upper classes tend to date more widely and more frequently than do those from the lower classes, reflecting the tendency of the higher socioeconomic classes to postpone any serious commitments, such as marriage, until the individual has reached sufficient maturity to handle the economic and social responsibilities demanded by such a commitment.

However, it should be noted that the motivation for dating tends to differ according to sex. Girls seem to date more frequently with an eye toward marriage and are more likely to become emotionally entangled. Boys, on the other hand, are more often motivated by recreational interests and are less apt to become deeply involved (Skipper & Nass, 1966). It is quite possible that many girls perceive dating as a means to marriage more often than do boys, since, traditionally, their socioeconomic future and their life chances will be mainly determined by their husbands (Coombs & Kenkel, 1966).

Some psychologists believe that initial dating is motivated primarily by a desire for companionship rather than by sexual attraction (McKinney, 1960). Other psychologists feel that there is an element of sexual attraction underlying every adolescent heterosexual relationship. But it is apparent in many adolescent friendships that young people relate to each other as individuals regardless of the sex of their companion (Staton, 1963).

Primary Functions of Dating

Although current American dating patterns possess many negative aspects which will be discussed shortly, dating does serve a number of positive functions. Certainly, it provides an easier, less abrupt transition from unisexual to heterosexual relationships than courtship alone would be likely to afford (Burchinal, 1969). It supplies an opportunity for the adolescent to establish and test his psychosexual role. Dating also offers numerous occasions for young people to learn many of the social graces demanded by adult society. It presents circumstances favorable for youth to engage in various sexual experiences and discovery. It provides an assessment of one's popularity and social success. Perhaps most important of all, it offers a combination of circumstances conducive to developing a love relationship and ultimately finding a mate (Skipper & Nass, 1966).

Problems in Dating

While serving many useful functions, adolescent dating does present a variety of problems, such as when to begin, the problems of the delayed dater or nondater, going steady, and the inadequacies of dating as a preparation for marriage. Many young people are exceedingly unhappy in their social relationships, and there is a need to take a serious look at some of the difficulties that are caused or exacerbated by dating norms and expectations.

Early Dating

During the past quarter of a century, young people have begun dating at an earlier and earlier age (Morgenstern, 1961; O'Dwyer, McAllister, & Davis, 1967). A study by Kuhlen and Houlihan (1965) compared heterosexual interest in 1942 with that in 1963. They noted that there is a greater display of heterosexual interest during grades six to twelve, with boys being a bit less reticent than they were a generation ago.

Several psychologists have expressed considerable concern over the trend toward earlier dating (Morgenstern, 1961; Douvan & Adelson, 1966; O'Dwyer et al., 1967). These social scientists feel that an early dating pattern can have many unfortunate consequences. Early daters, especially among girls, seem to become socially precocious, showing early development of pseudosophisticated versions of such social traits as poise and nonchalance, while at the same time lagging in their psychosexual development. Precocious dating tends to bring a premature ending to childhood and to force young people to try to behave like an adult before they are ready. There are often gaps left in their development, and the formation of deeper character traits, such as the postponement of immediate gratification for long-range goals, is often hindered. Early dating can also lead to premature "steady" relationships, an overemphasis on sex, and frequent, often unfortunate teenage marriages. (See Chapter 8.)

Numerous explanations have been offered for this trend in early dating: (1) There is too much emphasis on sex and romance, especially by the mass media. (2) There is a strong desire for success in our competitive society; during the adolescent period success is gauged by the attainment of popularity. (3) There is considerable peer-group pressure for individuals to conform to certain norms of heterosexual activity. (4) There is excessive permissiveness among many parents, who are reluctant to say "no" and find it difficult to apply sensible limits to the behavior of their children. (5) Many mothers try to experience vicarious pleasures through their daughters, who they often fear will not achieve popularity (Morgenstern, 1961; O'Dwyer et al., 1967).[1]

Solutions to this problem of premature dating lie both with parents and with educators. Parents can demonstrate their love and affection by offering their time and attention and by serving as models for desirable behavior. Mothers and fathers can also set definite limits on behavior accompanied by logical reasons for such limits and can thus help their young people to accept certain responsibilities along with their acquisition of certain privileges. At the same time, parents can help by attempting to understand the problems of adolescents and by providing a sympathetic outlet for young people to safely verbalize their fears and anxieties without being ridiculed or criticized (O'Dwyer et al., 1967).

The fact that early dating and teen-age marriages are so much more prevalent in America than in Western Europe poses some interesting questions for educators. Young people in these other countries begin to date later, possibly because they attend separate schools for boys and for girls and therefore have less opportunity for heterosexual relationships. In fact, Blos (1971) has suggested we consider separating the two sexes during the early adolescent years, the years from 11 to 14. This is the period when boys tend to lag behind girls in their physical and social maturation and girls, in turn, often appear to push boys into opposite-sexed social activities for which they are not yet ready and for which they have little interest. It is yet to be proved whether such separation would delay the onset of initial dating, delay the practice of "going steady," and postpone many premature marriages, as well as whether it would be beneficial to the adolescents' social development.

---

[1]One of the authors recalls very clearly the case of a mother, who herself had married at the age of 17. With considerable concern in her voice, she related how her daughter, Ellen, aged 11½, had been invited to a dance, which she attended, at her mother's insistence, with considerable reluctance. The mother concluded her story with an expression of bewilderment at Ellen's lack of interest in boys. One could speculate about how the mother's attitude might have been different had her own social development been less precocious and had she had less need for vicarious satisfaction through her daughter's social life.

But if educators are going to continue the present practice of heterosexual classes during this period of early adolescence, there are still ways in which they might be able to discourage too early dating. They could offer social activities that involve group associations of both sexes, such as square dancing or bowling, and discourage twosome dating. The school curriculum could be set up in such a manner as to encourage maximum interaction between the two sexes through coeducational physical education and homemaking courses, through mixed-group projects, and through class discussions on topics of concern to both boys and girls. Through such intermingling, boys and girls might gain a better understanding of each other, while the aura of glamour and romance could be minimized with such close contact, a situation somewhat comparable to coeducational dormitory living on many college campuses today. Educators can also provide parents with pertinent material on topics such as "going steady" and work together with them to establish a practical set of codes for adolescent behavior (Morgenstern, 1961).

The Late Dater or Nondater

It should be noted that the norm for initial dating may vary according to several factors. It may differ from one geographic area to another with those from urban communities usually beginning to date earlier than those from rural areas (Burchinal, 1969). It will vary according to socioeconomic level. Young people from the lower classes generally begin dating sooner than those from the middle and upper classes. Variations in the onset of dating can also be seen according to educational level. School dropouts are likely to start dating at an earlier age than those who continue their education (Cervantes, 1965).

But regardless of these differences, those who do not begin to date at the time considered appropriate to their background are likely to suffer from several unfortunate social and emotional consequences. The late dater, the one who does not begin to date by the age of 16 or thereabouts, or the nondater is likely to become anxious and to develop feelings of isolation. The adolescent may feel he or she is missing certain crucial experiences afforded by the dating institution and may even experience difficulty in finding like-sexed friendships, especially of his or her own age. Social life will tend to be minimal, thereby retarding the youth's social maturation. Late dating may also cause the adolescent to remain more dependent on his family (Douvan & Adelson, 1966).

There are several plausible explanations for the failure of young people to begin dating at the usual time. Extensive research among nondating girls by Douvan and Adelson (1966) disclosed that they were socially immature, with little awareness of a boy's needs or how to demonstrate sensitivity and an understanding of others. They had no concept of what is involved in a stable, loyal, trusting hetero-sexual friendship. They were oblivious to the fact that young people tend to seek those who make them feel more secure and adequate, those who help enhance their self-concept (Staton, 1963). These girls tended to have distorted ideas about what traits lead to popularity, believing only good looks and social facility to be important. They were usually quite self-conscious, egocentric, lacking in confidence, and they lacked a sense of humor. They engaged in few extracurricular activities, organized social groups, or leisure-time recreation. They were generally just as attractive as those who dated, but they did tend to display fewer traits of femininity. Sometimes their delay in dating may have reflected a disturbed family situation or an over-dependence on their families (Douvan & Adelson, 1966).

If such late daters or nondaters display deviant behavior patterns or seem very unhappy about their lack of dates, they could probably benefit from counseling by sympathetic adults. Since parents are too likely to be emotionally involved with their children's failure to date, understanding teachers and young adults, who are not too remote from the problems of adolescence, often prove effective in working with these young people.

Going Steady

There are probably few adolescent social patterns that create more conflict between the generations than the widespread practice of going steady. According to Cervantes (1965), "Going steady is the heterosexual interaction pattern that is presently institutionalized throughout the whole span of the youth culture. From grade school through graduate school it seems to be the dating 'ideal' " (p. 168). Going steady usually involves a commitment not to date others and a degree of emotional involvement that is described as being "in love." It has been estimated that the proportion of eleventh- and twelfth-grade students who go steady at any given time varies from about 20 percent to 33 percent. By the time they have graduated from high school, between 50 and 75 percent of all students will have pursued this pattern of dating at some time during their high school days (Reiss, 1961; Broderick, 1967).

Definite arguments both favoring and rejecting this practice have been presented. Certainly, going steady does provide a degree of security and relative freedom from the fear of competition (Reiss, 1961). Going steady does ease conversation and other social interaction and eliminates the need for frequent adjustment to the new, unfamiliar habits and attitudes of many different dates. Whether this is entirely advantageous is debatable, however, for it often appears to be stultifying to the young person's social development (Staton, 1963). Steady dating also facilitates the association of sex and affection, which is less likely to develop in casual dating (Rogers, 1969). Many girls tend to believe that sexual behavior becomes more respectable when one goes steady and that under such circumstances it is easier to protect one's reputation (Ehrmann, 1959).

At the same time, particularly during early and middle adolescence, there are several arguments against the practice of going steady, which was once described as a "demi-marriage" in words, if not in deeds (*Newsweek*, March 21, 1966). Parents especially tend to disapprove of this dating pattern, because they feel it interferes with boys and girls getting to know all kinds of people. They also fear that it will lead to excessive sexual intimacy and/or to early marriage. Teachers, too, appear to condemn this dating pattern, for they often believe that scholastic interests are subordinated and that discipline problems arise as a result. Frequently, youths who go steady separate themselves from their peers and from group activities (Staton, 1963).

It should also be noted that although many young adolescents in the sixth, seventh, and eighth grades may describe themselves as going steady, the term may describe no more than walking home from school with the same partner day after day and conversing with him nightly on the telephone. According to Douvan and Adelson (1966), those adolescents in their early teens who form a serious, stable, exclusive association with one partner are likely to be quite socially immature and possess poorly formed concepts of unisexual friendships as well as of heterosexual relationships. For girls, going steady with one boy tends to remove them from associations with other girls as well as with other boys. They are likely to have misconceptions about friendship and popularity with other girls and often fail to acquire an awareness of the need for such traits as trust, confidence, and sharing. They experience a gap in their social development when they forego intimate like-sexed relationships which are necessary for the development of a strong identity and the formation of a full capacity for genuine object love. In other words, a girl's relationship with her steady is likely to be a relatively superficial one because she has not had the opportunity of learning genuine affection through unisexual friendships. Although she may be more poised and self-confident than girls who do not go steady during this early adolescent period, she tends to possess little interest in personal achievement and in education while demonstrating a strong interest in adult feminine goals, which include those of being a wife, homemaker, and mother (Douvan & Adelson, 1966).

This preoccupation with feminine goals may help to explain the relationship of early steady dating to teenage marriages. Broderick (1967) has described going steady as the "beginning of the end." He feels that this dating pattern leads to a social and emotional commitment, through which youths often slip and slide into marriage. He notes that about 80 percent of steady couples have given some serious consideration to marriage and about 40 percent have informally agreed to marry. And the longer two people go steadily together, the more likely they are to announce their intention to marry, with over one half expecting to marry each other after one year of going steady. If such steady dating begins in early or middle adolescence, it is not surprising that there is such a high incidence of teenage marriages. (See Chapter 8.)

At the same time, it should be pointed out that a socioeconomic class distinction does exist. Among those in high school who go steady and plan on attending college, few will be likely to marry their high school sweethearts. On the other hand, those who drop out of school or who terminate their education with graduation from high school are much more likely to marry their high school partners (Cervantes, 1965). Apparently those who defer marriage are willing to endure other delayed gratification, tend to minimize the romantic cult, and concentrate on educational and vocational preparation, while they acquire emotional maturity as well.

Other Difficulties in Dating

In addition to the problems just cited, the American institution of dating is also beset by other difficulties. Many young people, especially as they first begin to date, experience strong feelings of insecurity. They often report feeling shy and fearful of doing and saying the wrong thing. Filled with well-meant parental advice, both dating partners tend to play their respective roles with considerable clumsiness (Saxton, 1968). Even college students report considerable insecurity in their dating relationships (Skipper & Nass, 1966).

Dating frequently proves to be frustrating for young people in another way. Among boys especially, the natural culmination of sexual pairing off is sexual intercourse, a practice which until recently has been discouraged outside the framework of marriage, especially for girls.

Thus, dating can encourage certain behavior patterns that will prove very inappropriate in marriage. Habits of sexual restraint, found particularly among middle-class girls during their years of dating, may be quite difficult to relinquish in marriage, thereby creating potential difficulties in marital adjustment (Douvan & Adelson, 1966).

Current dating patterns also tend to discourage the formation of the intimate relationships necessary for a successful marriage. Boys and girls who are dating hide their true selves from each other, adopting a facade or assuming a role that they feel will meet with approval and acceptance. Dating often becomes so ritualized that couples remain on guard to avoid any deep interpersonal relationships (Hettlinger, 1970). Such behavior is not likely to be very conducive to enabling two people to learn to know each other. On the contrary, they will tend to seek in their future mates superficial traits such as gaiety and charm, which are pleasant to possess but "irrelevant to the needs of marriage" (Douvan & Adelson, 1966, p. 208).

During the past decade certain new practices and ideas have appeared which may counteract this failure to develop close, meaningful heterosexual relationships, especially among middle-class college-aged students. One of the most interesting and provocative innovations has been that of the commune, or tribal family, as it has been described by one author. Such relationships have generally consisted of ". . . persons usually not blood kin (other than children) who have a semipermanent economic, sexual, and dwelling relationship on the basis of common needs and interests" (Downing, 1970, pp. 120–121). These family units have been described as seeking freedom from middle-class norms, which they have come to regard as frustrating and inhibiting, growth and self-actualization through the selection of their own values, the right for each individual to determine his own conduct, including his sexual behavior, and to define his own sexual role, a deemphasis on work as a panacea for all social problems, a sharing of all property based on the belief that the rights to property should be subordinate to human rights and needs, and an acute awareness of one's social responsibilities.

A second new living pattern has been created in coeducational dorms, which have opened on several college campuses throughout the country (*Life*, November 20, 1970). At first glance, it appears that such living arrangements tend to deemphasize sex and place it in a more practical perspective. When a boy sees a girl every day, she becomes more of a friend and less of a sex object. Apparently, the familiarity of daily living breeds a nonromantic heterosexual friendship. Some have suggested that this intimate coeducational living might be a more practical preparation for marriage than the romantic dating and courtship patterns that have been pursued by most adolescents. Hopefully, research in this area will soon be undertaken.

Margaret Mead (1970) has suggested that the establishment of two stages of marriage might also help counteract the difficulty of developing close heterosexual relationships. She proposes that couples first engage in an *individual marriage*. This arrangement could even be called a "student marriage," except conceivably it could take place between older men and women. Such a marriage would be legally recognized and licensed but only for two people, and it would not include bearing children. The second stage would be that of a *parental marriage* with its goals being directed toward the formation of a family. A license would also be required for this relationship, but it would be more difficult to obtain and possible to acquire only after the parties involved in the individual marriage had demonstrated a successful adjustment at the first level. Whether such an approach to marriage and the formation of a family will ever become an accepted practice is debatable, but it certainly deserves serious consideration as a possible solution to the high incidence of divorce and the millions of children currently growing up in broken homes.

SUMMARY AND CONCLUSIONS

One of the most important aids to the adolescent's social development is his peer group, which offers a valuable means of transition from the warmth, safety, and intimacy of the family to the insecurities of adult society. The peer group serves many functions: it offers opportunities for youth to learn new social roles, facilitates the development of identity, encourages discovery about oneself and about others, contributes to a feeling of belonging and status, and provides an environment conducive to learning to communicate with other people.

Factors involving acceptance by one's contemporaries vary from age to age and from one socioeconomic and ethnic group to another, but numerous authorities feel that athletic prowess and popularity have been given too much weight by too many young people. Although being accepted by the group demands a certain degree of social skill, much of this skill is acquired through the adolescent's participation in the peer group. If he is initially rejected by it, he may fail to develop adequate poise in his social relationships with others, a factor which may affect other facets of his adjustment.

Normal social development during this period of transition generally moves from primarily unisexual or like-sexed friendships, which are centered around the clique in early adolescence, to both unisexual and heterosexual relationships in middle adolescence, first involving crowds and later paired dating. Those who deviate too widely from the normal pattern of socialization because of peer-group rejection, precocious dating, delayed dating, nondating, or prematurity in going steady are likely to show immaturity and gaps in their social development.

One of the most controversial questions about the peer group is whether a peer-group culture actually exists. Several points of view have been presented in regard to this issue, and the reader is free to decide how he feels about this matter.

Dating and courtship are often regarded as synonymous. Actually their goals differ, and there is a difference in the degree of emotional involvement. Although dating offers many positive values, it also presents such difficulties as widespread feelings of insecurity and the encouragement of certain behavior which tends to be inappropriate to successful marital adjustment.

REFERENCES

Ausubel, D. P. *Theory and problems of adolescent development.* New York: Grune & Stratton, 1954.

Bealer, R. C., Willits, F. K., & Maida, P. R. The rebellious youth subculture—A myth. *Children,* 1964, **11**(2), 43–48.

Blos, P. The second individuation process of adolescence. *The Psychoanalytic Study of the Child,* 1967, **22**, 162–186.

Blos, P. The child analyst looks at the young adolescent. *Daedalus,* 1971, 961–980.

Bowerman, C. E., & Kinch, J. W. Changes in family and peer orientation of children between the fourth and tenth grades. *Social Forces,* 1959, **37**, 206–211.

Brittain, C. V. Adolescent choices and parent-peer cross pressures. *American Sociological Review,* 1963, **28**, 385–391.

Brittain, C. V. An exploration of the bases of peer-compliance and parent-compliance in adolescence. *Adolescence,* 1967, **2**(8), 445–458.

Broderick, C. B. Going steady: The beginning of the end. In S. M. Farber & R. H. L. Wilson (Eds.), *Teenage marriage and divorce.* Berkeley, Calif.: Diablo Press, 1967, Pp. 21–24.

Burchinal, L. G. Adolescent dating attitudes and behavior. In M. Gold & E. Douvan (Eds.), *Adolescent development: Readings in research and theory.* Boston: Allyn & Bacon, 1969. Pp. 199–202.

Cervantes, L. F. *The dropout: Causes and cures.* Ann Arbor: University of Michigan Press, 1965.

Coleman, J. S. *The adolescent society.* New York: Free Press, 1961.

Coombs, R., & Kenkel, W. Sex-differences in dating aspirations and satisfaction with computer selected partners. *Journal of Marriage and the Family,* 1966, **28**, 62–66.

Douvan, E., & Adelson, J. *The adolescent experience.* New York: John Wiley & Sons, 1966.

Downing, J. The tribal family and the society of awakening. In H. A. Otto (Ed.), *The family in search of a future.* New York: Meredith, 1970. Pp. 119–135.

Dunphy, D. C. The social structure of urban adolescent peer groups. *Sociometry,* 1963, **26**, 230–246.

Ehrmann, W. W. *Premarital dating behavior.* New York: Holt, Rinehart & Winston, 1959.

Elkin, F., & Westley, W. A. The myth of adolescent peer culture. *American Sociological Review,* 1955, **20**, 680–684.

Epperson, D. C. A reassessment of indices of parental influence in the adolescent society. *American Sociological Review*, 1964, **29**, 93–96.

Friesen, D. Academic-athletic-popularity syndrome of the Canadian high school society (1967). *Adolescence*, 1968, **3**(9), 39–52.

Hettlinger, R. F. *Sexual maturity*. Belmont, Calif.: Wadsworth, 1970.

Hollingshead, A. B. *Elmstown youth*. New York: John Wiley & Sons, 1949.

Horowitz, H. Prediction of adolescent popularity and rejection from achievement and interest tests. *Journal of Educational Psychology*, 1967, **58**, 170–174.

Horrocks, J. E., & Benimoff, M. Stability of adolescent's nominee status over a one-year period as a friend by their peers. *Adolescence*, 1966, **1**, 224–229.

Kuhlen, R. G., & Houlihan, N. B. Adolescent heterosexual interest in 1942 and 1963. *Child Development*, 1965, **36**, 1049–1052.

Life. An intimate revolution in campus life. November 20, 1970, 32–41.

McGovern, J. D. The adolescent and his peer group. In A. A. Schneiders & Contributors (Eds.), *Counseling the adolescent*. San Francisco: Chandler Publishing, 1967. Pp. 14–28.

McKinney, F. *Psychology of personal adjustment*. New York: John Wiley & Sons, 1960.

Mead, M. Marriage in two steps. In H. A. Otto (Ed.), *The family in search of a future*. New York: Meredith, 1970. Pp. 75–84.

Midcentury White House Conference on Children and Youth. *A healthy personality for every child—Fact finding report: A digest*. Raleigh, N. C.: Health Publications Institute, 1951.

Morgenstern, J. J. Teenage dating patterns. *NEA Journal*, 1961, **50**, 8–11.

Newsweek. The teen-agers. March 21, 1966, **67**(12), 57–75.

Nixon, R. E. *The art of growing*. New York: Random House, 1962.

O'Dwyer, C., McAllister, R. J., & Davis, I. Special aspects of adolescent problems. In A. A. Schneiders & Contributors (Eds.), *Counseling the adolescent*. San Francisco: Chandler Publishing, 1967. Pp. 49–65.

Parsons, T. *Essays in sociological theory*. New York: Free Press, 1954. Pp. 89–103.

Reiss, I. L. Sexual codes in teen-age culture. *The Annals of the American Academy of Political and Social Sciences*, 1961, **338**, 53–62.

Rogers, D. Dating. In D. Rogers (Ed.), *Issues in adolescent psychology*. New York: Meredith, 1969. Pp. 376–377.

Saxton, L. *The individual, marriage, and the family*. Belmont, Calif.: Wadsworth, 1968.

Sherif, M., & Sherif, C. Problems of youth in transition. In M. Sherif & C. Sherif (Eds.), *Problems of youth: Transition to adulthood in a changing world*. Chicago: Aldine Publishing, 1965. Pp. 1–12.

Skipper, J. K., Jr., & Nass, G. Dating behavior: A framework for analysis and an illustration. *Journal of Marriage and the Family*, 1966, **28**, 412–420.

Smith, E. A. *American youth culture.* New York: Free Press, 1962.

Snyder, E. E. Socioeconomic variations, values, and social participation among high school students. *Journal of Marriage and the Family,* 1966, **28**, 174–176.

Staton, T. F. *Dynamics of adolescent adjustment.* New York: Macmillan, 1963.

Wiggins, J. A., Dill, F., & Schwartz, R. D. On "status-liability." *Sociometry,* 1965, **28**, 197–209.

III

Physical and Sexual Development in Adolescents

4

Physical Growth and Development in the Adolescent

Growing is not the easy, plain sailing business that it is commonly supposed to be: it is hard work—harder than any but a growing boy can understand . . .

Samuel Butler (1835–1902)
The Way of All Flesh

In order to understand adolescent behavior, one must become aware of the dramatic physical and *biochemical* changes taking place during this period. Actually adolescence is a developmental process which is unique to the human being,[1] for it encompasses its own specific patterns of physiological, psychological, and social development. This chapter will focus mainly on physiological maturation. (Social maturation was discussed in Chapters 2 and 3, and psychological and emotional development will be emphasized in Chapter 6.) However, one must take into account the fact that these different processes are closely interwoven and that each is dependent upon the other two to some extent.

[1]The growth of mammals other than man reveals marked differences in the ages at which various maturational developments occur. In some instances, these changes take place within a span of a few weeks or months. Lower animals have an even earlier attainment of a relatively complete adaptive and sexual capacity. These animals experience neither an adolescent period of growth nor a latency period of quiescence of sexual drives.

THE PREPUBESCENT AND PUBESCENT STAGES OF DEVELOPMENT

Prior to the beginning of adolescence, the individual experiences a period called *prepuberty*. Prepuberty, which occurs between late childhood and the beginning of puberty, is characterized by rapid changes in hormone levels, which produce intensified interest in sexuality but very little interest in the opposite sex. The prepubescent's sexual interest during this period centers primarily on his own body and genitals (Marshall & Tanner, 1968).

Puberty is the period of physical growth during which physical maturity is reached and the individual becomes capable of reproducing. This *pubescent* period generally spans about two years, ending when all *secondary sex characteristics* have appeared and reproductive ability is reached. The period is marked by development of the genital organs. For females, puberty encompasses the first menstruation (or menarche), although the appearance of the menarche does not necessarily indicate that the reproductive system is complete. It may be a matter of months or even years before a girl has regular *ovulatory menstrual cycles* and is capable of reproducing. For boys, the pigmenting of underarm hair is a fairly reliable indicator of the onset of puberty.

The term *adolescence*, however, is much broader and more inclusive than *puberty*, for it refers not only to the biological changes but also to psychological maturation, which will be discussed in more detail in Chapter 6. Research has shown that psychological changes during this period do not necessarily parallel the physiological changes; they may arise earlier or later, and they are likely to be rather widely spread out (Judd, 1967; Clifford, 1968). Adolescence encompasses the years between childhood and maturity and represents a continuation of the psychological, as well as the physical maturational process initiated by puberty. Both physical and psychological development characteristically proceed asymmetrically with diverse rates of maturing. Sometimes the period of adolescence is divided according to physical development into two stages: early adolescence (synonymous with the puberty period) and late adolescence (Kestenberg, 1968).

Early adolescence may continue only through the brief time of the first irregular menstrual periods. Late adolescence begins with the ability to produce a fertilizable egg in the female, but this ability does not necessarily indicate the simultaneous appearance of sexual or psychological maturity (Marshall & Tanner, 1968).

A case study of the kind of disparity that can occur between physical and emotional maturity follows. Sally, at age 16, thinks that she is very much in love with John, who has just graduated from high school. They decide to marry, and within a few months after their marriage Sally becomes pregnant. After the birth of their son, Sally becomes overwhelmed by the responsibilities thrust upon her by parenthood—the constant care of her baby and her home, the lack of freedom to come and go as she pleases, and a very limited income. A few months later she decides to leave her husband and return to the home of her parents, who she knows will care for both her and her baby.

Adolescence is characterized by a unique group of developmental problems, which may be physiological, psychological, or social in nature. Several of these topics were mentioned in Chapter 1. Some of the physiological problems which appear during this period and their impact on behavior will be reviewed in subsequent sections of this chapter. A more complete discussion of adolescent sexual behavior will follow in the next chapter.

THE SECULAR TREND

There is an increasing tendency, called a *secular trend*, for maturation to occur at a younger age over successive generations. This acceleration is characterized by today's youth growing faster, attaining their adolescent growth spurt earlier, and reaching adult height sooner (Muuss, 1970). The secular trend has been evident in human growth and development for several generations, but today's young people are not only taller and heavier than youth before the turn of the century; they are also reaching puberty and physical sexual maturity at an earlier age. At present, over one fourth of the adult male population is over six feet in height, and more than one sixth of adult women is five feet seven inches or more. During the year 1900, the average height for both sexes was two or three inches less than it is today. Furthermore, in 1900 individuals reached their maximal height during their midtwenties; today it is attained about the age of 16 or 17 for girls and around 18 or 19 for boys (Hathaway & Foard, 1960; Cone, 1961).

Another indication of this accelerated biological maturation has been the decreasing average age at which first menstruation has been occurring in girls. Research has shown that during the past century there has been a gradual lowering in the average age at which the menarche has appeared among western European girls and apparently among girls of the United States and Canada as well (Tanner, 1962). According to the Tanner report, the menarche has been taking place approximately four months earlier in the life of the adolescent with each passing decade for the past century. Today the average age at the first menstrual period lies somewhere between 12.5 and 13 years (Marshall & Tanner, 1968; Offer & Offer, 1968). This earlier age of menarche further substantiates the presence of a general secular trend, as does the accelerated rate of increasing body size (height and weight) and earlier somatic or bodily maturity. The fact that research has indicated that this trend is just as evident among girls in temperate climates as well as for girls in warm climates would also tend to destroy the myth that girls in the South mature earlier than girls in the North. It also seems probable that the secular trend applies to male development as well as to female development (McCandless, 1970).

Apparently the rate of adolescent growth and development is influenced by two groups of factors: those controlled by genetics and those related to nutrition. The effects of heredity are shown by the fact that Negroid infants are advanced over Caucasian infants in their skeletal development at birth. Negroid children are also able to sit and to walk sooner than Caucasian children (Huffman, 1968).

Better nutrition also seems to explain today's earlier rate of maturation among adolescents. Good nutrition is a primary requisite for normal growth and development; and conversely, malnutrition decelerates growth and delays, decreases, or prevents physical maturation, although females seem better able than males to resist the effects of malnutrition (Huffman, 1968). It has been found that chronic malnutrition retards skeletal growth and maturation, delays the menarche, and extends the growth period (Bojlen & Bentzen, 1968). Thus, the fact that nutritional conditions are closely related to standards of living and socioeconomic status may very well explain why children from lower socioeconomic classes tend to mature physically later than those from the middle and upper classes and why parents with a high economic or educational status rear adolescents who biologically mature earlier and become larger adults (McCandless, 1970). The effects of nutrition can also be seen when one compares children from economically advanced nations to children from poorer countries. It is likely that a 6-year-old child from Central America will be smaller than a 4-year-old child in the United States or Canada.

The trend toward earlier physical maturation has important psychological and sociological ramifications. For example, sexual activity and pregnancy may occur at an earlier chronological age. Further, youth who undergo this earlier physical maturity also have a commensurate need for earlier psychological and intellectual development, but this development often lags behind their biological maturation. These discrepancies in development, along with the prolonged economic dependence of so many young people, have contributed to the lengthening of the adolescent period and its accompanying problems.

VARIATIONS IN NORMAL PHYSICAL GROWTH AND DEVELOPMENT

The age at which adolescence begins, and the rate and the extent of progress through this period of development, varies significantly among the members of a race as well as among races throughout the world. Thus, there are wide differences in the rates of biological maturation that are considered normal. Such deviations usually fall within two years of the norm or average.

There is definitely a distinction to be made between "deviating from the average" and being "abnormal." Growth and development occur in a sequential manner, but there are many normal variations in the time, the rate, and the extent of physical maturing. Since there are different states, rates, and modes of growth, a deviation must show a marked departure from the normal growth pattern before it can be considered to have reached abnormal proportions.

The vast majority of adolescents ultimately attain satisfactory, mature, adult development, but their manner of arriving at that stage may vary appreciably from one individual to another. The developmental deviations from the "norm" often cause emotional stress, since most young people experience some difficulty in accepting any rate of physical growth which is noticeably different from that of their peers. Much of the anxiety and many of the psychosomatic difficulties arising during adolescence are caused by the maladjustment of youths who deviate from the "typical," as the following case study illustrates.

Fran, at age 15, is somewhat slow, but not abnormal, in her physical and sexual development, as compared with her peers in the tenth grade. She has not yet begun to menstruate, and her chest is still quite flat. As a consequence, she refuses to don a bathing suit and constantly develops various aches and pains, which prevent her from having to dress and take gym. Because of her feelings of physical inadequacy and her fears that she will never develop in a normal manner and catch up with her classmates, she has become a rather shy, withdrawn girl with very few friends.

Developmental Age versus Chronological Age

Because of the complex differential development of the various body organs at different times and at different rates of speed, the concept of "chronological age" provides an unreliable frame of reference for determining an individual's growth rate. A more valid measure is the adolescent's *developmental age*, which is usually determined by the degree of development of the various secondary sex characteristics or by the extent of bone ossification (*skeletal age*). Skeletal age, or bone age, may vary from what would normally be expected of a given chronological age. For example, an individual may have a skeletal age of 13 and a chronological age of 15, or conversely, he may be 13 years old with a skeletal age of 15. If a healthy adolescent is slow in his skeletal development, he will normally continue growing over a longer period of time. On the other hand, if he is advanced in his skeletal growth, he will usually cease growing at an earlier chronological age (Wijn, 1968).

In girls the menarche is so closely related to somatic growth that the age of first menstruation is more closely correlated with their skeletal age than with their calendar age. Ausubel (1954) has pointed out that one can usually predict the onset of menstruation by the sudden skeletal growth spurt that generally precedes it by about one year. Therefore, skeletal age appears to correlate more reliably with the appearance of other maturational phenomena than does chronological age.

Thus, the use of the concept of developmental age as an index of growth insures a more exact prediction when assessing the physiological and metabolic changes in adolescence than does the use of chronological age alone. Since girls are biologically older than boys from birth to 15 or 16, and since individual differences are so great within each sex, the developmental age has proven to be a more effective measure of the level of each adolescent's physical maturational development.

ENDOCRINE FACTORS IN ADOLESCENT DEVELOPMENT

More than at any other stage of development, except for the first year of life, the adolescent period is characterized by rapid changes, diversity, and considerable physical growth and psychological maturation. From a low and stable level during childhood, there is a gradual, but considerable, increase in hormone levels and sexual development. This increase is initiated by the *hypothalamus*, which in turn activates the pituitary gland to secrete *gonadotropic* hormones; the increased secretions of the growth and sex hormones follow, bringing the development of the secondary sex characteristics and ultimately the capability of reproducing. When a girl is 10 or 11, there is a marked rise in the level of the female hormone, *estrogen*, and by the time she is 12 or 14, the amount of estrogen secreted has increased to about twenty times that of her childhood level (Osofsky, 1968). In boys the increase in the level of the male hormone, *androgen*, occurs approximately two years later, and the change is about fourfold. At the same time, a pituitary-produced growth hormone increases height, weight, and muscle. These rapid and extensive growth changes bring greater nutritional demands, particularly for protein, calcium, and iron. Additional dietary demands also occur in the female with the advent of the menarche. These rapid changes in physical growth and development and the greater nutritional requirements that result, as well as the state of emotional development, often cause young people to become apathetic, listless, and fatigued.

For several months during prepuberty and before the menarche, there is some acceleration in genital growth marked by an increase in the secretion of estrogen. Lengthening and widening of the vaginal canal occurs at this time. However, genital development during adolescence does not begin suddenly. It begins quite slowly during the prepubescent period and accelerates during the adolescent growth spurt, which we will discuss shortly. The genital changes which lead to physical sexual maturity are the result of endocrine secretions produced by the ovaries, which are activated by the anterior pituitary gonadotropic hormones.

The anterior pituitary, the thyroid, and the adrenal glands all participate in varying degrees in the endocrine system and play various roles in sexual maturation and function. Genital growth and development is directly controlled by the pituitary, which releases the hormones estrogen and androgen. Genital function is also indirectly influenced by the pituitary. And although the relationship of the thyroid gland to sexual development is not clearly understood, it is generally agreed that the adrenals act indirectly on genital activity through their production of androgen-like substances (see Figure 4-1).

Pituitary gonadotropic activity initiates the adolescent growth spurt, which takes place under hormonal control (Osofsky, 1968). The sex hormones, as well as growth hormones, are responsible for this growth spurt. In females, the ovaries begin to mature and to secrete estrogen. During early adolescence, menstruation occurs in response to hormonal fluctuations without ovulation taking place. Estrogen is also responsible for vaginal and breast development. Adolescent breasts generally reach a mature shape in girls 13.5 to 14 years old, although they are likely to continue developing for an additional two or three years (Tanner, 1962). Estrogen also initiates early deposits of fat in both sexes, while androgen stimulates the development of pubic hair and axillary (armpit) hair and the increased activity of the sebaceous and sweat glands in both boys and girls. In males, increased secretion of androgen accounts for the increase in the size of the *penis*, and in the female these same hormones stimulate the development of the *clitoris*. Thus, one can readily see the close interrelationship between the increased production of the sex hormones and the development of both secondary and primary sex characteristics. It is also apparent that although estrogen is primarily a female hormone and androgen basically a male hor-

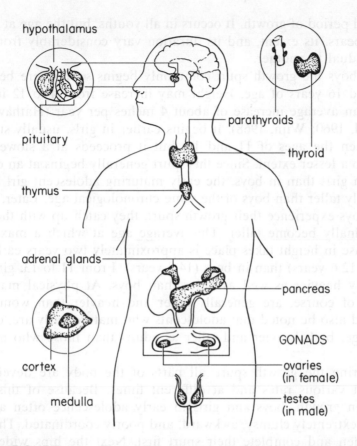

FIGURE 4-1.   The endocrine glands. (Diagram by Malcolm Le Jeune.)

mone, both are present in lesser quantities in members of the opposite sex and have a definite impact on various aspects of sexual development.

ANATOMICAL AND PHYSIOLOGICAL CHANGES

The Adolescent Growth Spurt

The rate of growth throughout life is not steady; it is most rapid during infancy, then declines, accelerates again between the ages of 6 and 8, then decreases, and finally once more starts to increase rapidly somewhere between the ages of 11 and 16 (Offer, 1966; Israel, 1967). This spurt during early adolescence is a markedly accelerated period of growth. It occurs in all youths, but the age at which it appears, its extent, and its duration vary considerably from one individual to another.

In boys the growth spurt commonly begins somewhere between 12 and 16 years of age. Height may increase from 4 to 12 inches, with an average increase of about 4 inches per year (Hathaway & Foard, 1960; Wijn, 1968). It begins earlier in girls, usually starting between the ages of 11 and 14, but it proceeds at a slower rate and to a lesser extent. Since this spurt generally begins at an earlier age in girls than in boys, the early maturing adolescent girl is frequently taller than boys of the same chronological age. Later, when the boys experience their growth spurt, they catch up with the girls and finally become taller. The average age at which a maximum increase in height takes place is approximately two years earlier in girls (12.6 years) than in boys (14.8 years). From 11 to 13, girls are usually heavier as well as taller than boys. At physical maturity, men, of course, are generally taller and heavier than women. It should also be noted that adolescents who mature early are, on the average, both heavier and taller as adults than those who mature late.

During the growth spurt, all parts of the body are developing but at various rates and at different times. Because of this very uneven growth, boys and girls in early adolescence often appear to be extremely clumsy, awkward, and poorly coordinated. The legs lengthen and complete their spurt first. Next the hips widen, although more noticeably for girls than for boys. This growth is followed by a broadening of the shoulders for both sexes, a change which is much more evident in boys than in girls. The fact that males do develop broader shoulders has been suggested as one explanation for their greater physical strength; apparently wide shoulders help to provide better leverage for the operation of their muscles (Horrocks, 1969). Subsequently, the trunk length and the chest depth increase; in the case of boys, the chest also broadens. In both sexes, excess childhood fat acquired prior to the growth spurt may disappear. After the skeletal growth has subsided, a second rapid increase in weight and muscle, particularly in boys, may take place.

As the trunk grows longer in comparison to the arm and leg length, the skeletal framework begins to change. The appearance of long-leggedness gradually disappears. The contours of the body become more rounded with the deposition of subcutaneous fat. The face fills out, and the skin becomes softer and often shows increased pigmentation.

Most of the somatic growth changes have occurred in girls and boys by the ages of 15 and 16.5 years respectively (Tanner, 1962; Offer, 1966). Since the rate of skeletal maturation is usually somewhat ahead of sexual development, many of the bodily changes have already taken place or are occurring by the time of menarche; however, many of the sex differences in biological structure and metabolic function make their appearance during the growth spurt. At this time the secondary sex characteristics begin to appear and develop.

Growth Sequence of Primary and Secondary Sex Characteristics

In boys there is a gradual increase in the size of the penis, followed by the appearance of pubic, facial, and then axillary hair, and the enlargement of the larynx and lengthening of the vocal cords. The voice takes on a deeper adult sound as a result of changes in the larynx. Boys show a more striking change in their voices than girls. The hallmark of male sexual development finally appears with the formation of spermatozoa (*spermatogenesis*), which is followed by the onset of seminal emission (*oligarche*). The appearance of pubic hair and the enlargement of the testicles normally occur between the ages of 12 to 16 years, whereas the enlargement of the penis and first ejaculation take place somewhere between 13 and 17 years of age (Young, 1961).

In girls there initially appears a budding of the breasts, next an appearance of pubic hair, then the first menstruation (menarche), and finally ovulation. Breast development and pubic hair first become visible about 10 to 11 years of age, whereas the menarche occurs on an average in the range of 11 to 13 years (Young, Greulich, Gallagher, Cone, & Heald, 1968). Reproductive maturity takes place from one to two years after the first menstruation, with maximum fertility developing in the early twenties (Offer & Offer, 1968).

The development of secondary sex characteristics in response to increased secretions of the sex hormones is a highly significant indicator of approaching physical maturity in both sexes. These organs develop in a sequential fashion, and their growth is correlated with height, weight, and genital growth.

TABLE 4-1. Sequence of pubertal development.

Female	Male
Initial increase in breast size	Enlargement of the testes
Growth of straight, pigmented pubic hair	Appearance of straight, pigmented pubic hair
Rapid physical growth	Growth of the penis
Appearance of kinky pubic hair	Voice changes
Menarche	Rapid physical growth
Growth of axillary hair	Development of the beard
Localized fat deposits	Growth of kinky pubic hair and axillary hair
Increased sebaceous gland activity	First ejaculation
Increasing maturity of reproductive organs	

The Menarche and Psychological Reactions to Menstruation

The average age of menarche is 12.5 to 13. However, some normal girls may begin to menstruate as early as 9, while others may not start until the age of 16 (Offer & Offer, 1968). The impact of variations from the average may be quite traumatic for some girls. For example, girls who unexpectedly start to menstruate before the usual age often experience marked surprise, stress, and anxiety. On the other hand, those who are noticeably delayed in the onset of their menstrual period may regard themselves as abnormal and suffer needless worry and concern.

Although the adolescent growth spurt is not an essential preliminary for the menarche to occur, the peak of accelerated growth usually has passed before the onset of the first menstruation. Actually the growth rate decelerates rapidly after the menarche, and there are few increases in height after the age of 16 or 17. Generally speaking, height increases only 2 to 3 inches after the menarche. Girls who menstruate early (before age 13) are usually taller and heavier throughout adolescence than girls who experience their menarche later (after 14 years). However, after the age of 15, the late maturers (at the time of their menarche) will be taller than early-maturing girls (Tooley, 1968).

An irregular menstrual cycle is quite common during the first few years of adolescence. Genital growth is usually not complete when menstruation begins, and it tends to continue slowly for several more years. Until a regular ovulatory menstrual cycle is established, the menarche is frequently followed by a period of sterility. The duration of this period varies considerably; the first ovulation may occur at menarche, or it may not take place until years later.

Menstruation serves as a profound landmark of psychosexual transformation for girls; boys do not experience this sort of demarcation point. The importance of the menarche as a biological marker should not be overlooked in understanding the psychology of adolescent development.

The menarche initiates a critical period of development which may elicit a wide variety of psychological reactions. It is a positive experience in that it represents the beginning of womanhood. Girls who are psychologically and intellectually prepared for this experience can accept this evidence of femininity, and the average girl regards it as a necessary inconvenience in achieving feminine maturity. She accepts menstruation as a normal, although perhaps somewhat disturbing, physiological activity. Normally, the major effect of menstruation is to enhance her perception of her role as a woman.

However, if a young girl is unprepared for her first menstrual period, she may experience psychological trauma and shock, which may continue with subsequent menses. Girls who are fearful or reluctant to accept this sign of female maturation are likely to exhibit various degrees of *denial* during their adolescent years. For example, they may pursue somewhat masculine, tomboyish interests and activities at this time, rather than show an interest in more feminine pursuits.

For several months following the menarche, there is usually a lack of regularity in the extent and timing of the menstrual flow. A high correlation between emotional flare-ups and hormonal changes has been noted to be associated with this irregularity in menstruation, particularly during puberty or early adolescence. Apparently, fluctuations in girls' moods and attitudes are rather closely related to various phases of the menstrual cycle. These changes usually occur premenstrually and take the form of anxiety, irritability, depression, disorganization, and a low frustration tolerance.

THE PSYCHOLOGICAL EFFECTS OF EARLY AND LATE PHYSICAL MATURATION

Considerable longitudinal research at the Institute of Human Development, University of California, has been undertaken on the psychological effects of early versus late physical maturing, especially among boys (Jones & Bayley, 1950; Mussen & Jones, 1957). The results have indicated that whether a youth physically matures early or late in the adolescent period seems to have a considerable influence on his psychological development during this transitional stage of life.

Eichorn (1963) has suggested that the reactions of both adults and peers to the development of the early maturer may have a marked impact on his behavior. Because he looks older, the early maturer may be accorded responsibilities and privileges which ordinarily would be reserved for chronologically older people. And since he is more physically developed, he is more likely to participate in athletics and thereby attain prestige and prominence, which may then extend to other roles of leadership and responsibility among his peers. Frequently able to meet such challenges and thereby reinforce the impressions of others, he enhances his skills and self-satisfaction, and, in turn, tends to have a higher self-concept than late-maturing boys.

Conversely, the late maturer, because he is delayed in his physical development may possess attitudes of inferiority, as well as excessive dependency upon others. Should he feel resentful about the childish status and treatment that have been accorded him, he may react in a rebellious, impulsive manner (Eichorn, 1963). It has also been noted by Weatherley (1964) that among college boys, late maturers more often than early maturers have failed to resolve certain conflicts characteristic of this period. They are less likely to assume roles of leadership and dominance over others, yet remain more reluctant to accept gracefully the discipline asserted by those in authority. Not surprisingly, such late maturers tend to have a low self-concept (McCandless, 1970).

As for girls, the effects of early versus late physical maturation are somewhat more variable and less conclusive (Rogers, 1969). Some researchers have suggested that girls who physically mature early tend to be more mature in their personality development and possess more favorable self-concepts (Jones & Mussen, 1958). Conversely, it has been noted that to a considerable extent the same traits associated with late-maturing boys would apply to late-maturing girls as well (Eichorn, 1963). On the other hand, the very early-maturing girl, the one who reaches puberty in the sixth grade, may feel physically conspicuous and develop an interest in the opposite sex, which is not reciprocated by boys her own age; nor is her emotional development sufficiently mature to cope with older boys at this time (Jones & Mussen, 1958; Faust, 1960). There is need for additional research on the psychological effects of early and late physical maturing in girls.

THE ADOLESCENT'S SENSITIVITY TO PHYSICAL CHANGES

Following the initial appearance of the secondary sex characteristics, young people develop an intense psychological need for physical sameness with their peers and considerable concern about any deviations from what they consider to be physically normal. Adolescents are much more sensitive to their growth and development than members of any other age group. And since they feel as they do about their physical development, unwarranted and erroneous beliefs about their bodily changes often arise.

Numerous adolescent difficulties may develop from sudden changes in height and weight. Margie began her growth spurt at the age of 11 in the sixth grade. By the time she reached the seventh grade, she was the tallest student in her class, towering above both boys and girls. Being the object of many jokes about growing like a weed and looking like a beanpole, she began to feel very inadequate and shy in the presence of her classmates, and she started to withdraw from her old friends.

Like Margie, most young people find it difficult to cope with so much change in such a short period of time (Mead, 1960; Young, 1968; Glaser, 1969). Consequently, if an adolescent discovers that he has grown 6 inches in one year, he may fear that there is something very wrong with his body. Or an adolescent who lags behind his friends in physical development may begin to wonder if he will ever mature. For example, a boy who remains shorter than his peers, has smaller genitals, or has less beard, and a girl who has smaller breasts, has not yet begun to menstruate, or who is very tall or skinny may tend to feel not only that they are abnormal but that they are also undesirable and unacceptable to their peers. Perhaps most stressful to these young people are deviations in sexual maturity or in height and weight. Likewise, obesity is a sensitive issue to both sexes. And as mentioned earlier, gangling arms and growing feet often produce self-consciousness as well as posture problems.

Commonly related to their compelling preoccupation with their physical appearance is a dissatisfaction with some of their own physical traits. This unwillingness to accept their changing bodies may tend to manifest itself in an obsessive wish to alter their appearance, possibly through plastic surgery to correct a real or imagined facial abnormality. Consider the following illustration of this sort of dissatisfaction.

At the age of 15, Mike first mentioned his concern about his nose to his parents, who said they felt it was all right. Shortly afterwards, he received his annual school picture and observed that his nose was quite crooked in the picture. About the same time he played the central character in a Sunday-school play about a boy with a long nose and he muffed his lines, although he had on other occasions memorized roles that he had played without an error. Six months following these two incidents he decided to undergo plastic surgery. Formerly a very shy, timid youth, especially with girls, he became much more outgoing and talkative after his operation. Socially, he seemed much more sure of himself. Not only did he begin dating regularly, but he also began to volunteer for group activities, which he had never done before. He showed some improvement in his academic performance, which had always been quite poor. It is reasonable to speculate that it may not have been the improvement in his appearance itself but rather his own perception of this alteration that brought about the modifications in his behavior.

It should also be noted that although such surgery may at times be indicated and perhaps may result in a much more favorable self-image, it is probably true that adolescents' perception of themselves tends to exaggerate such deviations, and in most instances time and physical maturity will correct some of the distortion.

Young people naturally want to be attractive in their personal appearance and devote considerable time and effort each day to their dress and grooming. Unfortunately, the adolescent period is often marked by the trying problem of skin blemishes. The increased activity of the sebaceous glands often causes acne to develop, which proves to be a source of considerable anxiety and embarrassment for many young people. The psychological effects of this condition should not be underestimated, since it almost invariably causes emotional distress. Various forms of medication, diet, frequent washing, plenty of physical exercise, adequate social activity, plus ample rest constitute its normal treatment. Generally speaking, the greater a youth's predisposition to acne, the larger the size of his sebaceous glands and the greater their secretions (which are produced by increased androgen levels that normally occur during this time). Since androgen stimulates sebaceous activity and estrogen decreases it, corrective hormone therapy is sometimes medically prescribed.

THE NEED FOR SEXUAL EXPRESSION

As the adolescent's body grows and secondary and primary sex organs mature, new sexual drives develop, which will be discussed in more detail in Chapter 5. However, it should be noted at this point that these increasing sexual urges, which are initiated by newly activated genital and hormonal stimuli, can become a disturbing matter to many young people.

It should also be pointed out that although girls have an earlier physical growth, boys develop earlier sexual feelings. Early-maturing girls, who are much taller than the boys of their age and more mature sexually, usually do not want to date boys of the same age and prefer males a few years older; however, these older boys tend to possess a sexual drive far in excess of that of the girls at this stage of their development. It is this difference in sexual feelings that contributes to many of the difficulties in adolescent dating, which we discussed in Chapter 3.

SUMMARY AND CONCLUSIONS

One cannot overemphasize the importance of physical and biochemical development in the dynamics of adolescence. From the moment of prepuberty, with its rapid increases in hormone levels and the beginnings of the growth spurt, through late adolescence, with its capability for reproduction, these swift changes play a major role in the social and emotional behavior of youth.

Any noticeable deviations from the norm or average of physical development are of considerable concern to young people.

Frequent and numerous changes are characteristic of youthful psychobiological development. These changes are often unpredictable and confusing: the fat become thin, the short become tall, and the immature become mature.

REFERENCES

Ausubel, D. P. *Theory and problems of adolescent development.* New York: Grune & Stratton, 1954.

Bojlen, K., & Bentzen, M. W. The influence of climate and nutrition on age at menarche: A historical review and a modern hypothesis. *Human Biology: An International Record of Research,* 1968, **40**(1), 69–85.

Clifford, P. L. Testing the educational and psychological development of adolescents: Ages 12–18. *Review of Educational Research,* 1968, **38**(1), 29–41.

Cone, T. E., Jr. Secular acceleration of height and biologic maturation in children during the past century. *Journal of Pediatrics,* 1961, **59**, 736.

Eichorn, D. H. Biological correlates of behavior. In *Child psychology: The sixty-second yearbook of the National Society for the Study of Education,* Part 1. Chicago: University of Chicago Press, 1963. Pp. 4–61.

Faust, M. S. Developmental maturity as a determinant in prestige of adolescent girls. *Child Development,* 1960, **31**, 173–184.

Glaser, K. Emotional problems of adolescents. *Maryland Medical Journal,* 1969, **18**, 51–54.

Hathaway, M. L., & Foard, E. D. Heights and weights of adults in the United States. Washington, D. C. Human Nutrition Research Division, Agricultural Research Service, United States Department of Agriculture, 1960, *Home Economics Research Report No. 10.*

Horrocks, J. E. *The psychology of adolescence* (3rd ed.). Boston: Houghton Mifflin, 1969.

Huffman, J. W. *The gynecology of childhood and adolescence.* Philadelphia: W. B. Saunders, 1968.

Israel, S. L. Normal puberty and adolescence. *Annals of the New York Academy of Sciences,* 1967, **142**(3), 773–778.

Jones, M. C., & Bayley, N. Physical maturing among boys as related to behavior. *Journal of Educational Psychology,* 1950, **41**, 129–148.

Jones, M. C., & Mussen, P. H. Self-conceptions, motivations, and interpersonal attitudes of early- and late-maturing girls. *Child Development,* 1958, **29**, 491–501.

Judd, L. L. The normal psychological development of the American adolescent: A review. *California Medicine*, 1967, **107**, 465–470.

Kestenberg, J. S. Phases of adolescence. *Journal of the American Academy of Child Psychiatry*, 1968, **7**, 108–151.

Marshall, W. A., & Tanner, J. M. Growth and physiological development during adolescence. *Annual Review of Medicine*, 1968, **19**, 283–300.

McCandless, B. R. *Adolescents' behavior and development*. Hinsdale, Ill.: Dryden Press, 1970.

Mead, M. Problems of the late adolescent and young adult. *Children and youth in the 1960's*, White House Conference on Children and Youth, survey papers. Washington, D.C.: National Committee for Children and Youth, 1960.

Mussen, P. H., & Jones, M. C. Self-conceptions, motivations, and interpersonal attitudes of late- and early-maturing boys. *Child Development*, 1957, **28**, 243–256.

Muuss, R. E. Adolescent development and the secular trend. *Adolescence*, 1970, **5**(19), 267–284.

Offer, D. Studies of normal adolescents. *Adolescence*, 1966, **1**(4), 305–320.

Offer, D., & Offer, J. L. Profiles of normal adolescent girls. *Archives of General Psychiatry*, 1968, **19**(5), 513–522.

Osofsky, H. J. Somatic, hormonal changes during adolescence. *Hospital Topics*, 1968, **46**(4), 95–103.

Rogers, D. (Ed.), *Issues in adolescent psychology*. New York: Meredith, 1969.

Tanner, J. M. *Growth at adolescence* (2nd ed.). Springfield, Ill.: Charles C. Thomas, 1962.

Tooley, K. A developmental problem of late adolescence: Case report. *Psychiatry*, 1968, **31**(1), 69–83.

Weatherley, D. Self-perceived rate of physical maturation and personality in late adolescence. *Child Development*, 1964, **35**, 1197–1210.

Wijn, J. F. Appropriate body weight for height and skeletal frame of adolescents and young adults. *Nutritio et Dieta*, 1968, **10**, 161–182.

Young, H. B. Special needs of adolescents. *International Journal of Psychiatry*, 1968, **5**(6), 494–495.

Young, H. B., Greulich, W. W., Gallagher, J. R., Cone, T., & Heald, F. Evaluation of physical maturity at adolescence. *Developmental Medicine and Child Neurology*, 1968, **10**(3), 338–348.

Young, W. C. (Ed.), *Sex and internal secretion* (3rd ed.). Baltimore: Williams & Wilkins, 1961.

5

Sexual Behavior in Adolescence

Sexual maturity is the capacity to enjoy sexual union as an expression of love for the partner, without needing to demonstrate one's power by dominating the other, and without doubting one's identity and worth as a sexual being.

Richard F. Hettlinger
Sexual Maturity

Sexual behavior probably elicits more interest, depression, activity, *displacement*, happiness, aggression, friendliness, frustration, anxiety, and humor than any other human activity. As in adults, sexual urges in adolescents can be expressed in a great variety of ways. But in young people the ultimate goal of sexual gratification is finding an appropriate identity for oneself.

Because adolescent physical changes are quite rapid, young people are not always completely prepared to integrate these changes and adjust to them as swiftly as they occur. Despite the stresses of adolescence, however, a majority of young people ultimately achieve an adequate sexual adjustment, usually by establishing a satisfying heterosexual relationship.

A mature sexual relationship is part of a profound interpersonal relationship in which both people can be themselves and freely express their sensitivity to each other's needs and desires. Often, however, for adolescents sexual intimacy takes on the nature of a battle, in which boys are concerned only with a successfully executed assault, while girls demonstrate a somewhat persistent resistance in defense of their virginity (Hettlinger, 1970). The fact that one out of every three teen-age marriages and one out of every four adult marriages in this country terminate in separation or desertion (Packard, 1968) is probably symptomatic of this kind of sexual immaturity.

Sexual exploration and experimentation have been traditionally restricted by arbitrary prohibitions in childhood. With adolescence, many parental and religious restrictions also prove to be in direct conflict with the young person's development of normal sexual desires; as a result, youths often develop feelings of uncertainty and guilt. Adolescents are usually given no adequate information or assistance in establishing positive sexual expression. Adult discussion on the subject is too often emotional, negative, and concerned more with prohibiting these activities than with helping young people understand their sexual drives. And while they fail to offer adequate guidelines, adults often reveal to the younger generation a hypocritical and contradictory set of rules and behavioral examples. For instance, society tends to place a blanket restriction on most adolescent sexual activity, while at the same time spending millions of dollars each year in advertising geared to arouse and stimulate sexual interest and desires in the teen-age market. Consequently, adolescents frequently find their parents to be oppressive and interfering and must find their own way to a meaningful sexual identity.

Research has revealed that certain behavioral patterns are typically associated with adolescent sexual development (Kinsey, Pomeroy, & Martin, 1948; Kinsey, Pomeroy, Martin, & Gebhard, 1953; Masters & Johnson, 1966; McCary, 1967). Since precise figures are difficult to obtain and the various reports differ in their estimates, specific investigations and their statistical results will not be cited in this chapter; however, the collective general findings of such studies will provide a basis for interpretation. In this chapter we will examine the incidence of different categories of sexual response that are characteristic of adolescent sexual expression at various ages.

MASTURBATION

Society generally decrees that sexual expression, if it is to be socially acceptable, must be prolonged several years beyond the time that sexual impulse reaches its peak in adolescents. Thus, boys and girls in the early period of adolescence find that sexual expression must be suppressed or alternatives to intercourse must be found if their sexual demands are to be satisfied. As a consequence, many adolescents use *masturbation* as their sexual outlet (Blaine, 1962).

The genitals, of course, are the leading erogenous zone of the body. As early as the first year of life, infants discover the pleasurable sensations of genital self-manipulation. During childhood, the clitoris and the penis remain the most accessible and susceptive erogenous zones. But it is primarily during puberty that there is a heightened readiness for genital stimulation for both sexes. At this time, the adolescent experiences a reawakening of sexual interests, partly through the onset of *nocturnal emissions*, that have remained primarily dormant throughout the latency or middle-childhood period. Consequently, masturbation becomes a central concern for young adolescents, particularly for boys.

A young adolescent male, unsure of his developing masculinity, may repeatedly try to reassure himself by masturbating. Doubts of masculinity, rebellious attitudes, feelings of unpopularity, fear of rejection by girls, as well as a need to explore his new sexuality, all contribute to this autoerotic phase of development (Spicer, 1968).

As a youth progresses through adolescence, masturbation begins to take on a deeper psychological significance than that of earlier exploratory behavior. He begins to fantasize as he masturbates, perhaps visualizing the sexual act with a certain desirable partner. This phase is a normal response to the adolescent's increasing psychosexual awareness, for it provides a means of learning how to control and integrate his new genital sensations.

Unfortunately, although many physicians have pointed out that masturbation is not weakening or dangerous in any way, some parents still hold to the myth that masturbation is a dirty act that can produce physical and mental deterioration or interfere with normal heterosexual development. Such parents often cause their children to carry unnecessary burdens of guilt and anxiety when they masturbate (Spicer, 1968).

For example, Sydney was referred to a guidance clinic because of his Peeping-Tom activities, or *voyeurism*. It was discovered that he engaged in this antisocial behavior whenever he was sexually aroused and felt tremendous guilt at his impulse to masturbate, a practice his mother had cautioned him was "dangerous and dirty."

During puberty teen-age boys have more sexual fantasies, engage in more masturbatory and homosexual experiences, and discuss sexuality more openly than do teen-age girls. Whether there is actually more male sexual activity or whether the activity is just more readily admitted by boys is open to debate. However, quite different developmental patterns of masturbatory behavior seem to exist between boys and girls; thus, they will be discussed separately.

The majority of boys first masturbate by the age of 10, with about 15 percent having engaged in this practice before this age. Evidence indicates that from that point the incidence begins to rise markedly so that by the time they are 12 or 13 years old, males engage in fairly regular masturbatory activity, with three out of four having done so by early adolescence (Gagnon & Simon, 1968). Masturbation remains the major source of sexual outlet for boys throughout the pubescent period.

Variations in the incidence of masturbation reflect differences in education and socioeconomic class. At least 75 percent of the males who terminate their education with elementary school and about 90 percent of those who go on to college masturbate (Reiss, 1960, 1965; Group for the Advancement of Psychiatry, 1966). In later adolescence (ages 17 to 21), it is estimated that approximately 90 percent of the male population engages in this practice from one to four times a week. By the end of the adolescent period most males have masturbated to the point of orgasm at least once in their lives (Kinsey et al., 1948; McCary, 1967). Accordingly, masturbation can be considered to be a typical behavior pattern of the adolescent male.

With the onset of regular heterosexual experiences, there is a marked decrease in the frequency of masturbation and its complex fantasy associations. In the late teens, males in the lower social classes and those with a more limited education begin to seek *coitus* as a source of erotic satisfaction, while those of higher socioeconomic and educational levels tend to focus on petting. Lower-social-class youths tend to experience coitus at an earlier age and to view masturbation as an immature practice (Rainwater, 1966).

For females, puberty is not significantly sexual, especially not in an overt way. Although female puberty begins with the onset of menstruation and the development of the breasts, there does not appear to be any correlation between the menarche and masturbation. Although there are individual differences, most girls do not seem to experience a marked need or desire for genital activity at this time, as do boys. It has been suggested that this later development of a strong sexual drive in the female is the underlying explanation of the double standard. In other words, the early strong sexual urge in males makes it more likely that they will actively seek sexual fulfillment during their teens than would females, who at this time generally experience more moderate sexual drives which don't demand overt expression. Also unlike her male counterpart, the female adolescent does not usually masturbate until late adolescence or early adulthood, and even then she masturbates sporadically and much less frequently than boys. However, it should be pointed out that current research indicates that adolescent girls may be masturbating earlier and more frequently (or talking about it more) than in the past (Gagnon & Simon, 1968; Simon, 1969).

It is estimated that by the end of adolescence, approximately two thirds of all girls have masturbated, but in contrast to boys, about one half of the girls who masturbate do so only after they have experienced orgasm in some form of heterosexual activity. Following adolescence, masturbation seems to be more common in women than in men.

In their late teens, girls from lower socioeconomic and educational backgrounds turn to coitus and away from masturbation as a source of sexual gratification (Rainwater, 1966), and by late adolescence, girls from all educational and socioeconomic classes tend to become more receptive to sexual intercourse. In early adulthood, females often regard genital self-stimulation as an inferior form of sexual activity, and masturbation is commonly superseded by a heterosexual relationship. Of course, there are adolescents who have never had sex dreams or fantasies, never masturbated, and never had heterosexual or homosexual relations.

Many young people consider masturbation normal and do not experience any anxiety or identity confusion. Guilt about masturbation usually develops as a result of erroneous and frightening information which has been handed down by adults. An acceptable program of sex education in the home and in the school can minimize the emotional conflicts associated with masturbation. Many of today's adolescents need reeducation to free them of the taboos they have learned in childhood.

HOMOSEXUAL BEHAVIOR

No male is completely masculine and no female completely feminine. Consequently, the conflict of *bisexuality* is normal in adolescent psychosexual development. With their rapidly developing physical sexual characteristics, most adolescents experience a rather intense identity struggle. The bisexual conflicts and strivings caused by such changes can initiate homosexual tendencies.

Young people normally experience some homosexual interests and tendencies while progressing toward heterosexual maturity. This transient sexual experimentation, which is common in childhood and adolescence, should not be confused with adult homosexuality, for the homosexual behavior of adolescent boys usually does not extend to sexual acts with grown men (Gebhard et al., 1967; Gagnon & Simon, 1968). It is important to distinguish between the adolescent attachment for and exploratory behavior with an individual of approximately the same age and that of the adult homosexual who prefers to achieve sexual gratification with members of the same sex rather than engage in heterosexual behavior.

Some adolescent boys have an occasional, casual homosexual experience before they become adults; others have a more extended erotic contact. Although homosexual experiences during adolescence are of psychological and social significance, they do not compare in incidence and frequency with other forms of sexual behavior. It has been estimated that about 30 percent of all males have had a single homosexual experience; of these, one half have continued to engage in adult homosexuality (Gebhard et al., 1967; Simon & Gagnon, 1967; Gagnon & Simon, 1968). However, it is not possible to make a diagnosis of a permanent homosexual condition prior to the age of 25 (Hettlinger, 1970).

The incidence of adolescent homosexuality for girls appears to be much less common than that for boys, and the contacts are relatively fleeting. About 15 percent of all women have indicated that they have engaged in such behavior (Freedman, 1965; McCary, 1967; Gagnon & Simon, 1968). Again, one can question whether a woman is perhaps less inclined to discuss this type of sexual activity than a man.

PETTING

A further step in resolving the identity conflicts of bisexuality is the adolescent's gradual progression from homosexual tendencies to overt heterosexual behavior, which includes petting for most and premarital sexual intercourse for some.

Petting includes various forms of physical contact designed to effect erotic arousal, excluding penile penetration. Petting can include any or all of the techniques of foreplay that are usually preludes to intercourse, such as kissing, breast fondling, genital stimulation, and mutual masturbation. Mutual petting to orgasm is becoming a more frequent solution to the relief of sexual tensions without intercourse (Hettlinger, 1970).

"Mom, if you really wish to talk to me about sex, just what is it that you want to know?"

Petting is extremely common among young people. Adolescents of today are petting at an earlier age and with greater frequency than was characteristic of past generations. This increase may reflect the earlier onset of puberty, the prevalence of early dating and going steady, and possibly the arousal of erotic urges by the mass media. Adolescents who pet, especially girls, may experience considerable conflict. Should one be "straight" or untouchable, or should one risk acquiring the reputation of being an "easy lay"? One pathway is likely to lead to a dateless existence, while the other may lead to a quick succession of short-lived, usually unsatisfying, romances (Blaine, 1962). To attain a balance between these two extremes is often a considerable problem to the average adolescent girl (Spicer, 1968).

There appears to be no correlation between the onset of puberty and the incidence of petting for either sex. Many boys and girls have been pubescent for some time before they begin to pet. Very few males have had any petting experience prior to puberty, in contrast to females, who begin dating at a much earlier age. A considerable increase in petting takes place about the age of 13 for both sexes. This increase continues throughout adolescence until by the late teens approximately one fourth of all girls and one third of all boys pet to the point of orgasm as a sexual outlet. During late adolescence, it has been estimated that over 80 percent of the females and nearly all of the males are petting to some degree of sexual arousal (McCary, 1967; Reiss, 1967; Gagnon & Simon, 1968).

PREMARITAL INTERCOURSE

It has been suggested that the achievement of complete sexual identity is difficult to attain without heterosexual experience and experimentation during late adolescence (Simon & Gagnon, 1969). Consequently, by late adolescence young people begin to move away from masturbatory behavior and toward shared sexual experience. Normal adolescents reach a point at which they are psychologically ready for intercourse, think about it, desire it, and often engage in it prior to marriage. Since only about one fifth of American adolescents in their teens are married, it is assumed that most youthful sexual behavior occurs in the nonmarital state; this seems to be particularly true of the young adolescent.

Due to increased knowledge of contraceptives and their accessibility to all age groups, fear of pregnancy is no longer a necessary reason for abstaining from intercourse, although it should be pointed out that one out of every five girls who have intercourse before marriage still becomes pregnant (Gebhard et al., 1958).

Despite these facts, it has been recently estimated that about one half of all male students and about two thirds of all female students are still virgins at the time of their graduation from college (Hettlinger, 1970). Research indicates, however that this difference in abstention between the sexes is diminishing as girls have become more self-assertive and have begun to feel less guilty about engaging in premarital sex (Kirkendall, 1961; Reiss, 1966; Bell, 1966b).

Even young girls are demonstrating more sexual precocity and aggressiveness than ever before, in many instances approaching the traditional male role in their courtship behavior. For example, it is much more common today for girls to phone boys and ask for dates than it would have been a generation ago. There are few statistics on the number of girls under 16 years of age who have had intercourse. The incidence of pregnancy is not a reliable indicator, since pregnancy among those under 16 is relatively uncommon; this period is often characterized by adolescent sterility.

With the large increase in the numbers of adolescents in their teens, the number of illegitimate births among teen-agers has also increased. One 1965 study by an Eastern urban social agency disclosed that among 750 predominantly white, middle-class, unmarried mothers, the median age was about 17 years (Young, 1967). At present, those still in their late teens contribute about 40 percent of the total illegitimate births (Crawley, Malfetti, Stewart, & Dias, 1964; Bell, 1966b).

Teen-age marriages, half of them due to pregnancy, now constitute over 40 percent of the nation's marriages. Thus, about one half of the women who ever marry have probably engaged in intercourse before marriage. However, it should be pointed out that among girls who have had premarital intercourse, about 50 percent limit their experience to the man they ultimately marry, and a rather large percentage of the remainder have relations with fewer than five males. Actually, it has been estimated that those who have had coitus with more than this number before marriage constitute less than 10 percent of all women (Gagnon & Simon, 1968).

Initial heterosexual experiences in middle adolescence are often sporadic and experimental. During the late teens, however, it is not uncommon for unmarried young people to approach the average frequency of intercourse for married couples. Thus, the patterns of adolescent sexual behavior are apparently well developed before youths ever leave home. The likelihood that an adolescent will have intercourse before marriage seems to be heavily influenced by such cultural factors as his socioeconomic status, his educational background, and his religious experience (Masters & Johnson, 1966; Couch, 1967; Reiss, 1967). For example, less-educated people begin engaging in coital behavior earlier than do those with more education.

Actually, many youthful sexual behavior patterns, as well as dating patterns, are determined by the culture in which one lives. Relatively fixed and specific sexual roles have characterized male and female behavior in various cultural settings, although recent years have witnessed some flexibility in these roles in some areas of the country. Nonetheless, for most individuals the relationship between the sexes has been ritualized, limited, and planned (Bernard, 1968). For instance, consider the fact that American society has generally decreed that the normal masculine role be one characterized by dominance and the initiation of sexual activity, while the female has traditionally been expected to fill the role of a passive submissive individual. Even the peer-group culture has contributed to such sex-role behavior. In fact, adolescents may even engage in sexual intercourse because they feel that such behavior is expected of them by their peers.

In their quest for love and happiness, many young people today are beginning to regard abstention as unnatural and to question the practicality of refraining from premarital intercourse. Of course, if the motivation for abstention is mutual and rational, then the decision is probably a wise one; however, if the motivation is guilt or fear, then harmful conflicts, frustrations, and anxieties are likely to develop.

The postponement of intercourse, particularly during an extended engagement, is apt to cause an overemphasis on the expectation of future sexual satisfaction in marriage, and the actual experience may then prove to be quite disappointing and much less satisfying than the partners had expected it to be. Many youths who engage in premarital intercourse that is associated with love and affection are not denouncing the desirability of marriage but are only indicating their belief that such a decisive step should not be taken without some preliminary experience with one's possible lifetime partner (Hettlinger, 1970). They feel that decisions of such finality and consequence should not be made without some assurance of the outcome, and that it is foolish to commit oneself permanently to someone who may turn out to be sexually incompatible. Many couples who are disappointed in their marriage learn too late that the wedding ceremony does not alter or remove previously acquired unconscious conflicts, anxiety, guilt, or inhibitions. Viewed in this perspective, premarital relations may help to prepare the adolescent for a more stable, happy marriage, in that by the end of the engagement period, sexual compatibility will not be an uncertain and primary concern.

The young people of today are more liberal and tolerant in their attitudes toward permissible sexual behavior than young people have been in the past (Reiss, 1967; Seward & Larson, 1968). Accompanying this attitude change is a marked increase in almost all types of sexual behavior and an appreciable decline in sexual inhibition. It is now estimated that by the end of adolescence, about three fourths of the male population and at least one half of the female population have engaged in premarital coitus (Hettlinger, 1970). This unprecedented sexual emancipation of many of today's young people apparently represents a significant trend toward open and honest sex as opposed to much of the old-fashioned hypocrisy of previous generations. Accompanying this noticeable trend toward fewer inhibitions has been a general feeling that adolescents should be free to decide for themselves about premarital intercourse. No longer is chastity viewed by all as a necessary prerequisite to marriage. In fact, many believe premarital intercourse to be acceptable when it takes place between consenting partners with affection for one another. Kirkendall (1961) has suggested that morality should be judged not on the basis of inflexible absolutes but rather on the basis of the consequences of an act upon the interpersonal relationship of two people. Within this context, many modern youth do not consider themselves to be promiscuous or immoral.

THE ABORTION REVOLUTION

Society has been traditionally punitive toward teen-age premarital or unwanted pregnancies and has generally provided only the alternative fates of a forced marriage, an illegitimate child, or back-alley abortion. Over the years illegal abortion has been tolerated as a necessary evil but has not been considered a subject for polite conversation. Women who terminated their unwanted pregnancies did so in fear and silence, often risking their lives and suffering much guilt and shame. However, since the 1965 United States Supreme Court decision declaring birth-control laws to be unconstitutional, many states have sought reform by liberalizing their statutes, by repealing some of their legislation, or by challenging the abortion laws in court. In addition, the sexual revolution, the population explosion, the decline in religiosity, and the demand for equality of the sexes have all contributed to changing attitudes about abortion. Today a woman is much more likely to die from pregnancy than from a hospital abortion. At present, one might even state that an abortion revolution in this country is well under way.

In this age of modern contraceptives, many women are beginning to regard sex without pregnancy as a natural and personal right, and when privately practiced, they feel it should not be the direct concern of society. Furthermore, many young people advocate the fundamental right of women to choose whether or not to bear children. Birth control, they feel, should be a matter of individual conscience, and if it is desired, legal abortion should be made available on request. Consequently, the pill, as a safeguard against unwanted pregnancy and abortion, is viewed as the simple solution to contraceptive failure that can be undertaken without adult interference.

SEX EDUCATION

As an adolescent learns about the anatomy and physiology of human reproduction he is also forming an attitude that will affect his future sexual behavior. When the acquisition of such knowledge is part of an organized program designed to provide instruction about sexual behavior or attitudes, the term "sex education" is commonly used.

The goals of sex education should include both the instillment of wholesome attitudes and the imparting of adequate and correct information about sex. More specifically, the objectives of sex education should encompass teachings that will facilitate good mental health and social adjustment and minimize the occurrence of emotional disorders and social maladjustment (Staton, 1968). For example, such attitudes of the past as "good girls don't, bad girls do" have often had an adverse effect on sexual adjustment in marriage (McCary, 1969). Thus, through sexual misinformation needless fears about sex have commonly arisen.

Sexuality is an attribute of human beings from the time of infancy. But even prior to school age many children are exposed, in one way or another, to distorted sexual attitudes from their peers, parents, and other adults. Long before youngsters reach adolescence, for instance, many of their parents have imparted to them the idea that their genitals are undesirable and are not to be explored (Hettlinger, 1970). Later during school and religious training, children and adolescents are often indoctrinated with Victorian or puritanical notions of sexual sobriety and premarital chastity. A sex-education program, which is presented to a youth previously well indoctrinated in this antisexual tradition, will in all probability fail in its objectives.

Effective sex education must work, therefore, not through the old modes of externally imposed controls by the church and society but by new modes of encouraging internal control in the adolescent based on what he feels is right as a result of appropriate parental guidelines and the outgrowth of his own experiences. "Society should offer to youth whatever information it requests regarding sex; it should then provide youth with freedom to experiment; and finally, it should stand ready to help pick up whatever pieces fall to the ground when the occasional drastic mistake blows off the roof" (Nixon, 1962, p. 100).

Unfortunately, the kind of sex education that has been found in our schools and colleges has tended to emphasize mainly the three R's—reproduction, repression, and religion (Ard, 1967), with the psychological aspects of sexual behavior falling by the wayside. The net result has been that young people usually acquire less knowledge of both physical and psychological factors than is desirable. Furthermore, it is often difficult to sexually "reeducate" an adolescent with only a short-term, superficial sex-education program. A frank and honest treatment of this subject, one that really comes to grips with the intimate practical problems of sexual behavior, is a rare, often nonexistent experience for today's youth. With masturbation and petting being commonly practiced and premarital intercourse rapidly approaching a similar status, there is an increasing need for a broader program in sex education than might have been necessary two or three decades ago.

Reliable information about what is known about sexual behavior and its effects on human relationships, however, is difficult for the average adolescent to obtain (Couch, 1967). Young people are too often exposed to adult society's own confusion and inconsistencies in its handling of controversial sex issues; hypocrisies, prejudices, myths, and taboos about the role of sex in human behavior seem to reign. Much that the average youth hears from adults is prohibitive and guilt-arousing mythology, while he receives quite opposite views (sometimes just as inaccurate) from his peer group. Seldom do adolescents have the opportunity to freely discuss sexual matters with a well-informed and willing adult.

Recently, however, adults have begun to reconsider, reevaluate, and reappraise the appropriateness and relevance of their traditional attitudes and sexual standards. Consequently, many contradictory and opposing opinions, practices, and attitudes exist about the proper place and importance of sex in our society. Of course, an erroneous assumption, too, has been that the sexual problem involves only the younger generation and not the elder.

Actually, sex education first begins when the preschool child asks such questions as "Where do babies come from?" At this point, it is the obligation of the parents to answer him honestly but simply, without endless elaboration beyond the immediate answers desired by the child. Unfortunately, however, many parents are unable to provide such answers at this stage and are even less prepared to cope with their child's crucial need for information when he reaches adolescence (Page, 1967). Thus, a young person with an intense curiosity and a need to pursue all possible sources of sex information, begins to observe and listen to others of the same age and sex, namely his "peer group." The peer group, by default, now becomes the most important factor in his sex education. Sexual interests are consciously experienced and discussed within the peer group and acted out in accordance with peer expectations and demands. Adolescents are then able to compare and test their own standards of morality with those of adult society; the result is that they often choose to compromise less with adult prohibitions (Bell, 1966a).

But adult society has a major responsibility to provide adequate sex education for the adolescent population. Young people should be instructed in the psychology as well as the physiology of sexuality. Physiological instruction should include material on the reproductive system and process, the effects of heredity, biochemical functions relating to sex, and differences in the anatomy of the sexes, as well as physiological changes from childhood to adulthood and the impact of these changes on behavior (Staton, 1968). Unfortunately, there is little material presently available on the effects of emotional stimuli, which may contribute as much to sexual arousal as any biological factors. There is a definite need for research into such topics as the role of love and romance in a girl's sexual desire as opposed to that of a boy's more erotic urges and the impact of conversation on sexual behavior.

The importance of a reality-oriented sex-education program should not be underestimated. There are presently about one and a half million cases of gonorrhea being treated each year in this country (Fleming, Brown, Donohue, & Branigin, 1970), and although the incidence of syphilis has declined during the past decade, it is still more prevalent in older adolescents than in any other age group (*Statistical Bulletin*, April, 1969). A survey of 346 youths in New York City disclosed that 32 percent were unaware of the fact that venereal disease can be cured when it is treated in time, while 60 percent of this group did not know that syphilis and gonorrhea are transmitted through sexual intercourse (*School Health*, 1963). Obviously, ignorance about these diseases should be of considerable concern to both the younger and older generations.

Another problem that should be faced by our society is indicated by the fact that about 40 percent of teen-age marriages are complicated by premarital pregnancy. Over 50 percent of all brides are under the age of 20, and about one third of these teen-age marriages will end in divorce within four years. Evidence from all of these figures indicates that many adolescents need advice on the responsibilities of sexual activities and information about birth-control methods.

An adequate sex-education program presented by those effectively prepared to teach such material would greatly minimize, if not avoid, adolescent misconceptions, misinformation, misbehavior, and anxiety about sexuality. Such a program, if it is to be successful, requires that adolescents receive an honest, factual, and relevant exposure to information that will help them understand that sexual awareness and desires are psychologically normal and that sex is an important part of the whole individual's development.

Rather than the traditional "They are going to learn in the street anyway" (Gagnon & Simon, 1969, p. 46) form of sex education, programs should be designed to keep pace with the current changes in attitudes and sexual behavior. A comprehensive sex-education curriculum should include relevant goals, methods, and content appropriate for different age levels—as well as suggestions on the role that the parents, the school, and the community can play in sex education (Bracher, 1967; Kinch, 1967). The recently formed Sex Information and Education Counsel of the United States (SIECUS) represents a start in that direction (Kirkendall, 1965).

SUMMARY AND CONCLUSIONS

Probably no greater problems confront the typical adolescent in today's rapidly changing world than those in the area of sexual behavior. Because of the wide gap existing between so many older generation attitudes and the current sexual attitudes and practices of the younger generation, young people are often beset with needless guilt and anxiety if they engage in certain sexual behaviors, which today are more or less commonly practiced.

A recent survey revealed that adolescents criticized their parents most of all for their failure to provide adequate information on sex (McCary, 1969). To fill this void, there is an emphatic need for a relevant sex-education program encompassing both the psychological and physiological aspects of sexuality. Such a program must focus its attention on the formation of healthy attitudes as much as on the biological forces, if young people are expected to become emotionally and socially well-adjusted individuals. Until adequate sex education becomes widespread, rising venereal disease rates, increasing numbers of premarital pregnancies and illegitimate births, and a growing incidence of unhappy teen-age marriages will continue to plague our society.

REFERENCES

Ard, B. Do as I do, be as I am: The bruising conflict. In S. M. Farber & R. H. L. Wilson (Eds.), Sex education and the teenager. Berkeley, Calif.: Diablo Press, 1967. Pp. 78–88.

Bell, R. R. Parent-child conflict in sexual values. Journal of Social Issues, 1966, 22, 34–44. (a)

Bell, R. R. *Premarital sex in a changing society.* Englewood Cliffs, N.J.: Prentice-Hall, 1966. (b)

Bernard, J. *The sex game.* Englewood Cliffs, N.J.: Prentice-Hall, 1968.

Blaine, G. B., Jr. *Patience and fortitude: The parents' guide to adolescence.* Boston: Little, Brown, 1962.

Bracher, M. The Martinson report: Implications for sex education. *Journal of School Health,* 1967, **37**, 491–497.

Couch, G. B. Youth looks at sex. *Adolescence,* 1967, **2**(6), 255–266.

Crawley, L., Malfetti, J. L., Stewart, E. I., & Dias, M. V. *Reproduction, sex, and preparation for marriage.* Englewood Cliffs, N.J.: Prentice-Hall, 1964.

Fleming, W. L., Brown, W. J., Donohue, J. F., & Branigin, P. W. National survey of venereal disease treated by physicians in 1968. *Journal of the American Medical Association,* 1970, **211**(11), 1827–1830.

Freedman, M. B. The sexual behavior of American college women: An empirical study and an historical study. *Merrill-Palmer Quarterly,* 1965, **2**, 33–48.

Gagnon, J. H., & Simon, W. Sexual deviance in contemporary America. *The Annals of the American Academy of Political and Social Science,* 1968. **376**, 106–122.

Gagnon, J. H., & Simon, W. They're going to learn in the street anyway. *Psychology Today,* 1969, **3**, 46–49.

Gebhard, P. H., Gagnon, J. H., Pomeroy, W. B., & Christenson, C. V. *Sex offenders.* New York: Bantam Books, 1967.

Gebhard, P. H., Pomeroy, W. B., Martin, C. E., & Christenson, C. V. *Pregnancy, birth, and abortion.* New York: Harper & Row, 1958.

Group for the Advancement of Psychiatry, Committee on the College Student. *Sex and the college student.* New York: Atheneum, 1966.

Hettlinger, R. F. *Sexual maturity.* Belmont, Calif.: Wadsworth, 1970.

Kinch, R. A. Adolescent sex education. *Annals of the New York Academy of Sciences,* 1967, **142**(3), 824–833.

Kinsey, A. C., Pomeroy, W. B., & Martin, C. E. *Sexual behavior in the human male.* Philadelphia: W. B. Saunders, 1948.

Kinsey, A. C., Pomeroy, W. B., Martin, C. E., & Gebhard, P. H. *Sexual behavior in the human female.* Philadelphia: W. B. Saunders, 1953.

Kirkendall, L. A. *Premarital intercourse and interpersonal relationships.* New York: Julian Press, 1961.

Kirkendall, L. A. Sex education. *SIECUS Study Guide No. 1.* New York: SIECUS, 1965.

Masters, W. H., & Johnson, V. E. *Human sexual response.* Boston: Little, Brown, 1966.

McCary, J. L. *Human sexuality.* Princeton, N. J.: Van Nostrand, 1967.

McCary, J. L. Why sex education? Paper presented at the Louisiana Psychological State Convention, Lafayette, March, 1969.

Nixon, R. E. *The art of growing.* New York: Random House, 1962.

Packard, V. *The sexual wilderness.* New York: David McKay, 1968.

Page, E. W. Physically adult, mentally unprepared. In S. M. Farber & R. H. L. Wilson (Eds.), *Sex education and the teenager.* Berkeley, Calif.: Diablo Press, 1967. Pp. 1–7.

Rainwater, L. Some aspects of lower-class sexual behavior. *Journal of Social Issues,* 1966, **22**, 96–108.

Reiss, I. L. *Premarital sex standards in America.* New York: Free Press, 1960.

Reiss, I. L. Social class and premarital sexual permissiveness: A re-examination. *American Sociological Review,* 1965, **30**, 747–757.

Reiss, I. L. The sexual renaissance: A summary and analysis. *Journal of Social Issues,* 1966, **22**, 126.

Reiss, I. L. *The social context of premarital sexual permissiveness.* New York: Holt, Rhinehart & Winston, 1967.

School Health, November 12, 1963.

Seward, G. H., & Larson, W. R. Adolescent concepts of social sex roles in the United States and the two Germanies. *Proceedings of the 76th Annual Convention of the American Psychological Association,* 1968, **3**, 435–436.

Simon, W. Sex. *Psychology Today,* 1969, **3**, 23–27.

Simon, W., & Gagnon, J. H. *Sexual deviance, a reader.* New York: Harper & Row, 1967.

Simon, W., & Gagnon, J. H. Psychosexual development. *Trans-action,* 1969, **6**, 9–17.

Spicer, F. Sexual problems in adolescence. *Proceedings of the Royal Society of Medicine,* 1968, **61**, 510–512.

Statistical Bulletin. Patterns of venereal disease morbidity in recent years. Metropolitan Life Insurance, April, 1969, **50**, 5–7.

Staton, T. F. Sex education for adolescents. In J. F. Adams (Ed.), *Understanding adolescence: Current developments in adolescent psychology.* Boston: Allyn & Bacon, 1968. Pp. 248–271.

Young, L. R. Emotional conflicts of young motherhood. In S. M. Farber & R. H. L. Wilson (Eds.), *Teenage marriage and divorce.* Berkeley, Calif.: Diablo Press, 1967. Pp. 85–94.

IV

Normal and Deviant Adolescent Emotional Development

6

Normal Development of Emotionality in the Adolescent

Don't laugh at a youth for his affectations; he's only trying on one face after another till he finds his own.

Logan Pearsall Smith (1865–1946)
Afterthoughts

Probably no other stage of life is characterized by stronger and more rapidly changing manifestations of emotionality than the period of adolescence. According to Stamell (1964), the typical youth "becomes easily disturbed by insignificant events and reacts out of all proportion to their insignificance" (p. 1020). Bewildered parents and teachers who are confronted by frequent, intense, and often abrupt mood swings in adolescents begin to wonder if they have failed them or if these young people have suddenly developed a serious emotional disorder.

What are some of the reasons behind adolescents' frequent display of intense emotionality? As we mentioned in Chapter 4, the many rapid physical and biochemical changes characterizing adolescence are usually accompanied by emotional changes. A second determinant is the adolescent's conflict between the desire to grow up and become independent and the wish to hold on to a childlike passivity and dependency (Daly, 1966). A third factor is the adolescent's search for identity, a term which has been used by Erikson (1963) to describe the feeling of being at home in one's body and possessing an awareness of where one is going. And recently Elkind (1967) has suggested

133

that the development of new *cognitive structures*, new ways of thinking, reasoning, perceiving, and feeling, makes possible *affective* or emotional experiences not previously experienced by adolescents.

EMOTIONALITY AND PHYSICAL CHANGES

When an adolescent experiences swift changes in body size and shape, his frequent reaction to his new image is a lowering of his self-esteem, which puts considerable strain on his already fragile *ego* (Daly, 1966). A girl in her early teens may compare her shape to that of a mature woman and become worried and concerned that she measures up second best. She may come to feel inferior and ashamed of her body and try to withdraw from social contacts to protect herself from such feelings. Because of their uneven physical growth and development both sexes may become sullen and depressed, often retreating to their own bedrooms for endless hours to worry about these rapid changes and what they signify and to daydream about a possibly brighter future.

Large increases in the secretions of hormones also appear to play a major role in the emotional development of the adolescent. The beginning of hormonal changes, marked by the menstrual rhythm, particularly influences their moods. Most young female adolescents, however, are at first unable to connect their mood swings with menstruation and hormonal fluctuations and become upset when their premenstrual behavior is quite atypical of their usual selves. Boys, too, experience many radical physical and hormonal changes to which they must become accustomed. Once such changes have taken place, however, and boys have become familiar with them, they are no longer confronted with change, although girls will continue to experience certain hormonal periodic changes every month, as the menstrual cycle becomes established (Bardwick, Douvan, Horner, & Gutmann, 1970).

Usually, however, by the end of the early adolescent period, the hormonal and biological processes have become somewhat stabilized, resulting in some stabilization in the emotions of the young person (Group for the Advancement of Psychiatry, 1968). They no longer tend to overreact with the intensity characteristic of early adolescence.

INDEPENDENCE VERSUS DEPENDENCY NEEDS

For most adolescents, "The level of emotional maturity fluctuates between attempts at independence and autonomy on one hand and childish demands for limitation and guidance on the other" (Karowe & McCandless, 1963, p. 237). Unfortunately, parents sometimes view this youthful search for independence almost as an insurrection rather than as a natural striving toward "maturity."

Blos (1967) has described this striving as the second individuation process, the first having been completed at the end of the third year of life. He points out that this process involves "the shedding of family dependencies, the loosening of infantile object ties in order to become a member of society at large or, simply, of the adult world" (p. 163). Failure to achieve this disengagement with a moderate degree of success prevents the young person from establishing new extrafamilial objects of affection in the outside world. He often reflects difficulties in resolving this situation in *acting-out* behavior, learning disorders, or patterns of procrastination, moodiness, apathy, and negativism.

The process of individuation is characterized by considerable ambivalence. The first exhilaration marking the realization of newly acquired independence from one's parents may even be accompanied by a depression almost comparable to a state of mourning upon the death of a love object (Blos, 1967).

When the dependency-autonomy conflict is most intense, the adolescent is most likely to engage in deviant behavior, perhaps as a cry for help or a plea for attention to the stress and strain he is undergoing. Frequently it is difficult to determine whether such behavior is transient or permanent, normal or pathological (Blos, 1967). During the period of early adolescence this behavior is likely to be characterized by a rebellion against and withdrawal from adults and their values. At first, this rebellion is primarily verbal, but it gradually may involve more and more acting-out behavior. While adults frequently offer severe criticism, dire predictions, and sweeping negative generalizations about the younger generation, youth, in turn, becomes more questioning and rebellious against the rules, standards, and values of adult society. (It is of interest to note that the adult's experiences in adolescence usually have little or no value in aiding him to understand, communicate, and relate to those who are now adolescents [Gallatin, 1968; Personality and Growth Series for Adolescents: An Evaluation, 1969]).

Although he may verbalize and act as if he rejects any need to be dependent upon his parents or other adults, the young person is often secretly relieved when the older generation places certain firm but fair limitations on his behavior. Such limits make him feel more confident and secure and less frightened in exploring areas within these boundaries (Josselyn, 1967).

For example, Donna, 16, was told by her mother that she would not be permitted to drive alone in the family car after dark and that when necessary her parents would escort her to her destination during the evening. Although vehemently protesting that among other things this would interfere with her freedom to attend community little-theatre activities and that most of her girl friends were permitted to drive at night, Donna relented. Despite the fact that she was quite vocal in her complaints about this "injustice," her mother overheard her remark to a close friend that she had been somewhat fearful of being alone in the little-theatre parking lot following rehearsals or of possibly having car trouble on her way home.

THE SEARCH FOR IDENTITY

Erik Erikson (1956) has described the stage of late adolescence as the period of the *identity crisis*. During this developmental stage young people engage in a personal redefinition of their role in society, a process which may take the form of intense self-awareness or exist at a less conscious level. A combination of psychological and environmental factors initiates this search for identity and facilitates its development, presenting the adolescent with a complex, often confusing variety of *self-images* (Bronson, 1959).

Erikson (1968) has used the term "identity confusion" to depict the psychological chaos and conflict arising in many young people of this age. In the process of evaluating his past self-image, assessing his present assets and liabilities, reformulating new ideals and goals, and testing new interpersonal relationships, the adolescent may often wonder who he really is (Bronson, 1959). Accustomed to a comparatively stable *self-concept* throughout childhood, the lack of such a sturdy sense of self in adolescence causes the individual to develop fluctuating appraisals of his social environment and to exhibit wide variations in his interpersonal behavior. Not surprisingly, this "identity confusion" is likely to be accompanied by considerable inner tension and increased anxiety.

In one study of 46 college students, composed mainly of coeds, all but seven showed behavior designed to resolve this problem of "identity confusion" through transient periods of social withdrawal or through commitments to various social or religious ideologies (Bronson, 1959). It is possible that many high school and college students who participated in *activist* movements were also searching for meaningful commitments that would help them resolve their "identity confusion" by delineating the identity of the younger generation from that of the "Establishment" or parent generation.

Erikson has suggested that our rapidly advancing technology, which has lengthened the period of adolescent dependence and delayed the acquisition of an occupational identity, has also added to the identity crisis. To compensate for this delay, a young person may temporarily overidentify with his peers and with the leaders of the peer group to the point that he appears to lose his own individuality. Such behavior may be indicative not only of an attempt to resolve the identity crisis but it may also reflect the transference of adolescent dependency needs from adults to the peer group. Even "falling in love" may represent an attempt to solve the problem of who one really is. A young man who becomes a young woman's steady is acquiring status in a certain role. Furthermore, adolescent love can serve as a means of projecting one's diffused self-concept on another and gradually through its reflection clarify his own identity (Erikson, 1963). Unfortunately, clannish, intolerant behavior and exclusion of those who are "different" from the group may also serve as a temporary defense against identity diffusion.

Some young people may find it necessary to declare a *psychological moratorium* in order for them to achieve healthy identity development (Blaine, 1965; Erikson, 1968). For instance, a student may temporarily drop out of high school or college in an attempt to reestablish a state of psychological equilibrium and a satisfying identity of his own. The apathy and listlessness, which are so often disturbing to parents at this time, may very well be masking much anxiety resulting from a concern about the void within, which develops through old values being discarded but new ones not making themselves apparent.

"The process of dropping-out often makes the difference because the student is able to get the feeling afterwards that he has made a real change from the established pattern that had been set down for him since early in life. When he comes back he feels that he is now going to college for his own reasons. This improves his ability to perform. The other great advantage of dropping-out of college is the feeling of accomplishment which may result from doing a job. . . . This gives him a feeling of confidence which he can carry back into college work" (Blaine, 1965, p. 394).

Larry Stevens was such a "drop out." He began his studies at the state university in the field of premedical training, a goal which apparently represented the ambitions of his physician father, rather than Larry's wishes. After a year and a half of college, Larry dropped out of school because of low grades and a general disinterest in preparing for the medical profession. He joined the United States Air Force and began training as a radar technician, an area which he found to be interesting and gratifying to him. After his tour of duty, which was spent mainly in the field of radar, Larry left the service and decided to return to school. With his satisfying experiences in the Air Force behind him and the feeling that he had achieved on his own (he had been promoted to staff sergeant before his separation from the service), he developed a new enthusiasm for completing his education. This time, however, with the results of vocational testing, which he sought as an aid in helping him to select his future occupation, Larry discontinued his premedical training and entered the college of engineering. Pursuing his own selected goals, his grades rapidly soared and he ultimately graduated from the university with honors.

Identity formation does not begin nor end with adolescence, for it is a lifetime development (Erikson, 1956). However, by the time a youth has graduated from college, or possibly within a few years following graduation after he has achieved an occupational status, the typical adolescent will have fairly well resolved the identity crisis. He will have acquired a sense of who he is and his role in life, an achievement that requires incorporating into the self certain identifications with valued people in the environment. Sometimes this phenomenon occurs rather abruptly, surprising even the young person himself, but regardless of when it takes place, it is a necessary step on the road to maturity (Blaine, 1965).

COGNITIVE STRUCTURE AND ADOLESCENT EMOTIONALITY

According to Elkind (1968), adolescence is accompanied by the simultaneous appearance of new cognitive structures and new affective or emotional experiences. He cites the example of prejudice, which he feels is not usually manifested until the adolescent period, when adolescents form small cliques based mainly on socioeconomic class. It has been suggested that these new affective displays are not necessarily the result of the emerging cognitive structures they parallel but that the cognitive changes are necessary for their occurrence.

Elkind bases his hypothesis about the interrelationship between *cognition* and adolescent emotionality on Piaget's theories of cognitive development (Inhelder & Piaget, 1958). According to Piaget, each individual goes through the same sequence of intellectual development although not necessarily at the same rate of speed nor the same chronological age. The highest stage of cognitive development is the stage of logical reasoning, which usually emerges about the beginning of adolescence and lays the setting for certain typical adolescent reactions. This cognitive stage is characterized by the ability to introspect and to think hypothetically at an abstract level. The adolescent who has reached this stage is able to perceive and to think about many different possibilities in his decision making. For instance, he becomes cognizant of several alternatives to his parents' directives and becomes reluctant to accept them without question. He also wants to learn not only where his parents stand but why, and he is usually prepared to debate these parental decisions and compare them with those chosen by himself and by his peers. Paradoxically, although perhaps troubled by having to arrive at decisions himself and often finding such decision making to be quite a burden, he still does not want adults to make up his mind for him. As a matter of fact, some adolescents seem to demand that their parents take a stand, if only so that they can rebel against it.

It has been suggested that in primitive cultures, where these more advanced cognitive structures may not develop, there may be little of the storm and stress commonly experienced by adolescents in our Western society (Elkind, 1968). Perhaps the presence of a more advanced cognitive framework makes it possible for a person to "construct" various alternatives in his problem solving. The development of the cognitive tools needed for such decision making also appears to set the stage for the typical conflicts erupting between parents and their adolescent children. As they become more and more adamant in arriving at their own decisions, young people tend to become more rejectant of parental values, thereby creating greater dissonance between the two generations.

OTHER ASPECTS OF EMOTIONAL DEVELOPMENT

Egocentrism

The whole universe of the preschool child is that which he directly experiences (Piaget, 1963). Although there are certain differences in the adolescent's perception of the universe, he is nonetheless just as ego centered as the preschooler. He typically fails to distinguish between what others are thinking about and his own preoccupations and consequently assumes that other people are as obsessed with his behavior and appearance as he himself is (Elkind, 1967).

Because the typical young person believes that the attention of others is focused on him, he reacts as though he were performing before an assemblage of people. Elkind (1967) has described this phenomenon as one's perception of having an "imaginary audience;" it is an audience because the adolescent feels that he is the focus of attention, yet it is imaginary because there is usually no audience in actual social situations (unless an individual behaves in such a manner as to create one). This perception of an "imaginary audience" probably explains much of the self-consciousness characteristic of so many young people. They perceive themselves with a critical eye and believe that their audience will view them just as critically. An adolescent's desire for privacy and his reluctance to reveal his private thoughts to others may also reflect this feeling of being under close scrutiny by a critical assemblage.

At the same time, adolescents are often self-admiring, and again the "imaginary audience" plays a role (Elkind, 1967). Youthful boorishness, loudness, and faddish dress may mirror the discrepancy between what a young person believes to be attractive and what others admire. It is not surprising that a member of the younger generation often fails to comprehend the older generation's disapproval of his dress and his manners. A similar manifestation of egocentrism may be seen at heterosexual gatherings in which young people seem to be more concerned with being observed than observing (Elkind, 1967). Thus, the young adolescent becomes both an actor to himself and an audience to others. This behavior is especially noticeable at parties during early adolescence. Boys tend to gather at one end of a room and girls at the other, each group gawking quite self-consciously at its opposite with the boys frequently displaying boisterous behavior and the girls giggling with embarrassment.

An adolescent's egocentrism is also reflected in his belief in the uniqueness of his own emotionality. As Elkind (1967) puts it, "Only he can suffer with such agonized intensity or experience such exquisite rapture" (p. 1031). At a slightly different level, this feeling of uniqueness becomes what Elkind has described as a "personal fable," exemplified by an adolescent's belief that he is immortal or an unwed girl's conviction that pregnancy happens to others but will surely never happen to her.

By the age of 15 to 16 this egocentrism, which is so characteristic of early adolescence, begins to diminish (Elkind, 1967). Apparently the process of *reality testing* takes the place of performance for an "imaginary" audience, and the adolescent begins to develop a genuine concern about the reactions of an authentic audience. This process first occurs at a cognitive level at which the individual learns to differentiate between his own thoughts and the thoughts of others and then at an affective level at which he gradually learns to integrate the feelings of other people with his own emotions.

Self-Consciousness

Closely associated with egocentric behavior in the typical young person are his experience of considerable self-consciousness and his strong need for self-confidence (Galdston, 1967). A young person is extremely conscious not only of his body but also of his mind. He is often aware of a sharp discrepancy between the self that he is and the self that he wishes to become, or his *ideal self.* With the onset of puberty most adolescents undertake a thorough assessment of themselves, comparing not only their body parts but also their motor skills, intellectual abilities, talents, and social skills with those of their peers and with those of their ideals or heroes. It is not surprising that this critical self-appraisal is accompanied by self-conscious behavior, which makes adolescents especially vulnerable to embarrassment, slight, and shame, as we can see in the following illustration.

Fifteen-year-old Laura, a tall, rather obese girl with a pretty face, is so self-conscious about her body image that she is reluctant to walk alone down the school corridors between classes or even to obtain a drink from the water fountain by herself. Apparently she feels that if a companion or two accompany her, she will be less conspicuous and her body size will be less noticeable.

The Quest for Self-Confidence

When his self-inventory is reasonably complete, the typical adolescent compiles the results and then directs his energies toward correcting his shortcomings and undesired traits. Galdston (1967) describes the situation quite vividly: "Adolescence is a time for discarding unwanted attributes and for building up others in a 'psychological spring housecleaning' " (p. 165).

It has been suggested that the deviant behavior displayed by many youths is often an attempt to nullify a major discrepancy existing between his self-assessment and the ideal self toward which he strives (Galdston, 1967). His rebellion may very well be a manifestation of his feelings about certain unpleasant facts about himself. For example, a young man who aspires to become an athletic hero may discover that he doesn't possess the skill, the stamina, nor the courage demanded of a star athlete. To silence his doubts about himself and his feelings of weakness and inadequacy, he may *overcompensate* by turning to patterns of behavior characteristic of a "tough" individual, in order to demonstrate the physical strength and courage he in reality lacks.

Although such behavior can fulfill a need, if it is carried to extremes, it can become dangerous to the individual adolescent and to his community, leading in extreme cases to vandalism and to promiscuity (Galdston, 1967). The amount of behavioral deviation is generally proportionate to the disparity between the childhood fantasies of the self-to-be and the adolescent self he ultimately becomes. If he falls too far short of his ideal, the young person may eventually discard it altogether, relieving the painful tension aroused by the wide discrepancy between self and ideal self but at the same time destroying the motivation which might have enabled him to reach his goals or to achieve satisfying alternate aims. The discarded dream leaves a void, which the adolescent often misperceives as being solely the result of factors beyond his control rather than the consequence of any of his own actions. Becoming cynical, he may seek relief through sensory stimulation by turning to drugs, which provide the temporary illusion of filling the void.

As development toward "maturity" progresses and the adolescent gradually acquires certain social skills and improved physical coordination, his self-confidence begins to rise. With this increasing assurance in himself, the young person usually develops a greater capacity for social self-responsibility, enabling him for the first time to develop an integrated system of personal values and a set of self-determined goals for his future (Karowe & McCandless, 1963). Prior to this stage of growth, his values are frequently outgrowths of his defiance of the older generation or in imitation of his peers.

Idealism

Adolescence is a period of intense idealism. The adolescent's capacity to construct ideals often leads him to regard his family, his religion, and society in general in a derogatory manner because of the wide contrast between ideal situations and the facts of cold reality. Often he *intellectualizes* and *rationalizes* his ideals (for instance, the practice of hippies loving everyone), but he displays little practical knowledge about how such ideals might become reality and even less interest in working toward their fulfillment (Elkind, 1968).

During this stage of development the older generation comes under fire for having failed to put certain professed ideals into practice. Few human beings can reach the pedestal on which the adolescent has placed the ideal person (Elkind, 1968).

Concurrently, young people often fail to demonstrate compassion for human weaknesses, both within themselves and in others. Because of their limited experience, their perspective is often narrow and their patience with the foibles of humans is extremely short.

Generally as he approaches his middle twenties, the typical young person begins to adapt to the cold realities of life (Elkind, 1968), and he begins to recognize that he will not be able to change the world overnight. This acceptance may reflect the fact that he has given up trying to change society because he has been defeated too many times, or it may be the result of his reassessment of the limitations of the older generation and his recognition of his own shortcomings. In any case, he gradually appears, at least overtly, to become more acceptant of both.

ADOLESCENT DEFENSE MECHANISMS

As a young person reaches adolescence, he starts to show changes in his emotional expression, such as increased intensity in his reactions, more extensive acting-out behavior, and changes in the defenses he uses to cope with his problems and conflicts.

As the adolescent period is reached, the defenses and adaptive behavior patterns that were developed to cope with childhood stresses begin to disintegrate. Such disintegration is important in that it enables the adolescent to seek new patterns of behavior that will be compatible with the demands of adulthood (Josselyn, 1967).

That is, the young person begins to modify his approach to life through changes and modifications in his *defense mechanisms.* Let us take a look at some typical adolescent defensive reactions to the numerous frustrations, conflicts, and pressures with which he is confronted.

Fantasy

The adolescent's devotion to idealism is closely tied to his reliance on fantasy. In fact, the adolescent period has often been described as a period of dreaming, a time when one can take refuge from the many demands of life by creating, in a childlike manner, an ideal world (Stamell, 1964). A young person engages in fantasies that are frequently unrealistic and antisocial in nature (Piotrowski, 1962). Such daydreams, often lively and characterized by strongly colored emotionality, can serve as substitute gratification of many adolescent needs and desires, such as sexual urges, which perhaps cannot be satisfied directly.

Unfortunately parents and others working with youth too often assume that such fantasies will inevitably be acted out (Piotrowski, 1962), but antisocial fantasies are only indicative of future delinquent behavior if one or both of two conditions exist: (1) that the adolescent regards his fantasies as realistic representations of "the way things are" or even as actual "rehearsals" of future behavior; and (2) that he possesses weak self-control allowing such fantasies to spill over readily into acting-out behavior. It is essential to distinguish between aggressiveness that serves purely as a defense against emotional stress and that which has become deeply entrenched as a character trait, as would be found in the *psychopath.* Actually fantasy can often prove to be a satisfying and acceptable outlet for channeling emotions at all stages of life. Provided an individual is able to distinguish his imaginative activity from reality and provided his control is adequate, he can indulge in many antisocial fantasies with little danger of his acting them out. Indeed, the crucial point is not the fantasy itself but the role it plays in an individual's motives and drives (Piotrowski, 1962).

As he grows toward emotional maturity, the adolescent will normally learn to impose self-limitations on his own behavior. However, this ego control need not cancel out his freedom to think about or to fantasize and ultimately discuss many ideas that would be unacceptable if they were translated into behavior (Karowe & Mc-Candless, 1963).

It can be beneficial to the adolescent to learn to discuss his fantasies and feelings in a supportive atmosphere. This may sometimes be accomplished through family councils and parent-child dialogues when the younger generation evinces an interest. Within the framework of the classroom, through class discussion and even "bull sessions," the authors have encouraged this emotional ventilation on numerous occasions. Gripes about difficult instructors, problems with parents, and other issues may enable students outwardly to express their feelings, alleviating considerable pent-up hostility and permitting them to assume a greater degree of objectivity in their attitudes toward some of their problems. Unfortunately, however, far too many adults tend to chastise or belittle young people who do ventilate their feelings, condemning them for possessing such thoughts rather than accepting and reflecting their ideas back to them.

Defenses against Fear and Anxiety

The fears and anxieties of adolescence, although less overtly expressed than those of childhood and sometimes subtly hidden behind a mask of indifference or apathy, are very much present and often quite intense. What types of fears are of the greatest concern to the adolescent in today's world and what kinds of individuals are most likely to possess these fears? Croake (1967) reported on a study of 98 male and 83 female ninth-grade students of low and high socioeconomic status from both a small town and a large city. His results disclosed that the girls possessed more fears than the boys, and lower socioeconomic class young people had more fears than those from the upper class. Interestingly, the most frequently cited fears were of a political nature, perhaps reflecting concern about our present instruments for self-annihilation.

In an earlier study by Angelino and Shedd (1953), 589 young people, 10 to 18 years of age, from regular public-school classrooms were asked to choose from a list of 10 the fears and worries they felt were most commonly held by their peers. The 13- and 14-year-old youngsters seemed to be most concerned with school problems. Personal-conduct fears—for example, fear of making mistakes in social behavior—assumed the second greatest importance for the 13-year-olds, and political and economic fears took second place among 14-year-old boys and social relationships second place among 14-year-old girls. However, by the age of 16, political and economic fears appeared to be predominant in both sexes. It is very possible that our rapidly changing, uncertain world, accentuated by the mass media and the long drawn-out Vietnam war, may explain the recent trend for political fears to emerge at an earlier age.

Such feelings can be expressed in a number of ways. They may be manifested through *asceticism*, wherein the adolescent puts stringent prohibitions on his instinctual impulses and urgent desires—for example, the hippies' expression of love for all people, regardless of whether they feel threatened or angered by any given individual. Or an adolescent may cope with his fears through intellectualization or compartmentalization of his emotional involvement and his intellect, thus reacting to threats as if he were devoid of feeling. Another defense is the *reaction formation*, in which an individual consciously builds up one attitude in order to contain or overpower a conflicting repressed emotion. Through *projection*, one attributes to others attitudes and behavior which one actually possesses oneself but which one needs to deny. An adolescent is likely to adopt a wide range of defense mechanisms before arriving at a combination that best protects his self from outside scrutiny (Hornick, 1967).

As it is in most human beings and higher animal species, adolescent emotionality is often accompanied by physical manifestations of heavy perspiring, muscular tension, increased heartbeat, varying pulse pressure, and experiences of overwhelming fatigue. Because he may be unaware of the precipitating causes of his anxiety, a young person may mistakenly regard these physical signs as conclusive evidence of physical illness. Consequently, his preoccupation with his physical condition may become a defense against his real anxieties and fears, as in the following case history.

Betsy, a high-school senior, went steady with her boyfriend for two years. Toward the end of this period they began to engage in heavy petting. Suddenly Betsy became aware of a general aching in her breasts and was immediately convinced that she had developed breast cancer. Reluctant to go to her mother and tell her about the pain or to phone their family physician for an appointment, she became so preoccupied with her physical condition that her grades began to slip. Her homeroom teacher, to whom Betsy was quite attached, noted this sudden drop in grades and requested that she come in one day after school for a visit. At first, Betsy denied that anything was wrong. Finally she broke down, admitting her fears. With her homeroom teacher's encouragement, Betsy told her mother, who, in turn, promptly made an appointment with the family physician. A competent, understanding man, he examined her and found no physical basis for her complaint; he suggested that there was often a *psychogenic* explanation for many aches and pains, that emotions often affect one's physical well-being. Betsy reflected on what he had said and finally began to see a possible relationship between the heavy petting, in which she had recently engaged, and her aching breasts. Raised in a rather strict home, where she had been warned about the potential dangers in such activity, she had developed feelings of anxiety and guilt about engaging in this behavior. In further discussion with her family doctor, Betsy soon gained insight into her problem, her pain disappeared, and her grades subsequently improved.

Boredom and Apathy

Adolescent boredom, which seems to be more prevalent in recent years, can be considered an outgrowth of the egocentrism characteristic of this period (Josselyn, 1967; Schonfeld, 1967). The following causes for this increasing incidence of boredom have been suggested: (1) an educational system that has frequently failed to meet the needs of many youth and that too often has lacked relevance to the rapidly changing world in which they live; (2) a culture that has failed to grant status and recognition to its young people; and (3) an affluent society, which has given the younger generation too much too soon, depriving them of the experience of anticipating and working toward the fulfillment of their own wants and needs.

But regardless of the etiology, or causes, of boredom, it has become a major problem for many of today's younger generation, as well as for many of their elders. Often possessed with too much leisure time or feeling that they are not really an integral part of today's society and that they are not recognized or accepted, both young and old have turned to criminal and delinquent behavior, excessive alcohol consumption, or drug abuse (which we will discuss in more detail in Chapters 7 and 8).

Although often used interchangeably with boredom, *apathy* describes a slightly different way of defending oneself against one's anxieties. Whereas boredom is a condition of wandering attention and impaired working efficiency, which simulates a type of fatigue, apathy is an apparent absence of feeling or emotion or an attitude of indifference, which may or may not exist in boredom (Drever, 1952). Boredom and apathy affect those from all socioeconomic classes (Blaine, 1966). These reactions often serve as masks for the anger and resentment experienced by many youths in their striving for status in the community, where they are often shunted aside and regarded as second-class citizens (Brown, 1968). The most extreme example of apathy can be found in the "alienated youth," a subject which will be elaborated upon in Chapter 8.

THE DEVELOPMENT OF LOVE AND AFFECTION

The acquisition of genuine love, which is significant in the life of any individual, is of very great importance in the emotional development of the adolescent. Unfortunately, many youths, as well as numerous adults, tend to confuse the concepts of love and sex and regard them as synonymous. The consequence is often impulsive premarital or extramarital sexual relationships or hasty marriages based on biochemical attraction rather than on genuine love. Another erroneous assumption is that love is one distinct emotion. The authors, on the other hand, would define genuine love as comprising many emotions which can occur between individuals of the same or opposite sex, of similar or widely different ages, with or without any erotic overtones.

Green (1970) has suggested that an individual must go through four rather broad stages if he is to achieve a mature affectional relationship called love. During the first stage, infancy, a child must learn to love himself, a situation which is possible only if he receives adequate love from the important "others" in his life, those within the family circle. This stage continues into childhood, when he begins to move from his initial egocentric love of self to a degree of compassion and fondness for others. The second stage, which is characterized by the development of an affinity for and a love of a peer of the same sex, should occur in early adolescence. During this time two young people can become quite inseparable, confiding their innermost thoughts and feelings to each other and reflecting the beginning of a sense of trust in others. The third stage, which occurs in middle and late adolescence, is marked by the emergence of an affinity for and a love of another of the opposite sex, a relationship in which two people gradually begin to trust themselves to each other, striving for a comfortable heterosexual relationship. The final stage occurs only with true maturity. According to Erich Fromm (1955), it is the stage in development ". . . in which man relates to man lovingly" (p. 362), or in other words develops an affinity for and a love of all mankind.

Far too many people never achieve a mature degree of love. Adolescents, like their elders, will at times suffer rebuff, ridicule, and even abuse, and because of these adverse experiences, they will tend to develop a distrust and cynicism in their relationships with others. Often lacking faith in themselves, they may come to believe that others will not give them total affection without some string attached (Green, 1970). As a consequence, many young people are reluctant to display any genuine overt affection, a tendency which may continue throughout their lives. Others may very well overcome this barrier in due time through the process of trial and error and the acquisition of wisdom gained through numerous experiences in interpersonal relationships with a wide variety of people.

SUMMARY AND CONCLUSIONS

The intense, frequently uninhibited, rapidly fluctuating emotionality in the typical adolescent is often a source of considerable difficulty and misunderstanding for his parents and teachers. Explanations of this erratic emotional development include (1) the swift biological changes occurring during early adolescence; (2) the conflict between the desire to become independent and to remain dependent; (3) the search for identity, especially during the late adolescent period; and (4) the possibility that cognitive changes at that time facilitate certain variations in emotional expression.

Among other aspects of emotional development are a propensity for egocentric behavior, a high degree of self-consciousness, a strong desire to improve oneself in order to enhance one's self-image and attain greater self-confidence, and a definite emphasis on a philosophy of idealism. But as in individuals of all ages, although perhaps differing in underlying causes or etiology, the defense mechanisms of adolescents, including those of fantasy, intellectualization, denial, reaction formation, projection, and others, serve to protect them from the many fears and anxieties so prevalent during this stage of life.

Adolescence is also a period characterized by the growth and development of genuine love and affection in the individual, a process normally beginning in infancy and continuing through maturity. One of the greatest problems confronting the young person is learning to distinguish between the biochemical phenomenon of sex and the genuine reality of love.

REFERENCES

Angelino, H., & Shedd, C. Shifts in the content of fears and worries relative to chronological age. *Proceedings from Oklahoma Academy of Science*, 1953, **34**, 180–186.

Bardwick, J. M., Douvan, E., Horner, M. S., & Gutmann, D. *Feminine personality and conflict*. Monterey, Calif.: Brooks/Cole, 1970.

Blaine, G. B. Some emotional problems of adolescents. *Medical Clinics of North America*, 1965, **49**, 387–404.

Blaine, G. B. *Youth and the hazards of affluence*. New York: Harper & Row, 1966.

Blos, P. The second individuation process of adolescence. *The Psychoanalytic Study of the Child*, 1967, **22**, 162–186.

Bronson, G. W. Identity diffusion in late adolescents. *Journal of Abnormal and Social Psychology*, 1959, **59**, 414–417.

Brown, W. N. Alienated youth. *Mental Hygiene*, 1968, **52**(3), 330–336.

Croake, J. W. Adolescent fears. *Adolescence*, 1967, **2**(8), 459–468.

Daly, M. J. Physical and psychological development of the adolescent female. *Clinical Obstetrics and Gynecology*, 1966. **9**(3), 711–721.

Drever, J. *A dictionary of psychology.* Baltimore: Penguin Books, 1952.

Elkind, D. Egocentrism in adolescence. *Child Development*, 1967, **38**, 1025–1034.

Elkind, D. Cognitive structure and the adolescent experience. *Adolescence*, 1968, **2**(8), 427–434.

Erikson, E. H. The problem of ego identity. *Journal of the American Psychoanalytic Association*, 1956, **4**, 56–121.

Erikson, E. H. *Childhood and society* (2nd ed.). New York: W. W. Norton, 1963.

Erikson, E. H. *Identity: Youth and crisis.* New York: W. W. Norton, 1968.

Fromm, E. *The sane society.* New York: Holt, Rinehart & Winston, 1955.

Galdston, R. Adolescence and the function of self-consciousness. *Mental Hygiene*, 1967, **51**(2), 164–168.

Gallatin, J. E. The development of the concept of rights in adolescence. *Dissertation Abstracts*, 1968, **28**(12-B), 5204.

Green, L. B. *An essay on love: Its character and development.* Unpublished report, University of North Florida, 1970.

Group for the Advancement of Psychiatry. Committee on Adolescence. *Normal Adolescence*, New York: Group for the Advancement of Psychiatry, February, 1968, **6**(68).

Hornick, E. J. The adolescent crisis today. Emergencies, anxiety and adolescence. *New York State Journal of Medicine*, 1967, **67**, 1979–1981.

Inhelder, B., & Piaget, J. *The growth of logical thinking from childhood through adolescence.* New York: Basic Books, 1958.

Josselyn, I. M. The adolescent today. *Smith College Studies in Social Work*, 1967, **38**(1), 1–15.

Karowe, H. E., & McCandless, F. D. Emotional problems of adolescence. *Postgraduate Medicine*, 1963, **33**, 237–248.

Personality and growth series for adolescents: An evaluation. *Journal of the National Medical Association*, 1969, **61**(1), 93–95.

Piaget, J. *The origins of intelligence in children.* New York: W. W. Norton, 1963.

Piotrowski, Z. A. Treatment of the adolescent. The relative pessimism of psychologists. *American Journal of Orthopsychiatry*, 1962, **32**, 382–387.

Schonfeld, W. A. The adolescent crisis today. Socioeconomic affluence as a factor. *New York State Journal of Medicine*, 1967, **67**, 1981–1990.

Stamell, B. B. Emotional growth in the adolescent. *Medical Times*, 1964, **92**, 1019–1023.

Kasper, H. K. & Rae, . . . J. D. Unionunal patterns of behavioral
alterations . . . . 14, 213–236.

Bernstein and Fisher . . . .
disturbed visual . . . .
1965.

Friedman, Z. W. Devel . . . .
of psychologists . . . .
19, . . .

McDonald, W. A. The Welfeldine . . . .
a theoretical view . . . .
Smuth, R. J. . . . .
92, 101–102.

7

Juvenile Delinquent Behavior

Of all the adult male criminals in London, not two in a hundred have entered upon a course of crime who have lived an honest life up to the age of twenty. . . . Almost all who enter on a course of crime do so between the ages of eight and sixteen.

Sir Anthony Ashley Cooper Shaftesbury (1671–1713)

Many youths find it difficult to cope with the adolescent period of development in a manner that is emotionally satisfying to them and yet socially acceptable to society. Each year thousands of these young people become alienated from the adult world; they turn to delinquency, to drugs, or to teen-age marriages, all of which serve as means of escape from a society that too often has failed to accord them adequate status and a sense of their individual worth and value. In this chapter, we will consider the ever-increasing problem of juvenile delinquency and its many facets, including its prevalence, the degrees and types, various causes, means of prediction and prevention, and a few of the recent innovations in its treatment. (The topics of drug use and abuse, political alienation, and teen-age marriage and divorce will be discussed in Chapter 8.)

The term "juvenile delinquent" is very broad. Depending on state and local laws, the term encompasses youths ranging anywhere up to a maximum age of 16 to 21 and includes those committing offenses that would be considered criminal performed by an individual legally classified as an adult. Also considered delinquent are acts in violation of specific ordinances applying only to juveniles, such as violations

153

of curfew regulations, school-attendance laws, and restrictions on the use of alcohol and tobacco. And last, youths judged as uncontrollable, ungovernable, incorrigible, runaways, or needing supervision can also legally be termed juvenile delinquents (The President's Commission on Law Enforcement and Administration of Justice, 1967).[1]

Juvenile delinquency is not a new phenomenon, for research indicates that the juvenile offender has been prevalent among adolescents in the United States, Canada, and other Western civilized countries for more than a half century. However, until recently delinquency was usually thought to be confined mainly to the lower socioeconomic classes. For example, during the depression of the 1930s, although almost everyone felt its impact, the brunt of this economic disaster was borne by the lower classes. Unemployment in the slum areas, which had always been high, became so widespread that a majority of household heads in the slums ultimately lost their jobs, a trend that was accompanied by a mounting problem of juvenile delinquency in these areas (Tappan, 1949).

Current investigations, however, suggest that only a very small percentage of those who commit delinquent acts are ever apprehended (Gold, 1970). Juveniles from more economically secure homes are less frequently detected, and rural offenders are less likely than urban offenders to be arrested because of a shortage of courts and legal authorities in rural areas (Robinson, 1960). Because only a fraction of those engaging in delinquent behavior are ultimately taken into custody, one must be cautious in his interpretation of all statistics dealing with its prevalence, its differing degrees, and the various types of delinquency.

THE PREVALENCE OF JUVENILE DELINQUENCY

It is apparent that juvenile delinquency has become one of the primary domestic problems existing in the United States and Canada today. In 1965, 697,000 delinquent cases were handled by juvenile courts in the United States (Schafer & Polk, 1967). Since that time each year has witnessed a steady increase in incidence, which has more than offset the rise in population within this age range. Studies

[1]All subsequent references to this source will be cited simply as "(President's Commission, 1967)."

on file in the Office of Juvenile Delinquency and Youth Development in Washington, D.C., attest to the fact that in inner-city slum areas "up to 70 percent or more of all youths find themselves in trouble with the law at some point in their adolescence" (Burns & Stern, 1967, p. 362). During any given year about 2 percent of all individuals between the ages of 10 and 18 are apt to appear in juvenile court, and of those who turn 18, at least 17 percent of the boys, or one out of every six, have been summoned to appear before court (Wheeler, Cottrell, & Romasco, 1967).

Not only are these figures disturbing now, but they also tend to serve as a prophecy for rising criminality in the future. For example, a follow-up study by Glueck & Glueck (1968) disclosed that of 438 youths originally judged delinquent in the 1940s, more than 80 percent had had subsequent criminal arrests between the ages of 17 and 25.

TYPES OF JUVENILE DELINQUENT ACTS

The use of the term "juvenile delinquency" is presently being questioned, for it tends to infer that delinquent acts of any variety should be classified in a homogeneous manner. Recent investigators have suggested that almost all individuals actually break the law at some time during their lives but that there are wide variations in the frequency and seriousness of these violations (Horrocks, 1969; Gold, 1970). They also point out that only a small number of these are likely to be legally recorded as delinquent acts.

Kvaraceus (1958) classified delinquents as pseudo- or quasi-delinquents and as true delinquents. In the first group he placed youths who, in acting out on one occasion, commit acts that might be judged as delinquent but for whom it would be harmful and undesirable if society so judged. These are adolescents who impulsively commit an offense, usually within the framework of peer-group activity, that may cause damage to property but not usually to people.

One of the authors recalls a student who related an incident that took place one day when he and four or five other boys were out driving in a car with nothing much to do, "time to kill," and a desire for a bit of excitement. He remembered that they came to an attractive suburban area where a large sign, which identified the section, seemed to beckon to him and his friends to remove it from its location. It was especially interesting that he recalled that no one spoke or suggested that they remove the sign. Apparently the driver stopped the car, and without a word being uttered but as if on cue, all of the boys piled out of the automobile and simultaneously began taking down the sign. Surely they were defacing property, but it was obviously an unpremeditated act committed impulsively in a search for "kicks," and whether it should be classified as a delinquent act or as a youthful prank is debatable.

On the other hand, Kvaraceus describes true delinquents as those adolescents who exhibit a characteristic pattern of misbehavior. Kvaraceus (1958) further divides this group into three subtypes. First, there is the emotionally disturbed delinquent, who is usually characterized by considerable anxiety and strong manifestations of dependency. He is the overinhibited individual whose compulsive behavior may be expressed through delinquent acts, or he may be an *"acting out neurotic"* whose release of tension and conflict is reflected in his "overt aggressive misconduct." Second in the *socialized delinquent*, whose entire mode of behavior is characterized by delinquent acts. He and his peers regard such behavior as "right" or "smart," and they generally experience few pangs of conscience about these offenses. Last, is the youth described as the *unsocialized delinquent*. Generally a "loner" who has difficulty relating to others, he reacts overtly and aggressively against those whom he regards as hostile or threatening. He is an individual whose behavior demands that firm limitations be placed on him and on his conduct, but who violently resists any such restraints imposed on his behavior.

In addition to the above method of classification, delinquent acts can also be characterized according to the seriousness of the violation. Although these classifications may vary from one state to another, the term "felony" is generally used to describe such severe crimes as murder, robbery, arson, and serious theft. "Misdemeanor" denotes less serious offenses, such as shoplifting or stealing money or merchandise valued at less than fifty dollars. Often the severity of the transgression may be determined by the presiding judge and by the circumstances under which the violation occurred.

Another distinction in juvenile delinquency may be found in the categories of misbehavior committed by girls versus the classes of misconduct committed by boys. For example, girls are more likely to be apprehended for sexual offenses than for any other delinquent acts. They are usually brought to the attention of legal authorities through venereal infection or premarital pregnancy. Boys, on the other hand, are seldom arrested for sexual misconduct, unless a complaint of rape is filed by a girl's family (Reiss, 1969). Actually, however, of those adolescent boys and girls arrested for stealing, most have also violated sexual-conduct norms, and conversely, those apprehended for sexual offenses generally have a background of other law-breaking activities.

There are two types of delinquent behavior with which school administrators and teachers come in especially close contact— truancy and vandalism—which we will discuss in some detail.

Truancy

Generally the school's closest contact with delinquency is through the delinquent act of truancy, or staying away from school unlawfully. And while engaged in truant behavior, a youngster often participates in other illegal activities, such as vandalism and theft, as well. However, it should be noted that although truancy is a violation of school regulations and legal norms, it may also be symptomatic of some normal behavior patterns. According to Kvaraceus (1966), ". . . truancy may be: a healthy rebellion of a normal adolescent who is willing to pay the price for this once-in-a-lifetime indiscretion; a representation of demand behavior of gang members who hold the school in low esteem; a brief emotional recess period from a confusing and unfriendly classroom climate; an indication of a serious conflict with parents who pressure a child to succeed and who are attacked by this act; or a symptom of a child's inability to face and cope with the realities of his daily life" (p. 59). Where truancy is symptomatic of delinquent behavior, however, it appears that the school is often a major contributing factor through its provision of so many frustrating experiences and so few satisfying ones, through its failure to maintain student interest, and through its neglect in providing suitable channels for the release of adolescent energy and tension (Moore, 1964).

The most important point to be made about truant behavior is that in the history of the delinquent adolescent there is almost invariably a pattern of repeated truancy. Glueck & Glueck (1950) noted in their studies of delinquents that 94.8 percent had been involved in truancy at some time during their school careers, in contrast to only 10.8 percent of nondelinquents. Of 474 delinquents who had been truant, two thirds had been truants persistently, while one third had skipped school occasionally. It was also pointed out in this same study that a high proportion of these delinquents began to be truants even before their eleventh birthday with an average age of 10 for the first act of truancy.

Vandalism

Another category of delinquent acts which should be of particular concern to educators is vandalism. School vandalism in recent years has increased to the extent that it is presently estimated by the United States Office of Education that damage to public elementary and high schools by vandals runs about $100 million each year (Cunniff, 1970).

Clinard and Wade (1969) have defined vandalism as "the deliberate defacement, mutilation, or destruction of private or public property by a juvenile or group of juveniles not having immediate or direct ownership in the property so abused" (p. 257). Such delinquent behavior is sometimes referred to as "malicious mischief," "destructiveness," "disorderly conduct," or even "assault." But regardless of its label, such destruction of property, which is especially common among adolescent boys, has begun to prove more costly to the American public than the combined cost of all other types of offenses against property. How serious an act of vandalism is considered to be is determined by a number of factors, including the relationship of the property owner to the offender, the danger of punishment to the vandal, the possibilities of real injury to the owner, and the type of property involved and its value. Too often such behavior is looked upon as a youthful prank, because at one time or another most American males, who generally have more freedom and less parental supervision than girls, are involved in this type of activity (Clinard & Wade, 1969). In general, when such vandalism is displayed by an adolescent, it is considered to be deliberate and malicious, even though it may represent a spur-of-the-moment urge, as illustrated by the case cited earlier in this chapter. And although society may look upon him as a "vandal," the youngster engaging in such activity is more likely to regard himself as merely a "prankster," describing his own behavior as mischievous rather than malicious. It should also be noted that vandalism does not usually involve theft.

What factors underlie the current widespread display of such behavior? Clinard and Wade have suggested that "Property destruction
appears to function for the adolescent as a protest against his ill-
defined role and ambiguous status in the social structure" (p. 262).

In many instances, vandalism directed against the schools may
also reflect youth's disenchantment with his educational experiences.
And among adolescents of lower socioeconomic status, such acts could
very well be manifestations of rebellion against what is regarded
as symbolic of the middle-class establishment. To prevent or reduce
the incidence of such extensive vandalism demands the concerted
efforts of both educators and society as a whole. They will need
to join in attempts to make education more relevant and meaningful,
to provide young people with some positive means of attaining the
status and recognition they so desperately seek, and to enable them
to find more socially acceptable means of channeling youthful frustration, energy, and spirit into less destructive outlets.

TYPES OF DELINQUENTS

Up to this moment we have been talking mainly about delinquent
acts rather than about delinquent youths per se. At this point we
should stop and take note of the fact that the incidence of delinquency varies according to socioeconomic class and that there are
also differences in the types of delinquent acts in which adolescents
of different social classes tend to engage.

The Lower-Socioeconomic-Class Delinquent

There is little question that recorded delinquency is most prevalent
in the slums, where it is characterized by an extremely high number
of serious offenses (Reiss & Rhodes, 1961; President's Commission,
1967). The underlying factors of this high incidence will be discussed
under the topic of causes of delinquency. However, it should be
stressed here that it is not the poverty and deprivation alone that
have contributed to the increase in the number of delinquent offenses
among this group. Rather it is the resentment of poverty in the midst
of an affluent society, an attitude manifested much less frequent!
among the deprived who live in a basically poor country. The present
distinctions between the "haves" and "have-nots" have also been

magnified by our mass media, which has come to stimulate the desire for a life of luxury among all socioeconomic classes (Toby, 1967).

Actually the vast majority of crimes committed by youths from the lower socioeconomic classes involve crimes against property rather than crimes against people. "The preponderance of crimes against property sheds light on the tendency of crime rates to rise in the most affluent countries. People steal, not because they are starving, but because they are envious, and they are more likely to be envious of the possessions of others in countries with rising standards of living" (Toby, 1967, p. 132).

However, other factors play a role in determining whether a low-socioeconomic-class youth becomes a delinquent. If a lower-class boy lives in a middle-class neighborhood where the crime rate is low, he is much less likely to become a delinquent. Or if he attends a primarily middle-class school rather than a slum-area school, he is less apt to pursue illegal behavior. Apparently the lower-class boy is least likely to become a delinquent when he is in a minority. "What seems more apparent is that the largest proportion of delinquents for any status group (low, middle, or upper-class) comes from the more homogeneous status areas for that group and that the delinquency-life chances of *all* status groups tend to be greatest in the lower status area and in the high delinquency rate areas" (Reiss & Rhodes, 1961, p. 729). Perhaps this trend can be explained by the fact that there are generally fewer desirable models to copy in such neighborhoods.

Actually there may be less discrepancy between the extent of lower-class delinquency and the extent of middle- and upper-class delinquency than statistics would indicate. Youths from lower socioeconomic classes are much more likely to be apprehended, held for legal action, judged delinquent, and have their records made public by legal authorities than are those from more affluent groups (Reiss & Rhodes, 1959; Cavan, 1969); middle-class parents are usually in a better position to help their children out of their difficulties.

The Affluent Delinquent

From 1948 to 1960 the number of juvenile delinquents between the ages of 10 and 17 increased 100 percent, although the number of youngsters within this age range in the total population increased only 19 percent during the same period. These statistics may reflect the rising incidence of delinquency among middle-class adolescents (England, 1969), or they may reflect the fact that in the past middle- and upper-class parents have shielded delinquent behavior from unfavorable publicity, so that society was simply not aware of its prevalence (Pine, 1966). Such affluent delinquents are less likely to become official statistics not only because their detection is less common, but also because if they are apprehended, their rehabilitation is more likely to fall into the hands of psychiatrists, psychologists, guidance clinics, or other private facilities, all beyond the framework of legal institutions.

For example, one of the authors recalls the incident of a middle-class boy and girl, each about the age of 15, who ransacked a summer camp, inflicting considerable damage to the recreation hall, including the total destruction of a piano. Apprehended by the authorities, both young people were released by the juvenile-court judge with the provision that they be seen regularly for psychotherapy by the local guidance center. In this case, as in many others, such emphasis on rehabilitation is often a more effective means of combating delinquency than commitment to a reformatory or inadequate supervision by an overworked probation officer.

Several additional explanations have been suggested for the rise of delinquency among the affluent (Pine, 1966). The adolescent period has become extended even more for the youth in the middle and upper classes than for those in the lower classes. These young people generally go on to college, which often necessitates their remaining economically dependent for an extended period of time and delays their acquisition of an occupational status. This prolonged transitional period tends to cause many young people to feel that they are living in an "existential vacuum," in which life lacks purpose and meaning. As a consequence, they often resort to deviant and rebellious behavior in attempts to establish their identities and develop some status. The affluent delinquent may also be subject to extreme pressures to achieve by his middle- or upper-class parents. Such pressures can create much anxiety in these adolescents about the discrepancy between their aspirations and the reality of their achievements. Delinquent behavior in such cases often serves as a means of calling attention to youthful distress over problems with which they feel unable to cope. In addition, the middle-class emphasis on the desirability of deferring immediate gratification for long-range goals is losing its importance for many affluent adolescents.

Taking its place have been impulse buying and long-term payments, practices formerly confined mainly to the lower socioeconomic classes. And lower-class traits such as type of dress, music, fads, and behavior are also being borrowed and adopted by middle-class youths. All of these trends may help to explain why affluent delinquency appears to be on the increase.

Several investigators have suggested factors other than those we have cited as being primarily responsible for the rise in affluent delinquency. For example, Lelyveld (1964), in a *cross-sectional* study made of juvenile delinquents from suburban well-to-do or middle-income families in two Ohio and New York towns, concluded that these adolescents had committed crimes because: (1) they were bored, and (2) they felt that their parents were not concerned about them.

Another study of 100 delinquents and 100 nondelinquents from middle- and upper-middle-class families from a midwestern suburban community disclosed that both groups agreed upon three factors as being contributory to delinquent behavior: (1) the influence of friends, (2) boredom, restlessness and a lack of activity, and (3) a lack of parental guidance or interest (Tobias, 1969). This same study revealed that nondelinquents tended to participate more frequently and in closer relationships with their parents, were responsible for more household chores, held part-time jobs more often, and had a clearer and more concise image of whom they would emulate as adults. Affluent delinquents, on the other hand, were more preoccupied with money, financial security, and a job, but at the same time they were less certain about their future goals.

These findings would suggest that many affluent parents tend to feel that by providing all of the material needs and desires for which their progeny clamor they are demonstrating their love, affection, and concern for them. Fairfell (1965) has suggested that delinquency among upper-class suburban boys reflects a tendency of parents to give their children too much freedom and insufficient guidance and attention. It is of interest to note that many of these youths commit their infractions against the law in such a way as to call attention to their misconduct; one could hypothesize that such behavior may actually be "a cry for help."

The types of delinquent acts committed by affluent adolescents also differ from those committed by lower-class youths. Often their delinquency centers around the automobile, which to them represents a status symbol. In fact, Crumbaugh (1968) has said that "The automobile is such a constant companion in American culture that it has, in many segments of society, become part of the body-image. Children grow up in such an intimate relationship with the car that it parallels clothes, jewelry, hair style, make-up, and the like as a personal attribute that delineates the individual's status and identity" (p. 349). Consequently, it is not surprising that it becomes the focal point for considerable adolescent misconduct, especially among the affluent. If he has access to an automobile, such a youngster may violate speed limits, mix alcohol and driving, or race his friends in their cars. As a consequence, he is much more likely to be apprehended for traffic violations than are lower-class boys who are much less apt to own a car (Reiss & Rhodes, 1969). If his parents have provided him with a car but he has no funds to maintain it, he may turn to pilfering gasoline, tires, and other articles essential for its maintenance. Or if he does not own a car at all, he may "borrow" one for joy rides, a violation of the law that can fall into the category of a felony (England, 1969; Schepses, 1969).

PRIMARY CAUSES OF JUVENILE DELINQUENCY

No case of juvenile delinquency is ever the result of any one single factor; it is the outgrowth of many variables. However, there are certain contributing causes that appear with greater frequency than others, and which fall into five general categories: (1) socioeconomic factors, (2) the family, (3) educational factors, (4) the peer group and/or gang, and (5) personality factors.

Socioeconomic Factors

It is common for poverty to be transmitted from one generation to the next. In fact, among numerous lower-class families the third successive generation is now receiving welfare benefits. This program of relief has tended to discourage fathers from remaining in the home and facing their responsibilities; and it has not provided the necessary training, skills, or job opportunities enabling youth to secure gainful employment with possibilities for advancement (President's Commission, 1967). As a consequence, a general attitude of hopelessness, defeat, and despair tends to pervade lower-class families.

In addition, poverty-stricken neighborhoods are commonly characterized by bars that sell liquor to minors, by extensive gambling, and by organized adult crime, which may be the setting for an adolescent to learn to emulate antisocial behavior, such as the consumption and pushing of illicit drugs (Leinwand, 1968). The model for a lower-class youth is often a successful criminal or gangster. Lacking the traditional exemplary citizen after whom to pattern his life, the lower-class adolescent may seek out a criminal of prestige, who is highly regarded in the neighborhood as a "model of power and affluence" (President's Commission, 1967).

Since lower-class parents are frequently illiterate or have gone no further than grammar school, they are likely to feel inferior to their offspring who go further in school. Consequently, they may be reluctant to discipline their children because they feel that the younger generation knows so much more than their parents about life (Cervantes, 1965).

The Family

Probably of greater impact on the development of delinquency than socioeconomic class per se is the family. Although many people may assume that a broken or one-parent home is the main familial factor contributing to juvenile delinquency, it is not the only one (Sheppard, 1965; Leinwand, 1968). Indeed, a broken home may result in a disorganized family life marked by a lack of parental supervision and control (President's Commission, 1967; Leinwand, 1968). Perhaps the most influential factor is that many broken homes tend to be matriarchal in structure, thereby failing to provide the male adolescent with a suitable masculine figure with whom to identify. As a result, he develops conflict over his sexual role and an obsessive concern with his masculinity, and his delinquent acts often function as a means of resolving this sexual role conflict (Bacon, Child, & Barry, 1963).

The Gluecks (1950) have also reported a higher incidence of delinquent boys, compared with nondelinquents, stemming from homes "broken by desertion, separation, divorce, or death of one or both parents, many of the breaches occurring during the early childhood of the boys" (p. 280). In addition, it was noted that delinquents have fathers with a greater tendency toward family and work irresponsibility than the fathers of nondelinquents. If they are unemployed, this factor may also tend to discourage their sons from identifying with them (President's Commission, 1967).

In fact, it has been noted that most delinquents do not identify with anyone, a fact which reflects a lack of close relationships and shallow emotional ties to their families (Baugh & Carpenter, 1962). Also a part of such family relationships is the degree of parental affection or rejection manifested toward adolescents, especially by their fathers (President's Commission, 1967). One study by Bandura and Walters (1958), for example, noted that antisocial boys tend to experience a lack of paternal affection along with rejection, which is likely to prevent identification with their fathers and limit internalization of parental standards and values. Another report by Allen and Sandhu (1967) of 179 institutionalized delinquents versus 178 nondelinquents disclosed that low family affect or little display of affection was characteristically reported by the delinquents.

Family structure and cultural patterns are also of extreme importance in the development of delinquent behavior. Slocum and Stone (1963), in a study dealing with delinquent-type behavior but not with adjudged delinquents, had students fill out identical anonymous questionnaires. The results disclosed that: (1) adolescents from democratic and cooperative families are less apt to become delinquent and are more prone to conformity, (2) those regarding discipline in the home as fair are less likely to become delinquents, and (3) students from unaffectionate families are more apt to become delinquent and less likely to conform.

Often parents, both in the suburbs and in the slums, may label their children early in their lives as "wicked," "troublemakers," or "bound to turn out bad." Ultimately the *self-fulfilling prophecy* takes over, and young people so labeled do become delinquents, especially in the slums where professional counseling and guidance are usually unavailable (President's Commission, 1967).

Before leaving familial causes of juvenile delinquency, one interesting phenomenon, which may well be a contributing factor, should be mentioned. This is the "faint smile syndrome," a facet of nonverbal communication by parents often betraying unconscious approval of a consciously condemned act. Concerned parents who consciously prohibit certain behavior in their offspring may actually vicariously enjoy their children's misconduct and reveal their underlying approval in many ways, including their facial expressions (Leland, 1961). Consider the following example.

Ted, a high school senior from an upper-middle-class suburban neighborhood, was caught in the process of returning a neighbor's car, which he had "borrowed" without permission and had proceeded to take for a "joy ride" into the surrounding countryside. Although the neighbor declined to press formal charges, he did tell Ted's father about the incident, who politely expressed his regrets and said he would discipline his son. Later, however, he remarked to his wife that it was just a kind of "prank" he himself would have committed as a youth, and although he eventually reprimanded his son for his questionable behavior, it was fairly evident from his facial expression and tone of voice that he did not really regard the offense as a very serious one.

Delinquency and the Schools

In recent years there has been increasing evidence of a high correlation between the failures of our educational institutions and the prevalence of delinquency. For example, one study disclosed that among "blue collar" boys, or those of the lower-middle and lower classes, the rate of delinquency was almost seven times as high for those who failed in school as for those who did not fail (Polk & Richmond, 1966).

For slum-area children, the teacher may represent their first genuine encounter with authority. If they have lacked supervision at home, unlike closely supervised middle-class youngsters, and have previously been left to their own devices, these lower-class youths may rebel against this new authority. The ways in which the school authorities and classroom teachers react to such rebellious behavior may well determine whether or not such children will opt for a career in delinquency.

Teachers who adopt a firm but positive attitude based on their understanding of the factors causing the rebellion may encourage such students to learn and perhaps, in time, to discover the benefits of possessing a good education. Other instructors, however, who choose to ignore the disruptive child in an attempt to avoid direct and open conflict are unlikely to elicit trust or intellectual curiosity in those they ignore. Further, teachers who regard any infractions of their rules as an affront to their position and label as "misbehavior" any violations of their often rigid regulations, quickly classifying certain youths as "troublemakers," are likely to enforce the tendency of these young people to rebel against the school and its authority. A vicious cycle ensues, and it becomes increasingly difficult to modify the behavior of these students. They find a way of gaining "recognition" through their unacceptable, disturbing behavior; and since it is the attention and notice that they crave, they continue to engage in such behavior until ultimately they become the delinquents that the schools have claimed them to be all along (President's Commission, 1967).

In other cases, teachers and school administrators may label a student as deviant because of his friends, his appearance, or his reputation rather than because of his actual behavior. And once again the self-fulfilling prophecy takes hold, and the student begins to see himself as deviant and to adhere to the behavior of others similarly labeled (Schafer & Polk, 1967).

Nor can one overlook the impact on blacks, Spanish-Americans, and other students from minority groups of unconscious attitudes on the part of many classroom teachers. Although they may consciously deny it, educators often unknowingly demonstrate considerable intolerance and lack of understanding for those from non-Anglo-Saxon homes. Raised in middle-class homes with middle-class values, they find it difficult or almost impossible to be acceptant of many of the youths who come from homes with values that conflict with those of the teacher. Not surprisingly, young people from minority groups may fail to develop a healthy self-concept, and their rebellious behavior becomes their only way of releasing the tensions that arise from the many frustrations, conflicts, and pressures with which they are confronted each school day.

School buildings in the inner cities are often deteriorating and poorly equipped. Inadequate facilities and teaching resources, a limited number of textbooks and library books, inexperienced and incompetent teachers, overcrowded classrooms, as well as racial and economic segregation all contribute to the poor education and ultimate dropout of so many lower-class adolescents (President's Commission, 1967). But perhaps a more serious disadvantage in such schools is their failure to provide supervised study and recreational facilities after school hours. Many youths in the slums come from homes in which there are no books or other implements for learning, no educated parents to give them assistance, and no quiet places to study, while their only playgrounds are likely to be the streets of the city or the corner pool hall.

"Habits of failure and feelings of inferiority are characteristic of delinquency" (Kvaraceus, 1945, p. 140). This pattern is evident in the reasons given by delinquents for their dislike of school: inferior clothing compared to that of other students, frequent ridicule by their teachers, incompatibility with other youngsters, and consistent placement in slow classes with a lot of other "dumb" students.

In summary, the following educational factors appear to be primary contributors to the development of delinquency: (1) the cumulative effects of academic failure combined with a thirst for success and no satisfying means of attaining it, (2) an education perceived as possessing no relevance to later life, (3) a lack of commitment to the accepted values of both the community and the school, values that represent middle-class standards which the lower class often find alien and undesirable, and (4) ineffective management and a lack of understanding and tolerance by teachers and administrators of students who frequently resort to misconduct in school (Schafer & Polk, 1967).

The Gang and Delinquency

Not all gangs are necessarily delinquent gangs (Horrocks, 1969). However, it has been estimated that from 60 percent to 90 percent of all delinquent acts occur in the company of others (President's Commission, 1967). Such statistics certainly indicate that the gang plays an important role in the commitment of most delinquent acts.

According to Cohen (1955), membership in a delinquent gang is "a result of ineffective family supervision, the breakdown of parental authority and the hostility of the child toward the parents; in short . . . the delinquent gang recruits members who have already achieved autonomy" (p. 31).

Such delinquent subcultures apparently fulfill two essential functions for their members: a sense of belonging and a certain status. Belonging may be achieved by a youth who demonstrates an awareness and a desire to adhere to certain standards and values established by the gang. Status may be acquired and maintained by those who show that they possess certain traits valued by the lower-class culture, such as toughness and smartness or the ability to "dupe" others (Miller, 1958). Such delinquent gangs can also be found among the middle classes, but they are most prevalent among lower-class youths.

The stealing patterns of many gangs support this hypothesis that delinquent behavior is a function of a need to belong and be respected by fellow gang members. It seems that gang members do not particularly need or want the articles they steal but rather steal for "kicks." In certain delinquent subcultures stealing actually becomes a type of status symbol (Cohen, 1955). Youths shoplift in order to obtain recognition and acceptance by their peers.

An associated characteristic of delinquent gang behavior is what Cohen (1955) describes as "short-run hedonism." Members act impulsively, doing whatever offers excitement to them at the moment. They strongly reject organized and supervised recreation, much preferring spur-of-the-moment "fun," which even among the most delinquent groups turns into delinquent behavior only a small percentage of the time.

Group cohesiveness is important to delinquent gangs. Gang members are encouraged by their peers to resist pressures from any "outsiders," including family, school, other regulatory agencies, and even other gangs. Often relationships with other delinquent subcultural groups are marked by indifference, hostility, or even rebellion (Cohen, 1955). In fact, most gang violence involves rival gangs who fight in order to protect or obtain territory or status (President's Commission, 1967).

Probably the most prevalent basis for gang cohesiveness is the gang members' deliberate and extensive repudiation of middle-class values. Because they perceive a certain amount of hypocrisy and phoniness in the preachings of the older generation, gang members consciously pursue goals that are in opposition to adult middle-class values. They refuse to compromise with middle-class morality and want it clearly understood that they conform to no standards but their own. Consequently, they turn more and more to the gang for their values, which in turn leads to greater alienation from adults and to antisocial or delinquent behavior. It has been suggested that the destruction of property by delinquents is a reaction formation that serves as a direct attack on the middle and upper classes. Since property is perceived as the main status symbol for upper socioeconomic groups, gang members attack it as their most vulnerable point.

However, for most delinquent adolescents, delinquent behavior would not be chosen as a way of life if it were not "socially legitimized"—that is, if it were not given a certain degree of respectability, at least within a limited group (Cohen, 1955). According to Reiss and Rhodes (1961), very few delinquents are consciously interested in careers as criminals but mainly tend to conform to peer expectations. Cohen (1955) offers a similar hypothesis: ". . . there is a certain chemistry in the group situation itself which engenders that which was not there before, . . . group interaction is a sort of catalyst which releases potentialities not otherwise visible" (p. 136).

Personality Factors and Delinquency

The personality traits of juvenile offenders have been studied for years by numerous psychologists. In general, it has been concluded that the true delinquent does possess certain deviant personality patterns that contribute to his delinquent behavior.

According to Kirkwood (1955), delinquents can often be divided into two major categories: the *sociopath* and the *psychoneurotic.* The sociopathic personality lacks an ability to visualize the results of his actions or to care about the consequences of his behavior. In addition, he does not seem to experience deep emotional feelings and appears indifferent to the culture and its customs and mores. Yablonsky (1962) noted that core members of violent gangs are especially prone to *paranoid psychopathic* or sociopathic personality patterns, acting as if they believe almost everyone is against them. The psychoneurotic individual, on the other hand, is characterized by a high degree of anxiety, which he finds difficult to channel into healthy, satisfying outlets.

Baugh and Carpenter (1962) agree that delinquents are pathologically disturbed. According to one of their studies, a majority of boys institutionalized at least twice for delinquent offenses displayed serious emotional disorders which apparently resulted from the early frustrating experiences of a childhood characterized by lack of love, emotional and/or maternal deprivation, and excessive punishment.

Their delinquent behavior appears to represent attempts to master the instincts within them through the process of projection. In other words, they tend to attribute to others their own antisocial, aggressive feelings and thoughts, a defense mechanism often underlying an individual's belief that he is being persecuted by other people. They lack a sense of trust in themselves and therefore project this feeling that others are not to be trusted as well.

And while it is evident that the juvenile offender acts out much of his aggression, he also appears to turn much of his hostility inward in what seems to be an atonement for his underlying guilt and need for punishment (Baugh & Carpenter, 1962). Thus, the delinquent behavior typical of the sociopath is designed to call attention to his misbehavior and perhaps reflects his unconscious desire for punishment.

The use of the Rorschach ink blot test has also revealed certain personality traits that distinguish delinquents from nondelinquents (Glueck & Glueck, 1950). For example, delinquents are more socially assertive, defiant, and ambivalent toward authority than nondelinquents. They are also more resentful, hostile, and suspicious of other people; and they are more destructive, often to a sadistic extent. In addition, they show greater impulsivity and vivaciousness and decidedly more extroverted behavior.

At the same time, Glueck and Glueck (1950) point out, these delinquents are less concerned about failure and defeat than nondelinquents. They are also less cooperative with and dependent upon other people. They display more unconventional ideas, feelings, and behavior than do normal youths. And they are less self-punitive and demonstrate less self-control.

Scarpitti (1965) administered a structured questionnaire to 515 boys (285 white and 230 black) from an Ohio Boys Industrial School for Delinquents, 61 white ninth-grade boys from a lower-class Columbus, Ohio, school, and 68 white ninth-grade boys from a middle-class school in the same city. The results disclosed that delinquents, regardless of age, race, and grade level tend to reject middle-class values and to be aware of their limited access to opportunity. Because of inadequate socialization, these juvenile offenders have a poor image of themselves and of others, and it is this low self-concept that appears to be the crucial factor differentiating these delinquents from the other two groups. Apparently a favorable self-concept serves as a shield, protecting lower-class boys as well as middle-class boys from the effects of an adverse environment.

Jaffee and Polansky (1962) note that verbal inaccessibility is another personality trait of many delinquents. They suggest that due to parental inconsistency and emotional neglect, young delinquents demonstrate a tendency to be more primitive in their ways of discharging their drives. They tend to "act out" rather than verbally express their feelings. It has also been hypothesized that their adherence to pseudomasculine traits inhibits verbal expression of their emotions. Such verbal inaccessibility may even be a conscious attitude on the part of these delinquent youths, for it is questionable that young people with delinquent trends would even trust their inner thoughts to other people. Apparently they are reluctant to look inward at their feelings and to share them with others.

Despite common beliefs to the contrary, delinquents do not differ appreciably from the range of intelligence-quotient scores found among nondelinquents (Prentice & Kelly, 1963). However, because standardized paper-and-pencil intelligence tests tend to rely so heavily on verbal skills and reading ability, which are likely to be below average for delinquents, it has been the authors' experience that such youths often appear to possess a lower level of mental ability than they actually have.

THE PREDICTION OF DELINQUENCY

Authorities have often suggested that if future delinquency could be accurately predicted, much of it might be prevented through early treatment. Because most juvenile delinquency is likely to begin shortly after the age of 8 (Thomas, 1967), some investigators have recently suggested that every child between the ages of 6 and 8 should be evaluated through the use of projective techniques in order to detect those children most likely to develop antisocial behavior.

Perhaps a bit less dramatic but nonetheless outstanding has been the research undertaken by Glueck and Glueck (1950; 1959). These criminologists, too, feel that early prediction is the most rational approach to the problem of delinquency. By assessing certain predictive factors even before a child enters school, they believe it is possible to determine who is most prone to delinquent behavior before it actually begins. If such early detection is then followed by preventive measures, the number of juvenile offenders should ultimately be reduced, especially among those who might have a slightly more than even chance of becoming delinquents (Glueck & Glueck, 1959).

Maintaining that there are many traits and factors in the early life of a child that foretell the development of delinquent behavior, Glueck and Glueck (1950) developed the Glueck Social Prediction Table, which is designed to be used by trained social workers to identify potentially antisocial behavior in boys at the time of their entrance into school. This table includes five factors, all pertaining to the family: (1) discipline of the boy by his father—whether it is too strict, inconsistent, or lax, or firm and kindly, (2) supervision of the boy by his mother—whether it is unsuitable, fair, or suitable, (3) affection of the father for his son—whether it is indifferent, hostile, or warm and possibly overprotective, (4) affection of the mother for her son—whether it is indifferent, hostile, or warm and possibly overprotective, and (5) the cohesiveness of the family—whether it is unintegrated, partly intact, or strong in its unity.

According to Glueck and Glueck (1959), delinquents are most likely to come from a family in which the father's discipline is harsh, unreasonable, or inconsistent and the mother's discipline unsuitable because of her careless supervision in leaving her son to his own devices or in the hands of an incompetent substitute, in which both parents are indifferent or hostile toward their male offspring, and in which there is little cohesiveness.

If a child has a high possibility of becoming a delinquent according to the Glueck Social Prediction Table, but only a slight chance according to the results of the Rorschach ink blot test and a study of the personality dynamics, the possibilities of deterring the onset of antisocial behavior through modification of the familial environment are favorable. On the other hand, if the reverse were true and the Social Prediction Score was low but the Rorschach and the personality dynamics were unsatisfactory, preventive action would not likely be successful. In such instances the problem would probably be too deeply rooted, and prevention of delinquency would be difficult, since it would demand a basic reorganization of the entire character structure (Glueck & Glueck, 1950).

Two constitutional factors have recently been added to a revised Glueck Social Prediction Table: infant destructiveness and resistance to authority. Dr. Eleanor Glueck now feels that it may be possible to identify a potential delinquent as early as the age of 3 (Brown, 1965).

Kvaraceus (1958) devised a measurement entitled the Delinquency Proneness Check List, which can be used by classroom teachers to locate the predelinquent early. The list is made up of eighteen factors, which should be perceptible to any observant teacher. It can be checked "yes," "no," or "not sure" and provides a fairly accurate assessment of delinquent proneness (see Table 7-1).

TABLE 7-1.   Delinquency proneness checklist. (From Kvaraceus, William C. *Juvenile Delinquency*. What Research Says to the Teacher Series, No. 15. Washington, D.C.: Association of Classroom Teachers, a department of the National Education Association, 1958, p. 17.)

Yes	*No*	*Not Sure*	
			1. Shows marked dislike for school.
			2. Resents school routine and restriction.
			3. Disinterested in school program.
			4. Is failing in a number of subjects.
			5. Has repeated one or more grades.
			6. Attends special class for retarded pupils.
			7. Has attended many different schools.
			8. Intends to leave school as soon as the law allows.
			9. Has only vague academic or vocational plans.
			10. Has limited academic ability.
			11. Is a child who seriously or persistently misbehaves.
			12. Destroys school materials or property.
			13. Is cruel and bullying on the playground.
			14. Has temper tantrums in the classroom.
			15. Wants to stop schooling at once.
			16. Truants from school.
			17. Does not participate in organized extracurricular activities.
			18. Feels he does not "belong" in the classroom.

Educators need to exercise caution in evaluating the results of this table. Rash judgments that a student is a potential delinquent, based solely on the answers to this checklist, should be avoided.

THE PREVENTION OF DELINQUENCY

"The traditional institutions of America—the family, the school, the church, the law—have become decreasingly responsive to the realities of people's lives. The traditional sanctions, services, and structures which they have provided and the stability which these have represented no longer illustrate either the aspirations or the needs of a growing number of Americans" (Office of Education, U.S. Department of Health, Education, and Welfare, 1967, p. 280). If delinquency is to be prevented or at least reduced, the institutions cited in this quote will have to be modified.

Perhaps the single most important factor demanding alteration is the family. Society must find ways of reducing the number of broken homes, cementing family interpersonal relationships, and strengthening the role of the father in the familial structure in order to facilitate the positive socialization of its children. Many parents today need assistance in establishing or reestablishing their roles of authority within the family. Far too often they tend to relinquish this authority to their offspring and then wonder why their adolescents refuse to heed any of their advice. Parents also need to be helped to learn how to become actively involved in the academic lives of their children and to participate in the affairs of the educational community, which, in turn, must establish a closer liaison with the family.

The public school today is responsible for many more aspects of a child's life than his education. Thus, the school facilities should be open longer hours as well as the year round, serving not only as a center for the education of children, but also as a place for recreation, for adult education, and possibly even for counseling (Schafer & Polk, 1967). Teachers and administrators need to find new methods for effectively disciplining recalcitrant youths. For example, suspension from school of a student already on legal probation may only lead the youth to commit additional delinquent acts.

Educators must avoid placing the blame for misconduct on an individual student, when the fault may lie with the school's handling of the situation. For example, teachers may fail to provide the students with the necessary information, materials, or forms to carry out certain demands or regulations. To cite one example, a high school art teacher assigned students work which they had trouble in completing because of the difficulty of obtaining some of the required material. The teacher's lack of consideration for the students is quite apparent in the fact that some of these items were almost impossible to locate, and when available were exorbitantly expensive to purchase.

Efforts must also be made to avoid labeling students as troublemakers, and thus burdening them with a negative reputation that is passed on from year to year, from one teacher to another. Ultimately such young people begin to live up to the name by which they have been branded. They then discover what they have in common with other misbehaving adolescents and wind up with a deviant peer group, which is bound to establish its own standards and openly flaunt the regulations of the school (Schafer & Polk, 1967).

Since dropping out of school and delinquency are so closely related, some communities are experimenting with "store-front schools" for dropouts. Even the United States Post Office has become involved in this plan, having opened "store-front academies" in several cities for the purpose of educating ghetto-area school dropouts, aged 16 to 21, through a four-month program of vocational training and part-time jobs with the Post Office (*Today's Education*, 1970).

There is also a need for special youth agencies, to which other agencies can make referrals and to which parents and their children can go for help on their own. Such agencies could offer services ranging from diagnosis and counseling to vocational training, job placement, and family-life education. With a staff including youths, adult volunteers, and professionals possessing a wide range of skills, such centers could meet the needs of many potential delinquents (Burns & Stern, 1967). To provide the greatest benefits, however, these agencies should be located in close proximity to the neighborhoods they serve. In fact, it has been suggested that store-front quarters in slum areas would attract far more people than would stiff, antiseptic treatment centers located in more pleasant surroundings.

Adolescents also need help in learning to find meaning in life and in learning to care what happens to them and to society as a whole. Interest may be sparked by encouraging young people to participate in community activities through helping to plan, organize, operate, and develop programs for other youths (President's Commission, 1967). This was demonstrated in the late 1960s when a few riot-torn cities successfully mobilized youngsters from inner-city areas to serve as police aides and junior patrols to assist patrolmen in putting down violence.

Although juvenile courts have existed in the United States since 1899, they have generally failed in the functions for which they were initially created. According to Paulson (1967), "A contact with the juvenile court not only is unlikely to assist a youngster to become a better citizen but, according to respectable theory today, the contact is likely to lead him into further delinquency" (p. 70). "Recidivism [recommitment to a correctional institution] among young people who have been institutionalized is extremely high" (Burns & Stern, 1967, p. 355). And court records, although supposedly confidential, often prevent delinquents from being employed, cause them to be excluded from membership in labor unions, prohibit them from participating in certain apprenticeship training, or from being licensed in certain occupations (President's Commission, 1967). It has been suggested that certain types of delinquency, such as truancy, should be handled by the schools rather than by the courts (Schafer & Polk, 1967). This would probably prove to be a more effective means of dealing with such behavior; otherwise, at the present time few positive approaches to the *legal* handling of delinquency have come to the fore.

THE TREATMENT OF DELINQUENCY

Current practices in dealing with juvenile offenders usually include one or more of the following: (1) there is a court hearing with no final disposition of the case, a method sufficient to deter some from future delinquency; (2) the court assesses a fine and restitution of any property damaged or destroyed, a mild form of punishment, provided it is paid by the offender and not by his parents; (3) the youth is placed on probation, which may range from friendly counseling to serious surveillance; (4) an adjudged delinquent is placed in a state institution for an indefinite period of time (Wheeler et al., 1967).

As alternatives to commitment to a reformatory or a training school, however, several new treatment programs have been introduced throughout the United States and Canada, many of them centered in the community where the juvenile offender resides. Some programs involve a treatment center where adjudged delinquents participate in daily group therapy while living at home and working or attending school. Other programs encourage the delinquent himself to help bring about change in other law-breaking youths, the philosophy being somewhat comparable to Alcoholics Anonymous (Wheeler et al., 1967).

Shore and Massimo (1969) have suggested that the identity crisis is more severe for lower-class boys who realize their limited opportunities than for those of the more affluent classes; they also note that these youths often entertain unrealistic fantasies about their abilities but lack the academic skills demanded by even lower-level jobs. Thus, they suggest that treatment of delinquency among lower-class youths should include comprehensive vocational training.

In 1963 Massimo and Shore reported on one such program—a ten-month experimental vocationally oriented psychotherapeutic program undertaken with 20 adolescent boys (10 in an experimental group and 10 in a control group) ranging in age from 15 to 17, with intelligence quotients from 85 to 110. A single practitioner served each youth in the experimental group in all therapeutic capacities, starting when the subject was expelled from or dropped out of school. Contact was initiated through offers to help the youth obtain a job. Pre-employment counseling with emphasis on job readiness was undertaken. Because the program was not compulsory, it encouraged and helped alleviate fears of dependency in the young people who participated. It was flexible and geared to the needs of each youth with a focus on his acquiring a sense of responsibility. The job was mutually selected by the boy and his therapist according to the boy's interests and abilities. Following placement, the counselor's emphasis shifted from job readiness to work problems. Remedial education was initiated according to work performance; it was introduced when the subject was ready to improve his skills on the job.

The results of this interesting study were that those in the program tended to improve first in their self-image, second in their control of aggression, and last in their attitude toward authority. In addition, they improved academically and showed a much better employment record than the control group, with seven out of ten still in jobs and the other three back at school at the end of the ten-month period. On the other hand, in the control group three boys remained unemployed during the entire ten months and a fourth boy was unemployed at the time of the final contact; this group also held more jobs for shorter periods of time than did the experimental group (Massimo & Shore, 1963).

The positive results of this study suggest that the delinquent's experience of success reduces his need for aggressive dealings with the world and its frustrations. Perhaps most important of all, however, it indicates the need for training people who can work with delinquents in multidimensional activities (Massimo & Shore, 1963). It might prove feasible to initiate a special education course of study to teach people to work with these youths on an individual basis with an extensive knowledge of each student's strengths and weaknesses, as teachers are taught to work in special education with the retarded or physically handicapped.

If it is necessary that delinquent youths be sent away from the community, one approach that is certainly preferable to the usual reformatory is the Vermont Weeks School. Although it appears to be a boarding school for upper-class children, it is actually a training school for court-committed delinquents ranging in age from 10 to 19. The school is designed to help its young people acquire the education they have failed to acquire in the public schools. Small classes provide individual attention. No grades are given and no students are failed; instead they are encouraged to like what they learn and to continue learning. When they acquire a basic foundation, they are permitted to attend the public high school in the community, with all of the obligations and most of the privileges of regular students, including extracurricular activities except for sports. Weeks School has its own athletic program, and its teams compete against other local teams. Adolescents of sufficient age are encouraged to seek jobs in the community in order to have spending money. They are also permitted to mix socially with students from town, and after a few months they are allowed to go home for weekends and vacations, provided their home is a stable one. Discipline involves the withholding of privileges, and although there are occasional runaways and some returnees, there is more success than failure (Levine, 1968).

In another institution for delinquent girls, a three-month pilot project was undertaken which was based on the theory that much antisocial behavior is the result of educational failure due to a *learning disability* (see Chapter 9). Both remediation of the academic deficits and a modification of the maladaptive behavior were stressed in this program. Referred to as *educo-therapy*, the program was undertaken with ten of the institutionalized delinquent girls who were considered to have educational or learning disabilities and/or a behavior disorder possibly related to such disabilities. The philosophy underlying the treatment was fourfold: (1) each girl should experience success in school, especially in reading; (2) each one should learn socially acceptable modes of behavior; (3) each should achieve an enhanced self-concept; (4) each girl should learn to assume responsibility for her behavior and its consequences (Rice, 1970).

As a result of this three-month educationally oriented therapeutic project, the girls improved their reading skills in from 2 to 13 months, with a corresponding increase in their intelligence quotients. There was also improvement in the girls' personal appearance and social behavior, less hostility and aversive behavior, and more positive cohesiveness among the ten, with each helping one another. "It was felt that the aversive gang or peer influence, which so often determines delinquent behavior, had changed somewhat to encouragement of socially adaptive behavior" (Rice, 1970, p. 23). As a result, three girls were released from the institution at the end of the three-month program. Another encouraging outcome of this project was the tendency of the other institutionalized girls to copy the behavior of those in the educo-therapy program.

SUMMARY AND CONCLUSIONS

Youths who have difficulty achieving a satisfactory emotional adjustment during the adolescent period may turn to drugs, militant movements, or delinquency or a combination of these behavior patterns as a means of escaping from a world which they often consider intolerable and frustrating. The rapid increase in delinquency since World War II is the outgrowth of many factors: socioeconomic conditions with a wide gulf between poverty and wealth and an emphasis on affluence by the mass media, the disintegration of the family, and the failure of the schools to provide an education relevant and suitable to the needs of all young people. It also reflects a high incidence of delinquent behavior among the affluent classes, but whether this is the result of parental failure or better detection and record keeping is debatable.

To prevent or reduce the incidence of juvenile offenses demands the concerted efforts of federal, state, and local governments, the schools, and the parents. Educators need to be particularly concerned about truancy, which is often a forerunner of more serious delinquent acts, and about vandalism, which is costly and frequently reflects the failure of our schools.

Certainly incarceration is failing as a deterrent to delinquency. In fact, it may even be a contributing factor to a higher incidence. However, new innovations in prevention and treatment are being introduced throughout the United States and Canada. These encompass various therapies, including psychological, vocational, and educational approaches. Several of these programs show promise of proving much more effective than the traditional reformatories and training schools.

REFERENCES

Allen, D. E., & Sandhu, H. S. A comparative study of delinquents and nondelinquents: Family affect, religion, and personal income. *Social Forces*, 1967, **24**(1), 263–269.

Bacon, M. K., Child, I. L., & Barry, H. A cross-cultural study of correlates of crime. *Journal of Abnormal Psychology*, 1963, **66**(4), 291–300.

Bandura, A., & Walters, R. H. Dependency conflicts in aggressive delinquents. *Journal of Social Issues*, 1958, **14**(3), 52–65.

Baugh, V. S., & Carpenter, B. L. A comparison of delinquents and nondelinquents. *Journal of Social Psychology*, 1962, **56**, 73–78.

Brown, V. Future delinquents can be seen at age 3. *Alexandria Daily Town Talk*, December 20, 1965, B-1.

Burns, V. M., & Stern, L. W. The prevention of juvenile delinquency. In The President's Commission on Law Enforcement and Administration of Justice, *Task force report: Juvenile delinquency and youth crime.* Washington, D.C.: U.S. Government Printing Office, 1967. Pp. 353–408.

Cavan, R. S. The concepts of tolerance and contraculture as applied to delinquency. In R. S. Cavan (Ed.), *Readings in juvenile delinquency* (2nd ed.). Philadelphia: J. B. Lippincott, 1969. Pp. 5–19.

Cervantes, L. F. *The dropout: Causes and cures.* Ann Arbor: University of Michigan Press, 1965.

Clinard, M. B., & Wade, A. L. Juvenile vandalism. In R. S. Cavan (Ed.), *Readings in juvenile delinquency* (2nd ed.). Philadelphia; J. B. Lippincott, 1969, Pp. 257–263.

Cohen, A. K. *Delinquent boys: The culture of the gang.* New York: Free Press, 1955.

Crumbaugh, J. C. The automobile as part of the body-image in America. *Mental Hygiene*, 1968, **52**(3), 349–350.

Cunniff, J. School vandalism on rise. *Alexandria Daily Town Talk*, March 26, 1970, D-4.

England, R. W., Jr. A theory of middle class juvenile delinquency. In R. S. Cavan (Ed.), *Readings in juvenile delinquency* (2nd ed.). Philadelphia: J. B. Lippincott, 1969. Pp. 106–115.

Fairfell, W. *Delinquency in the United States.* Boston: Beacon Press, 1965.

Glueck, S., & Glueck, E. *Unraveling juvenile delinquency.* Cambridge, Mass.: Harvard University Press, 1950.

Glueck, S., & Glueck, E. *Predicting delinquency and crime.* Cambridge, Mass.: Harvard University Press, 1959.

Glueck, S., & Glueck, E. *Delinquents and non-delinquents in perspective.* Cambridge, Mass.: Harvard University Press, 1968.

Gold, M. *Delinquent behavior in an American city.* Monterey, Calif.: Brooks/Cole, 1970.

Horrocks, J. *The psychology of adolescence* (3rd ed.). Boston: Houghton Mifflin, 1969.

Jaffee, L. D., & Polansky, N. A. Verbal inaccessibility in young adolescents showing delinquent trends. *Journal of Health and Human Behavior,* 1962, **3**(2), 105–111.

Kirkwood, J. The nervous child, personality characteristics of the juvenile delinquent. *Dissertation Abstracts,* October, 1955.

Kvaraceus, W. C. *Juvenile delinquency and the school.* New York: New World Publishing, 1945.

Kvaraceus, W. C. *Juvenile delinquency.* Washington, D.C.: National Education Association, 1958.

Kvaraceus, W. C. *Anxious youth: Dynamics of delinquency.* Columbus, Ohio: Charles E. Merrill, 1966.

Leinwand, G. (Ed.) *Crime and juvenile delinquency.* New York: Washington Square Press, 1968.

Leland, T. W. The faint smile syndrome. *American Journal of Orthopsychiatry,* 1961, **31**, 420–421.

Lelyveld, J. The paradoxical case of the affluent delinquent. *The New York Times,* October 4, 1964.

Levine, R. A. The personal touch. *American Education,* 1968, **91**(4), 14–17.

Massimo, J. L., & Shore, M. F. The effectiveness of a comprehensive vocationally oriented psychotherapeutic program for adolescent delinquent boys. *American Journal of Orthopsychiatry,* 1963, **33**, 634–642.

Miller, W. Lower class culture as a generating milieu of gang delinquency. *Journal of Social Issues,* 1958, **14**(3), 5–19.

Moore, B. M. The schools and the problems of delinquency: Research studies and findings. In R. S. Cavan (Ed.), *Readings in juvenile delinquency.* Philadelphia: J. B. Lippincott, 1964. Pp. 182–197.

Office of Education, U. S. Department of Health, Education, and Welfare. Delinquency and the schools. In the President's Commission on Law Enforcement and Administration of Justice, *Task force report: Juvenile delinquency and youth crime.* Washington, D.C.: U.S. Government Printing Office, 1967, Pp. 278–304.

Paulson, M. G. The role of juvenile courts. *Current History,* 1967, **53**(312), 70–75.

Pine, G. J. The affluent delinquent. *Phi Delta Kappan,* 1966, **48**(4), 138–143.

Polk, K., & Richmond, L. *Those who fail.* Unpublished paper. Lane City Youth Project, Eugene, Oregon, 1966.

Prentice, N. M., & Kelly, F. J. Intelligence and delinquency: A reconsideration. *Journal of Social Psychology*, 1963, **60**, 327–335.

The President's Commission on Law Enforcement and Administration and Justice. *Task force report: Juvenile delinquency and youth crime.* Washington, D.C.: U. S. Government Printing Office, 1967.

Reiss, A. J., Jr. Sex offenses. In R. S. Cavan (Ed.), *Readings ir: juvenile delinquency* (2nd ed.). Philadelphia: J. B. Lippincott, 1969. Pp. 263–274.

Reiss, A. J., Jr., & Rhodes, A. L. A sociopsychological study of conforming and deviating behavior among adolescents. U. S. Office of Education Cooperative Research Project 507, 1959.

Reiss, A. J., Jr., & Rhodes, A. L. The distribution of juvenile delinquency in the social class structure. *American Sociological Review*, 1961, **26**(5), 720–732.

Rice, R. D. Educo-therapy: A new approach to delinquent behavior. *Journal of Learning Disabilities*, 1970, **3**(1), 16–23.

Robinson, S. M. *Juvenile delinquency.* New York: Holt, Rinehart & Winston, 1960.

Scarpitti, F. R. Delinquent and non-delinquent perceptions of self, values, and opportunity. *Mental Hygiene*, 1965, **49**(3), 399–404.

Schafer, W. E., & Polk, K. Delinquency and the schools. In The President's Commission on Law Enforcement and Administration of Justice, *Task force report: Juvenile delinquency and youth crime.* Washington, D.C.: U. S. Government Printing Office, 1967. Pp. 222–277.

Schepses, E. Boys who steal cars. In R. S. Cavan (Ed.), *Readings in juvenile delinquency* (2nd ed.). Philadelphia: J. B. Lippincott, 1969. Pp. 244–256.

Sheppard, B. J. The orbiting teenager—a seminar. The delinquent juvenile—1963 status. *Medical Times*, 1965, **93**(2), 209–210.

Shore, M. F., & Massimo, J. L. The chronic delinquent during adolescence: A new opportunity for intervention. In G. Caplan & S. Lebovici (Eds.), *Adolescence: Psychosocial perspectives.* New York: Basic Books, 1969. Pp. 335–342.

Slocum, W. L., & Stone, C. L. Family culture patterns and delinquent type behavior. *Marriage and Family Living*, 1963, **25**(5), 202–208.

Tappan, P. *Juvenile delinquency.* New York: McGraw-Hill, 1949.

Thomas, J. H. Lecture on the Louisiana Probation and Parole Program. Presented at Louisiana State University at Alexandria, April, 1967.

Tobias, J. J. Work activities and future goals of the affluent suburban male delinquent. *Vocational Guidance Quarterly*, June, 1969, 293–299.

Toby, J. Affluence and adolescent crime. In The President's Commission on Law Enforcement and Administration of Justice, *Task force report: Juvenile delinquency and youth crime.* Washington, D.C.: U. S. Government Printing Office, 1967. Pp. 132–144.

Today's Education. Journal of the National Education Association, 1970, **59**(3), 3.

Yablonsky, L. *The violent gang.* New York: Macmillan, 1962.

Wheeler, S., Cottrell, L. S., Jr., & Romasco, A. Juvenile delinquency—its prevention and control. In The President's Commission on Law Enforcement and Administration of Justice, *Task force report: Juvenile delinquency and youth crime.* Washington, D.C.: U. S. Government Printing Office, 1967. Pp. 409–428.

Toys of addiction and adolescent drugs. In *The Health 80's* (stimulation on Drug Enforcement and Administration). *Abuse*. New series: Juvenile delinquency and juvenile crime. Washington, D.C.: U.S. Government Printing Office, 1962. Pp. 432–34.

Tobias, Preventive Control of Drug Abuse. *Journal of Abnormal* 1916. 66.)

Yablonsky, L. *The violent gang*. New York: Macmillan, 1962.

Wheeler, S., Cottrell, L. S., Jr., & Romasco, A. Juvenile delinquency—its prevention and control. In *The President's Commission on Law Enforcement and Administration of Justice, Task force report: Juvenile delinquency and youth crime*. Washington, D.C.: U.S. Government Printing Office, 1967. Pp. 409–424.

8

Other Adolescent Problems

Adolescence is certainly far from a uniformly pleasant period. Early
manhood might be the most glorious time of all were it not that
the sheer excess of life and vigor gets a fellow into continual scrapes.

Don Marquis

No current text dealing with adolescent behavior can adequately
cover the topic of the development of youth in our modern society
without dwelling on some of the major problems confronting young
people today. In this chapter we will discuss various aspects of the
more prevalent problems, including those of the alienated youth,
drug abuse, and teen-age marriage and divorce. We will take a look
at some of the underlying causes and factors contributing to these
difficulties and suggest possible solutions for some of the disorders.

ALIENATED YOUTH

"Alienation can be defined as an estrangement from the values
of one's society and family and a similar estrangement from that
part of one's history and affectual life which links him to his society
or family. Subjectively, the alienated person experiences himself as
being detached from his own feelings as well as from those around
him" (Halleck, 1967, p. 642).

Matza has described three major categories of alienated young
people—radicals, bohemians or hippies, and delinquents. It is also
necessary to distinguish among the bohemian alienated youth or
hippie, the alienated radical, and the political activist who works

185

within the system. Alienated radicals have been described as young people who engaged in violence during the student demonstrations of the last decade and frequently advocated the overthrow of the Establishment. The political activist, on the other hand, is not considered to be alienated. He is the young person who in the early 1960s became aroused about the injustices endured by American minority groups and took it upon himself to go into the southern states to help with the implementation of civil rights for the blacks. Such young people are usually academically superior students from white, upper-middle-class professional families with whom they are generally in agreement about political values although more overt in "taking a stand" and in demonstrating their convictions than their parents. On the other hand, the alienated hippie is characteristically pessimistic and too firmly opposed to "the system" even to attempt to express his disapproval (Keniston, 1965). He dissents privately and passively through his nonconforming behavior, ideology, and dress and through his frequent dependence on drugs, in which he indulges in order to intensify his subjective experiences. In contrast to the radical activist, he exhibits a distaste and a disinterest in politics, and he is morbidly convinced that meaningful change of the social and political society is impossible. He perceives that his "dropping out" is the only possible alternative (Keniston, 1967). Too often such alienation has been equated with delinquency (Brown, 1968). More accurately it might be used to describe all of those who feel shut off, unprepared, unable, or unwilling to move into the mainstream of life.

Although such *alienation* is usually expected to be found primarily among college-age students, there has been evidence in recent years that this phenomenon has been filtering down to the high school and even to the junior high school level with the arrival on the scene of the so-called *teenybopper*. Nor has it been confined to middle-class adolescents, for many black youths from the urban slums have also become alienated from society. Although often desiring to attain the goals of the middle class, they have lacked the necessary resources and professional assistance needed to achieve such aims (Gottlieb, 1970).

The foundation for adolescent alienation is laid during the years of childhood and early adolescence. In addition to the failures of society and of the schools, certain factors in the family constellation appear to play a vital role. For example, Gould (1970) found that

the firstborn or only child develops feelings of alienation more frequently than later-born children. He suggests that this tendency may
be related to the less adequate emotional adjustment of the eldest
or only child, which was discussed in Chapter 2. Because alienation
has become a fairly common pattern since the early 1960s, educators
at all academic levels, as well as parents and other adults, need
to become cognizant of the factors contributing to adolescent feelings
of alienation.

The hippie movement is not a new phenomenon. Adler (1968)
points out that hippies are reminiscent of the Gnostic movement
which first appeared at the time of the downfall of Rome and kept
reappearing as new cults with new names throughout the Middle
Ages. Similar, too, was the nineteenth-century Romanticist movement, which rejected the values of the Industrial Revolution, the
French Revolution, and the Napoleonic Wars and emphasized self-
expression (Flacks, 1967). And in the 1920s, following World War
I, American literary expatriates, who rejected American values and
standards and returned to Europe to live as bohemians, had ideas
and life styles that were quite similar to those of modern hippies
(Berger, 1967). Such movements have tended to appear during periods
of transition—in stressful times of severe social instability and crisis
when morale is low and all sense of order is lost (Adler, 1968).

Actually, today as in the past, alienated youth view the "Establishment" as evil and corrupt and deplore what they regard as the aimless,
trivial preoccupations of family and business. Rejecting society's
forms and rituals as being empty and dead, they often seek fulfillment
through drugs or an emphasis on mysticism as a means of obtaining
peak subjective experiences, through sexual freedom and the challenging of traditional sex roles, and through new art forms such
as the "theater of the absurd" (Adler, 1968). Like many adults, their
behavior is based on a search for the meaning of man's existence
coupled with a desire for self-actualization. However, in striving to
achieve such goals, they tend to use means that differ considerably
from those of the older generation.

Adler (1968) has suggested that perhaps hippies are searching for
a Golden Age in which to experience a rebirth of the lost innocence
of childhood, which is characterized by the purity of the ancient
apostles and the integrity of the noble savage. This reasoning could
help to explain their adherence to Indian tribalism and their desire

to leave the cities and live in communes in the wilderness in search of the utopian society.

While the last chapter focused on alienated delinquents, the following sections of this chapter will deal mainly with the category of alienated youth classified as hippies.

Characteristics of the Alienated Youth

Because the traits of alienated individuals present a common behavioral pattern, alienation has come to be viewed as a distinct personality disorder of youth. Halleck (1967) has described seven characteristics which consistently appear in the personality constellation of these adolescents:

(1) They exhibit a tendency to live only in the present, avoiding any commitment to people, causes, or ideas, in contrast to political activists or protesters, who are generally concerned with all such facets of life. The alienated fail to relate their current problems to any of their past experiences and show reluctance to assume the responsibilities associated with the role of the adult. Although they may be available to activist movements, they are unable to sustain their interest for any length of time, possibly because of their chronic apathy, boredom, and unhappiness.

(2) They demonstrate an almost total lack of communication with their parents and with other adults. Because they are distrustful of the older generation, they are convinced that any close relationship with them is an impossibility. Their withdrawal from their parents is usually passive in nature and often accompanied by the exclamation that they just desire to be left alone. The resentment which they typically hold toward adult authority is reflected through such behavior as cheating on exams.

(3) Alienated youth tend to possess ill-defined self-concepts. They appear to be unable to resolve their identity crisis, continuing to exist in a chronic state of identity confusion, uncertain as to who they are or what their lifetime goals may be, long after the more normal adolescent has successfully come to grips with these problems in his life.

(4) They manifest tendencies toward severe depressions, which are often provoked by relatively minor stresses. Such profound emotionality may be accompanied by impulsive efforts at self-destruction. More than most adolescents, they experience difficulties

in understanding themselves and their own motivations. And as noted in Chapter 6, they tend to project their hardships on the world, blaming society for their failures and for its inability to provide them with more meaningful lives.

(5) Despite the fact that they are usually quite bright, they show an inability to concentrate or to study for any length of time. This behavior may reflect their commonly held belief that today's education is largely meaningless.

(6) Alienated youth tend to engage in promiscuous but usually ungratifying sexual experiences, from which intimacy, self-respect, and orgasm are generally missing.

(7) And the alienated have a tremendous reliance on drugs. These adolescents seem quite aware that their usage of these drugs is disturbing to their parents and enraging to the law; therefore, drug use represents a potent weapon of defiance and rebellion.

Antecedents to Alienation

Investigators in the area of alienation have attributed its development to a number of antecedents. These may well be divided into two subgroups: primary or familial factors and secondary or societal factors.

Primary or Familial Factors Leading to Alienation

Alienated youths typically feel that they are unloved by their parents and that their parents may talk about their love for their offspring but often fail to provide genuine love and affection, depending on material giving as proof of their love. Characteristically from white middle-class families in large urban areas, these young people generally have parents who are pseudosophisticated in their knowledge of psychology. Actually, however, one or both of the parents has probably at one time experienced emotional difficulties requiring psychiatric treatment (Halleck, 1967).

The fathers of adolescents who experience alienation are usually absent from their homes for extended periods of time, or their working days are such that they leave early and return late with little opportunity for time with their children. They are likely to be perceived by the alienated youth as passive, submissive individuals who have "sold out" to pressures for success and status.

Keniston (1965) describes the mother, on the other hand, as a talented individual who has sacrificed her career to marriage and her children. Because her life is so wrapped up in her family, she tends to discourage her son's development of independence, often being overprotective and oversolicitous of his welfare.

By late adolescence these young people have still failed to resolve certain childhood conflicts. This failure may be a reflection of permissive child-rearing practices, in which the parents neglected to place consistent limitations on their children's behavior. (The reader may recall the authors' belief, expressed in Chapter 1, that certain conflicts occurring during the late teens and early twenties result from the failure of young people to resolve these conflicts during early adolescence when they probably would have proved to be less difficult and much safer for both parents and society.)

Although their parents may have encouraged them to verbalize their feelings, alienated youth often perceive that their parents are actually wary of their children's expressions of anger. To counteract their fear of emotional outbursts, their parents try to create an environment of understanding and permissiveness, which makes direct confrontation between the two generations unlikely to take place. Their children therefore try to adopt a pose in which they appear to be sufficiently rebellious to appear normal according to the usual standards established for adolescents yet sufficiently conforming to please their parents (Halleck, 1967).

Thus, alienated young people soon learn that they possess considerable power. They come to discover that their inertia, apathy, and withdrawal give them greater control over their parents than overt rebellion and that passivity provides a powerful weapon for hurting the older generation (Halleck, 1967).

Secondary or Societal Factors Leading to Alienation

Rapid social change, widespread affluence, leisure, automation, the lack of opportunity for creative work, and a decline in utopian ideals have all contributed to young people's disenchantment (Keniston, 1965). Fromm (1955) has suggested that our highly technological, industrial society contributes to the depersonalization of man's work and thus lowers his feelings of self-worth. Such depersonalization makes men feel alone, isolated, alienated, and driven by forces beyond their control. Further, in an increasingly more complex culture, the government finds it necessary to wield greater control over the daily lives of its citizens, thereby creating more repression and discontent. Such restrictions are particularly resented by those who fail to fit into the mold imposed by a conservative majority (Rogers, 1969).

Not only are these societal factors conducive to youthful alienation, but also educational institutions reflect the problems of the society at large and are in a position to affect young people more directly. Youths in our society today tend to be overworked in high school, where considerable stress is laid on educational achievement and on getting into the "right" college. As a consequence, young people currently have little time for play and fantasy and limited opportunity for mild, wholesome forms of rebellion (Halleck, 1967). Thus, an overt expression of conflict may be delayed in the adolescent until it is too late for him to resolve it in a normal, wholesome fashion at the appropriate time in adolescent development.

As young people leave home for college, latent problems may become overt in the new atmosphere of almost unlimited freedom. And although they may protest any attempts by the college to serve as a surrogate parent, not all young people are able to cope with their new freedom. At the same time, in college they may realize that they are in a highly desirable position in that their affluence is unearned. However, as the gap between them and the "have nots" becomes more apparent, they are likely to develop strong feelings of guilt. Ultimately they may react to their new environment and their subsequent feelings of guilt with apathy and withdrawal, as they gradually come to perceive that in such a world where anything is possible to them, no goal is truly important. This assumption is reinforced as they begin to discover that the current "knowledge explosion" will quickly render much of their learning obsolete. As a consequence, they come to live only in the present with their emphasis on immediate gratification. The result of this kind of emphasis is often a loss of ability to feel compassion, to assume responsibility, or to take up any commitments.

The residential college is unique in that it creates an affluent ghetto. Living in an isolated society with those of the same age and often taught by those little older than they, students can go for months without conversing with anyone over 30. Such isolation tends to reinforce any developing deviant trends and creates a subculture that can powerfully influence students' lives toward the rejection of adult standards and values (Halleck, 1967).

The impact of the mass media and the arts is another potent contributor to youthful alienation. By focusing on the extremes manifested by alienated youth, the media present this deviant behavior as if it were the norm. Such emphasis can give deviants a certain amount of status and recognition, which they may have failed to attain through more positive behavior (Halleck, 1967).

In summary, it appears that the phenomenon of alienated youth is the result of many psychological and sociological determinants, including the family structure, governmental action, rapid technological and social change, the educational system, and the impact of the mass media. However, considerable research is needed to determine just which combination of factors and the extent of each that may be necessary to precipitate the development of culturally alienated youth. Meantime, however, it has been noted that certain stages of development are typical in the evolution of the alienated personality.

The Development of Alienation

Allen and West (1968) have noted that there are four distinct stages in the development of the alienated individual. First, the youth becomes dissatisfied with society and develops feelings of impotence in dealing with the world around him. Second, he starts to search for a more meaningful life within the framework of his superior education and financial affluence. Next, he begins to associate with others who are also searching for a more meaningful existence and subsequently discovers that apparently some of them have discovered a "way." And last of all, he "turns on" (through the use of drugs), he "tunes in" (on the hippie scene), and he "drops out" (from society).

Counteracting the Trend toward Alienation

Alienation is neither inevitable nor irreversible (Eisner, 1969). One means of counteracting it is through the process of encouraging young people to take an active role in the formulation of programs pertaining to them and to their needs.

For example, in 1965 several thousand northern California high school students were invited to meet at a conference sponsored by the governor. Delegates to this meeting proposed 64 recommendations, 10 of which especially pertain to the issues at hand. Eisner (1969) has summarized these suggestions as follows:

Education:
    (1) Provide students with more responsibility for student affairs.
    (2) Encourage young people to become more involved in establishing school standards and rules through an active Student Council.
Community action:
    (1) Invite schools and youth organizations to participate more actively in community action and in the solving of community problems.
    (2) Give youth a genuine voice in the government of the community, possibly through an elected youth official.
    (3) Encourage young people to become actively involved in civic projects, for which they would be given recognition.
    (4) Appoint adolescents to serve on committees with adults.
    (5) Invite students to serve in youth services agencies, where they could bridge the gap between agency adults and recipients of agency services.
Jobs:
    (1) Expand the school curriculum in order to expose students, especially college-bound youth, to the world of work.
    (2) Make job opportunities available to all adolescents, not just dropouts.
    (3) Include young people on school or district committees engaged in working with industry to facilitate the development of jobs for young people.

Another study was made of over one thousand principals from public and private, large and small junior high and high schools throughout the United States. A good many of these administrators stressed that there was an ever greater need for students, educators, and parents to get to know each other better and to develop new channels of communication (Trump & Hunt, 1969). (This topic will be discussed at some length in Chapter 11.)

A set of suggestions for the college level, which are somewhat similar to those reported for the northern California high school students, has been advocated by Masland (1969). He emphasized that young people should be given the opportunity to grow through a minimum of required courses and maximum acknowledgment of the student's ability to enhance his knowledge through extensive use of the library, participation in community affairs, and self-initiated creative work.

Generally, a young person chooses the pathway to alienation only after he has failed to be assimilated into society (Eisner, 1969). If the members of his society could provide him with a meaningful role, which gives him an opportunity for pertinent decision making, provides him a certain amount of status and recognition, and helps him feel that he is actively contributing to the community, he can be deterred in many instances from becoming a culturally alienated individual.

DRUG USE AND ABUSE

During the past decade probably few problems have aroused greater concern among adults than the problem of drug use and abuse. Traditionally, a "drug" has been considered to be a substance prescribed by a physician for the treatment or prevention of an illness or the alleviation of pain, with the law regarding such substances as habit forming or addictive and therefore necessarily subject to legal control. But within the framework of our discussion, a more precise definition of "drug" is "any substance that by its chemical nature alters structure or function in the living organism" (Modell, 1967, p. 346).

In some schools drug use has recently become so widespread that "turning on" has become the puberty rite for entry into the adult world (Ungerleider & Bowen, 1969). Especially disturbing to the older generation has been the fact that the use of drugs is generally considered illegal, and is more likely to be treated as a felony than a misdemeanor (*Time*, September 26, 1969). And while knowledge about the immediate and long-range effects of these substances is very limited, there has been a critical lack of scientific research undertaken to study the consequences of drug use and abuse.

A Brief History of Drug Abuse in the United States

Although the misuse of drugs has been evident almost throughout the history of mankind, not until the turn of the century did society begin to show concern about this practice. Kolb (1962) noted that there was a wave of drug usage between 1910 and 1920. In 1919 a special committee appointed by the United States Secretary of the Treasury reported that there were many heroin addicts under the age of 20 in this country.The use of drugs declined in the mid-twenties until after World War II, when there was a resurgence of drug abuse. This increase, which reached a crest during 1951 and 1952, may have reflected a favorable report on marijuana issued in 1944. In the early 1940s Mayor LaGuardia of New York City appointed a committee to study the effects of marijuana. This group issued the statement that this drug was not addictive, that physical dependence and tolerance did not develop nor lead to more serious drug addiction, even though heroin addicts often admitted to earlier indulgence in the substance (Mayor's Committee on Marijuana, 1944). A decline in drug use took place in the late 1950s. Then during the decade of the sixties another flareup occurred, greater than that of any previous era and characterized for the first time by the widespread indulgence in drugs of white, middle-class, college students as well as middle-class high school and even junior high school students (*Time*, September 26, 1969).

The Phenomenon of the Drug Myth

Perhaps never in history has there been a period when people have turned so readily to drugs as in the past decade (Zinberg, 1967). From every side the public has been besieged by the "miracles" of science and the wonders it can perform in relieving man's physical and psychological aches and pains. Mother takes her tranquilizers to "soothe her nerves" and often administers them as well to her hyperactive child to keep him reasonably tractable. Father drinks liquor "to relax" after the stresses and strains of a hard day's work. And the child, long before he learns to read, is given a rudimentary course in physiology and pharmacology by the advertisers who display their wares on television. As a result, in this chemical age (Forsythe, 1969), a myth about drugs has developed—a myth that states that "drugs, with the exception of the ill-defined group referred to as 'dope,' are to be used readily to combat and correct any personal or physiologic disturbance of equanimity; they are the miracles of modern science developed essentially to cure various afflictions which are bad, and therefore the drugs themselves are good and presumably safe" (Pollard, 1967, p. 613). In such a drug-oriented society, it is small wonder that young people in ever-increasing numbers from all socioeconomic classes have turned to drugs during the past decade in the belief that drugs can give meaning to and relief from an often humdrum, purposeless existence (Forsythe, 1969).

Why Do Adolescents Turn to Drugs?

The motivating factors underlying the consumption of drugs by adolescents are varied and numerous (Blaine, 1966; Pollard, 1967; Forsythe, 1969). Undoubtedly, one of the primary factors is youthful rebellion. Adolescents often like to do the opposite of that which is expected of them. Thus, taking drugs can serve as a means of getting even with parents, whom the adolescent tends to regard as hypocritical in their own dependence upon mood-altering substances (alcohol and tranquilizers) while vehemently disapproving the indulgence of their offspring in similar mood-altering drugs. Adolescent drug usage may also reflect a desire for adventure and flirtation with danger. Young people often try out drugs for the first time strictly as an experiment and to satisfy an urge for "kicks." Another explanation can be found in the adolescent's tendency to regard drugs as a means of improving communication with his peers. Under the influence of drugs he reports increased ability at participating and sharing in group experience. Fourth, he may optimistically believe that drugs can lead to favorable personality changes and can provide him with a means of enhancing his self-esteem. Another contributing factor is the frequent and overt use of drugs by certain admired artists, writers, musicians, and would-be messiahs. For example, rock musicians are well-known drug takers, and their compositions frequently contain references to drugs (*Time*, September 26, 1969). Modern communication through the mass media is probably a sixth cause of the rising incidence of drug use, for youths in one section of the country can instantly learn what those elsewhere are doing. And a seventh cause is the easy availability of drugs, especially in many large urban areas throughout the United States.

A Distinction in the Use and Abuse of Drugs

At this point, it should be noted that the vast majority of adolescents use drugs for "kicks" and for experimentation, taking a drug on several occasions and then quitting (*Time*, September 26, 1969). It is not these youths who distress us so much; rather it is those who develop a habituation or addiction to these substances with whom we are concerned.

We should also distinguish between the terms "addiction" and "habituation." The World Health Organization (1950) defined drug addiction as "a state of periodic or chronic intoxication detrimental to the individual and to society produced by the repeated consumption of a drug, natural or synthetic" (p. 6). Addiction is typically characterized by an overwhelming desire or need to continue using the drug and to obtain it by any means possible, a trend toward ever-increasing amounts of dosage in order to maintain the same level of effect, and psychological and physiological dependence upon the drugs' effects. It is the third factor that is probably the most important feature distinguishing addiction from habituation (Pollard, 1967), for habituation is characterized by a primarily psychological dependence on drugs (Hinsie & Campbell, 1960).

Psychological Traits of the Adolescent Addict

Laskowitz (1964) has suggested that addictive behavior develops primarily in a psychological context and that physiological dependence is of less importance. He points out, as have others who treat drug addicts (Saint, 1969), that in most instances addiction occurs in those individuals already reflecting various emotional disorders, often of a *schizoid* nature.

Without a doubt, one of the most striking traits found among drug addicts is the repeated pattern of emotional dependency on the mother or on a mother figure (Zimmering, Toolan, Safrin, & Wortis, 1951; Blaine, 1966). And evidence in the history of the addict indicates that this dependency has been fostered by the mother's undue pampering and overprotective behavior. Often this maternal protectiveness reflects an attempt to compensate for the frequent absence of a stable, significant man in the home (Laskowitz, 1964), for many addicts come from broken homes (Einstein, 1970). Since a similar familial background is usually found in the case history of the culturally alienated youth, it is not surprising that extensive drug use and addiction are commonly found among this segment of the youth population.

Other numerous personality traits tend to appear with considerable frequency among addicts. One study of 22 boys, aged 14 to 17, admitted to the adolescent wards of the Psychiatric Division of Bellevue Hospital in New York City, disclosed these drug addicts to be nonaggressive, soft-spoken, skilled in verbal expression, and not typically gang oriented (Zimmering et al., 1951). The absence of gang affiliation was also noted by Laskowitz (1964), who pointed out that addicts tend to show a preference for associating with one or two individuals with whom they may share the "risks" and "rewards" of obtaining drugs. Addicted youths also demonstrate a tendency to control social situations through their passive manipulation of those around them, resorting to such techniques as "sweet talk" (Zimmering et al., 1951). Consistent with this behavior is their preference for structured situations, which can be more readily sized up and controlled before making a response (Laskowitz, 1964). And although they demonstrate a preference for authoritarian attitudes, reflecting their need for control and their distaste for ambiguity, they do their best to manipulate authority into corrupt behavior, a fact about which teachers and others working with young addicts need to become cognizant.

Because of a low frustration tolerance or inadequate preparation for dealing with stress, the addicted adolescent tends to avoid overt displays of anger toward the object of his frustrations (Laskowitz, 1964). In one study reported by Gold (1960) 30 male addicts, ages 16 to 21, and 30 delinquent nonaddicts and 30 nonaddictive nondelinquents, matched for age and intelligence, were compared on the basis of the Rosenzweig Picture Frustration Test. The results revealed that adolescent drug addicts are typically more *impunitive* (seeking to avoid all blame) than nonaddicts. They seek solutions to their stress through techniques that involve a minimum of conflict with others. They minimize the expression of their emotions to such an extent that they fail to resolve their feelings of frustration.

Difficulty in deferring immediate gratification has also been observed to be common among addicts (Laskowitz, 1964). Since this trait is also typical of the alienated youth, we see in this behavior pattern another explanation for the high correlation between alienation and drug abuse. Both of these patterns of deviant behavior are characterized by the belief that waiting is intolerable because the likelihood of future gratification is uncertain. And both the alienated and the addicts express their lack of trust in authority, reflecting their feelings and doubts that significant individuals in their lives will live up to the expectations they have made for them.

Of special interest to educators is the addict's fear of failure and his attempts to resolve conflict through avoidance behavior, a pattern which has been manifested in his selection of his school program (Laskowitz, 1964). He shows avoidance of even a diluted academic course, preferring pleasurable and unpaced activities such as painting, physical education, woodworking, and music. On the positive side, while offering a refuge from more demanding academic selections, such a curriculum may at the same time provide opportunity for peer-group recognition and awaken latent interests and talents, of which the young person may have been previously unaware.

However, because of the addicted youth's limited vocational training and academic background, he is often restricted to routine, unstimulating jobs. Rarely finding that such work satisfies his demands for immediate gratification, the youthful addict is quickly diverted from vocational pursuits and seeks out the type of gratification so quickly available through drugs (Laskowitz, 1964). In this behavior once again we witness the emergence of a pattern common to both the alienated youth and to the drug addict.

Types of Drugs Used by Adolescents

The various substances, both synthetic and natural, used by young people are numerous. The Maryland Psychiatric Case Register listed 77 mood-altering drugs for an eight-month period (Klee, 1969). The imagination and ingenuity displayed by adolescents in their search for substances that will produce the desired psychic effects is at times amazing (Freedman & Wilson, 1964), although wishful thinking rather than pharmacologic facts has undoubtedly been reflected in such practices as the smoking of banana skins. And no doubt, the effects of certain drugs have been reinforced by an environment conducive to mood alteration, as well as by the user's expectations.

Zinberg (1967) has differentiated between two types of drug abusers, pointing out that the kinds of drugs consumed depend largely upon the group into which the individual falls. The first group he described as "oblivion-seekers"—those mainly from the lower socioeconomic class who use drugs as a means of escape from what they regard as an intolerable environment. The second group he classified as "experience-seekers"—those who indulge in drugs not to escape life but to embrace it.

Heroin

This addictive drug, a derivative of opium, is the most hazardous of all and is usually the choice of the first group of abusers. Heroin provides a greater kick but at the same time a greater pull toward physical dependency than any other drug to be discussed subsequently. The potential heroin taker knows that he will be breaking the law and becoming dependent on this drug.

Family patterns are rather distinctive for the potential "oblivion-seeker." More than half of them come from homes broken by a parental death before the child has reached the age of 16. Frequently, such addicts are only children or the youngest child in the family. And the dependency noted earlier in a description of the behavioral traits of addicts is reconfirmed in a study by Zinberg (1967), in which it was observed that large numbers of addicts in their twenties and thirties continue to live with their mothers or with other female relatives.

The dangers in the use of heroin cannot be overestimated. In New York City alone during 1969 more than 200 adolescents died from involvement with this one drug (*Time*, December 26, 1969). Such tragedies may have been due to a possible overdose, but more likely they were the result of unsterile conditions under which the drug was injected or the outgrowth of malnutrition and other disorders resulting from the addict's indifference to his physical well-being (Einstein, 1970).

Marijuana

Without a doubt, the greatest controversy has centered around a mildly *hallucinogenic* substance known as marijuana or by Western users as "pot" or "grass" (Pollard, 1967). Although "oblivion-seekers" may start their drug consumption with marijuana, its main appeal has been for the group of "experience-seekers," who come mainly from the middle and upper socioeconomic classes. First declared illegal and a narcotic in 1937 by the United States government, its use has generally been considered to be a felony, until recently punishable on the first offense by two to ten years in a penal institution (Ginott, 1969).

Actually this drug has a history of use dating back 3000 years, and according to the World Health Organization (1950) there are more than 50 million users scattered throughout the world, most of them illegally indulging in marijuana.

Although the LaGuardia Committee (Mayor's Committee on Marijuana, 1944) declared this drug to be harmless, and pointed out that its use tends to result in nonproductive and apathetic behavior, the controversy continues to rage. Keeler (1967), in a study of eleven people reporting adverse reactions to marijuana, observed that taken in certain amounts by some subjects, it could precipitate an acute brain syndrome, panic, and delusional thought. Further, he noted that its use can set off changes in the life style of an individual, and that it is especially dangerous to those with a predisposition toward *schizophrenia*. According to Klee (1969), its use is far from harmless, for he sees the greatest danger to be the likelihood that a marijuana user will go on to other drugs. Other investigators (McGlothlin & West, 1968) have pointed out that thus far there is no evidence of long-term physical effects or physical dependence, and the clinical evidence of significant psychological dependence is debatable. At the same time, however, they observe that regular use may contribute to the development of such personality characteristics as apathy, passivity, a low frustration tolerance, a short attention span, lack of motivation, and impaired verbal facility. They also suggest that although the use of marijuana may not be a predisposing factor toward the use of heroin, it does play a role in initiating young people to other drugs, particularly LSD, which will be discussed shortly.

Weil, Zinberg, and Nelson (1968) reported on a study of seventeen volunteer males ranging in age from 21 to 26 (eight chronic marijuana users and nine nonusers who were cigarette smokers). All were administered pure marijuana, supplied by the Federal Bureau of Narcotics for experimentation purposes, and both low and high doses were used. To counteract any purely psychological effects, placebos were also utilized, and even the rooms in which the studies were being conducted were sprayed to mask the odor of marijuana. The results of the investigation disclosed that although marijuana does increase the heart rate moderately, it has no effect on the respiratory rate nor on the blood-sugar level. No changes in the size of the pupils of the eyes were observed, although dilation of the conjunctival blood vessels was evident. There also was evidence of its having some impact on behavior with subjects demonstrating impaired performances on simple measurements of intelligence and motor skills.

In any case, very little research has been undertaken to scientifically assess the effects of marijuana. In fact, until the spring of 1968, only three studies involving human subjects had been conducted and reported (Einstein, 1970). Perhaps this lack of research is due to the fact that one government agency controls both enforcement and research (McGlothlin & West, 1968). Or perhaps the fact that the medical profession has discovered no therapeutic use for marijuana may have caused it to pay little attention to it or to the need for research (Pollard, 1967).

Why do adolescents find "pot," or "grass," so appealing? Apparently, in small amounts this drug acts as a mild euphoric agent and sedative somewhat comparable to alcohol, whereas when taken in large doses its effects more closely resemble those of the hallucinogens or *psychedelic* drugs than any other group (McGlothlin & West, 1968). The eleven cases cited earlier (Keeler, 1967) reported that marijuana gave them feelings of positive pleasure, enhanced their creativity, provided insight, and enriched their lives. Nine of these eleven individuals felt that the benefits of the drug outweighed the unfortunate aspects, and they planned to continue using it. However, Keeler did not substantiate these claims with any objective evidence. Another explanation for its widespread use may be that young people are moved to defy laws they regard as unjust—a trend perhaps similar to the defiance of the prohibition laws of the 1920s. Many people feel that reducing the penalties for using this drug, as established by law, would reduce its appeal for young people.

Other Hallucinogenic or Psychedelic Drugs

Although psychedelic substances have not been used as extensively by young people as have other mood-altering drugs, they are considerably more dangerous (Pollard, 1967). Probably the best known among this group is LSD (Lysergic Acid Diethylamide). Such drugs are sometimes described as *psychomimetic* because of their tendency to create effects that mimic psychosis or severe emotional disorders in individuals not ordinarily emotionally disturbed. "Under the guise of bringing about increased creativity and greater feelings of harmony and loving kindness, many students have been given these drugs—with tragic results in some cases" (Blaine, 1966, p. 76). The temporary psychotic experiences induced by hallucinogenic substances even in apparently stable people have produced states of panic, in some cases even leading to suicide. In addition, episodes of psychosis may reappear weeks and even months after the individual has ceased taking the drug. Consider the case of Jonathan.

Jonathan, a 21-year-old college student, appeared one morning in the office of one of the authors. He was obviously quite disturbed and agitated and admitted that he was having hallucinatory experiences, although it had been a year and a half since he had last taken LSD. Not only does Jonathan illustrate the prolonged effects of such a potent drug, but he can also serve as an example of how a young person can be led to drug experimentation. Jonathan is an extremely bright young man with considerable literary talent, but he is very small. He is the son of a deceased Air Force officer; he and his family had lived all over the United States. Because of Jonathan's superior intellectual ability, he was skipped twice in the public schools. His low self-concept, which was still very evident, may well have stemmed from the fact that he was so much smaller than his older classmates and could not begin to keep up with their social development. Ultimately, he dropped out of school and drifted to the Haight-Ashbury district of San Francisco, where he began consuming LSD, perhaps with the hope that it would raise his image of himself in his own eyes as well as in the eyes of others.

Recently there has also been evidence that LSD may be damaging to human chromosomes and that the user takes a risk of passing on birth defects to his children (Cohen, Marinello, & Back, 1967; Ginott, 1969). For some young people, knowledge of this fact has proved to be a sufficient deterrent to using the drug. Unfortunately, however, LSD is easily made and readily available in many areas of the United States and Canada.

Stimulants, Sedatives, and Tranquilizers

Today there are many young people taking stimulants like *amphetamines* (such as Benzedrine) and *barbiturates* (such as Nembutal) strictly for "kicks." Unfortunately, the use of barbiturates can become as addictive as narcotics, while an overdose of Benzedrine, which stimulates the central nervous system, can lead to extreme excitement marked by hallucinations and delusions of persecution (Blaine, 1966).

Without a doubt, one of the most dangerous of the amphetamines is Methedrine, more commonly called "speed," which can kill (*Time*, September 26, 1969). Taken in moderation for a short time, stimulants are felt to be safe and helpful in treating depressions and in curbing appetites. Individuals wishing to elevate their moods, however, consume many times the medical dosage prescribed for weight watchers. Such overdosage, especially of the drug Methedrine, can provoke a psychosis similar to schizophrenia and in some cases raise the blood pressure to such a high elevation as to cause instant death.

Alcohol

Many authorities have classified alcohol as a drug (Blaine, 1966; Blum, Aron, Tutko, Feinglass, & Fort, 1969). Therefore, it would be unrealistic to conclude a discussion of various mood-altering drugs without including some mention of alcohol.

Alcohol, which is man's oldest drug dating back to the era before Christ, is a substance that depresses the central nervous system. This fact does not mean that excessive consumption of alcohol causes depression. Rather, alcohol tends to release one's inhibitions, a result which helps to explain why some individuals react as if they had really been stimulated. In moderation, such a release may be desirable, as in the case of an extremely shy person becoming somewhat sociable. In excess, however, he may become excessively aggressive and abusive. Alcohol is also an addicting drug, although the development of addiction, unlike that of other drugs, may take several years (Einstein, 1970).

During recent years, there has been an increasing awareness of teen-age drinking, for most adolescents experiment with liquor during high school (MacKay, Phillips, & Bryce, 1967). Offord (1965) has stated that by the tenth grade 50 percent of the boys and 20 percent of the girls have been introduced to alcohol. Unlike many adults, however, "An adolescent does not drink to relax or to get drunk as much as to discover just what kind of sensations drinking does produce" (Group for the Advancement of Psychiatry, 1968, p. 828). He appears to favor "party" drinking and engages in it, not to satisfy any inner cravings but in attempts to prove that he "belongs" or can conform to the group. In addition, drinking serves as a means of proving his manliness and of "sowing his wild oats" (Offord, 1965).

According to many observers, the primary factor in determining whether a young person will drink is the drinking behavior of significant adults in his life, particularly his parents (MacKay et al., 1967). The environment in which early drinking experiences take place is also important. Those who begin drinking in their own homes or at the homes of friends with adult supervision and approval generally remain more moderate drinkers than those who drink away from home without adult sanction or supervision. Actually most adolescents are moderate in their use of alcohol, although as they climb from the age of 14 to the age of 18, problem drinking increases from 2 to 5 percent.

In a study of twenty adolescents, referred to an alcoholism clinic for treatment, MacKay (1961) noted that these youths possessed the following traits in common: (1) Alcoholism was a frequent characteristic of their parents, especially among their fathers. (2) When they first started to drink, they were usually beset by uncertainty, ambivalence, and concern about their consumption of alcohol, knowing full well its effects on their parents, yet finding that it relieved some of their numerous tensions. Usually by the end of the first year of adolescence, they had begun to indulge in excessive consumption with occasional hangovers, shakiness, and blackouts. (3) The characteristic response among these young people was the display of considerable hostility toward their parents, whom they viewed as very inconsistent people lacking the ability to provide sufficient love and material needs for their children. (4) Drinking with their peers served as a partial substitute for the lack of close family relationships in the lives of these young people. (5) The use of alcohol at least temporarily relieved overwhelming anxiety and depression, as manifested by feelings of worthlessness, fear of the future, insomnia and suicidal attempts.

TABLE 8-1. The types, uses, and effects of drugs: A summary of significant factors related to drug misuse. (From *The Use and Misuse of Drugs* by Stanley Einstein. © 1970 by Wadsworth Publishing Company, Inc. Reprinted by permission of the publisher.

Drug	Addicting	Habit forming	Tolerance	Withdrawal symptoms	Manner used	Physical complications	Mental complications during use	Mental complications after use	Death by overdose	Conventional therapeutic usage in U.S.A.	Source of drug	Illegal manufacture and sale	Illegal possession
heroin	yes	yes	yes	yes	sniffing, injecting	related to manner of drug use, and kind of life user is living	intoxication	unknown	respiratory failure	none	Europe, Asia, Middle East	felony	felony
barbiturates	yes	yes	yes	yes	oral, injecting	drug related	intoxication	psychosis	convulsions, respiratory failure, shock	yes	U.S.A.	felony	felony
alcohol	yes	yes	yes	yes	oral	drug related, non-drug related	intoxication	brain damage, psychosis	coma, respiratory failure	yes	U.S.A.	felony	misdemeanor
cocaine	no	yes	yes	no	oral, sniffing, injecting	drug related, non-drug related	agitation, intoxication	psychosis? brain damage?	convulsions, respiratory failure	none	South America	felony	felony
amphetamines	no	yes	yes	yes	oral, sniffing, injecting	drug related, non-drug related	agitation, intoxication	psychosis, brain damage?	convulsions, coma, cerebral hemorrhage	yes	U.S.A.	felony	felony
marijuana	no	yes	no	no	oral, smoking	drug related	intoxication, rare panic or paranoid state	rare psychosis?	unknown	none	grows in almost all climates	felony	felony
LSD	no	yes	no	no	oral, injecting	drug related	panic, paranoid state	psychosis, paranoia, anxiety reactions, brain damage?	unknown	yes	U.S.A.	felony	felony
airplane glue	no	yes	yes?	yes?	sniffing	drug related?	intoxication	brain damage?	asphyxiation	none	U.S.A.	city and state laws	none, or state misdemeanor

The Present Incidence of Drug Use and Abuse in the United States

The current extent of drug use and abuse seems to vary according to geographical location and according to the age of the adolescents. Towns bordering Mexico, cities with large international airports, and seaports, where such substances are illegally smuggled into the country, provide relatively easy access to many drugs. And because they are more readily attained, their use in such cities is much more widespread than in other localities.

In the spring of 1968 a study of a suburban high school in the San Francisco Bay Area revealed some rather provocative facts (Blum et al., 1969). First, it was noted that the illegal use of drugs had increased two to four times over the rates disclosed by studies of other high schools in the same area 18 months earlier. This 1968 research also revealed that once drugs were started, the chance of their being continued was much more likely, particularly in the use of marijuana. The investigators hypothesized that the acceleration in drug usage reflected a considerable increase in exposure to such substances, greater experimentation with them, and widespread use among middle-class students in the San Francisco Bay Area.

In the case of marijuana, almost all of the students of this particular high school knew of users, 55 percent stated that they had tried it, and 41 percent of the boys and 37 percent of the girls described themselves as regular users. The incidence increased as students became upper classmen. Less than one third of these young people felt that there was anything wrong about using it, and of those who had tried it, a majority reported indulging in it for recreational purposes and for tension relief.

Two thirds of the students said they had had an opportunity to try hallucinogens, while 20 percent admitted that they had indulged in them, and 12 percent of the girls and 10 percent of the boys admitted that they had used them repeatedly. Once again it was noted that there was an increase in use among older students in the upper grades. About half of these young people saw nothing bad about using hallucinogenic drugs, but more than two thirds confessed that they could see no positive benefits to be derived from their use. About one third of the students reported that benefits included personal and social insight or a better understanding of oneself and of others.

In the use of amphetamines, 18 percent stated that they had tried them, although only 2 percent were regular users. Surprisingly, very few students saw anything wrong in the consumption of these substances, although neither could a vast majority find anything good in their use. Among students expressing positive feelings about these drugs, the most common reports were those of feeling good (euphoria) and of greater productivity (performance enhancement).

In the area of alcohol, 14 percent of the boys and 9 percent of the girls admitted that they regularly used alcohol, while 7 percent stated that they had never tried drinking. Eighty-seven percent described their parents as drinkers, but 61 percent regarded their peers as nondrinkers. Again it was noted that drinking increased with age and grade level in school. A large proportion felt that there was nothing wrong in the consumption of alcohol, although at the same time they admitted that they could perceive little good in it either. A majority of students pointed to recreational and social uses as the benefits to be derived from its use.

Although these figures, especially for marijuana, are quite high, the results of another study made at a medium-sized midwestern state university disclosed a much lower incidence (Sherwin, 1969). Of 260 students selected at random from a student directory, 78 percent stated that they had never indulged in "pot," 15 percent had experimented with it at least once or used it several times, and only 7 percent reported using it regularly at least once a month. From these statistics it can be seen that the vast majority were nonusers, some were occasional users, and only a small minority were regular users. At the same time, these same students overestimated the numbers of occasional and regular users and underestimated the numbers of nonusers. In other words, students believed that there was a greater consumption of drugs on campus than there actually appeared to be. Sherwin summarized his findings by stating that "it is more likely that student behavior with reference to marijuana use is similar to their behavior with reference to sex; there may be much more talk than there is action" (p. 21).

Regardless of the differences in these reports, it is quite evident that in many areas of the country a genuine drug problem does exist and the need for preventive action and remedial efforts is quite apparent.

Handling Drug Use and Abuse

From the widespread misuse of drugs, however, it is apparent that parents, teachers, and legal authorities have been very ineffective in their handling of the problem. Certainly, schools which expel drug-using students and parents who report their young people to law enforcement officials have not deterred these youths from their illegal consumption of such substances.

Actually, it seems that few students, either users or nonusers, shy away from the consumption of drugs because of moral reasons or fear of illegal activity and the disapproval of authorities (Blum, 1969). Those who abstain from drug usage often report that they do so because of their concern about possible physical damage that might result from drug use. Some adolescents feel that drug use is inappropriate for them, stating that they lack interest in drug-induced euphoria or in expanding their experiences and sensations through the use of such substances.

Ungerleider & Bowen (1969) have suggested that the wide variation in drug usage existing from school to school, especially at the high school level, appears to reflect, at least in part, the attitudes of the school administration. In certain schools where student response indicated low drug usage, there was an active educational program on drugs with outside speakers (former drug addicts being particularly successful in communicating with the student body) and the encouragement of active discussion on drugs. In fact, the key factor distinguishing these low-drug-usage schools from others was the opportunity afforded for such discussion. In other schools noted for extensive drug use, the administration often denied that they had a drug problem and said they did not believe in giving any emphasis to drugs through lectures, which they felt would only arouse youthful curiosity. Apparently, in prohibiting any discussion of the topic, they were merely making drug use more exciting and more appealing.

What can the schools do to counteract the rising incidence of drug consumption? Forsythe (1969) has made the following suggestions which educators might note in their attempts at handling the problem: (1) Educational programs should include discussions about the effects of drugs on those consuming them and the legal penalties under state and federal laws, as well as their possible impact on the students' lives. (2) Teachers should be honest in admitting what they do not know about drugs. (3) The schools should focus their attention on the students and their reasons for turning to drugs. (4) Attempts should be made to identify as early as possible those most likely to prove susceptible to drugs, and professional assistance should be sought to correct the root of the problem.

Perhaps the most interesting remedy for combating drug abuse has come from Ungerleider and Bowen (1969). They have suggested that each school employ an ombudsman. This term, of Swedish origin, describes an impartial referee who serves the student's interests without any obligation to the school administration. This individual would be one who is an "approachable" and understanding teacher with several months of special training and education in drug use and abuse. Ungerleider and Bowen define the role of this person in the following statement: "The ombudsman may best be described as a parent surrogate who is 'not square' (but who does not use 'pot,' 'acid,' or 'speed'), who is not afraid of discussing drugs, and who has some training in recognizing severe degrees of emotional disorder—enough to refer the chronic drug abuser (rather than the curious experimenter) for further help" (p. 1696). Such an ombudsman would be available to students just about any time. He would also be granted the right of privileged communication, wherein he would be under no obligation to reveal any confidence of any student to parents, to the police, or to the school authorities. Such an individual could not only counsel young people troubled about drug use but could also provide information to students requesting it, enabling many of them to take a firm position against drug usage for themselves. But whatever approach is to be used, it appears that in order to bring a halt to the rising incidence in drug use, youths should be reached at the earliest possible moment, when they first demonstrate an interest and curiosity about drugs.

TEEN-AGE MARRIAGE AND DIVORCE

Many adolescents might not view teen-age marriage as a problem. However, the fact that 40 percent of all brides in the United States are between the ages of 15 and 18, and 50 percent of all teen-age marriages break up within a period of five years (Farber & Wilson, 1967) certainly presents a set of serious problems for many young people, for their parents, and for society as a whole (see Table 8-2).

TABLE 8-2. The percentage of the population ages 14 to 18 classified as married by U.S. Census Reports for 1910 to 1960.

			Percentage of Age Group Married		
	Year	14	15	16	17	18
Males	1960	0.6	0.6	0.9	1.9	5.3
	1950	0.6	0.7	0.8	1.5	3.8
	1940	0.1	0.1	0.3	0.7	2.1
	1930	0.1	0.1	0.2	0.6	2.2
	1920	0.3	0.2	0.3	0.8	2.7
	1910	0.1	0.1	0.1	0.4	1.4
Females	1960	1.1	2.3	5.6	11.9	23.8
	1950	0.7	2.0	6.1	12.9	24.0
	1940	0.3	1.1	3.8	8.8	17.3
	1930	0.4	1.3	4.3	9.9	19.2
	1920	0.5	1.4	4.2	9.8	19.2
	1910	0.4	1.2	3.7	8.7	17.0

Of particular concern is the fact that about half of all teen-age girls are pregnant when they marry (Gagnon & Simon, 1968). One can only speculate about what percentage of these marital unions is solely the consequence of premarital pregnancy and what percentage is the result of genuine, mature love. This problem also raises the question of the wisdom in compounding one mistake (premarital pregnancy) with another (premature, hasty, and immature marriage).

Factors Contributing to the High Incidence of Teen-Age Marriage

In addition to premarital pregnancy there have been many other explanations offered for the widespread phenomenon of teen-age marriage in the United States (Broderick, 1967; Burchinal, 1960; Cadwallader, 1967; Ginzberg, 1967; Hechinger, 1967; Moss, 1965). Probably the most significant factors would include the following:

(1) There is a growing trend toward pushing youngsters into teen-age behavior at the age of 10 or younger.

(2) Along with this trend is an emphasis on going steady as early as junior high school. This dating pattern may lead to sexual experimentation often resulting in premarital pregnancy and a marriage by necessity rather than by choice.

(3) By the time they reach the late teens, adolescents will have undergone so many experiences in our affluent society that marriage may remain one of the few experiences that they have not yet tried. Having been denied little, they decide to try matrimony, often with the idea that if it fails, it can be easily dissolved.

(4) Physical maturity is occurring earlier in life than it did in previous generations, while at the same time the opportunity for sexual fulfillment has been delayed.

(5) The lack of clearly defined adult limitations on adolescent behavior has contributed to considerable insecurity among youth, who try to find this missing element in their lives through marriage.

(6) Our society tends to emphasize the pursuit of personal happiness and instant satisfactions, while at the same time overlooking the responsibilities demanded by marriage.

(7) Mass media often encourages early wedlock through its focus on the romance and glamour in marriage.

(8) The refrain that "Everybody is doing it" may push an adolescent into marriage before he is emotionally ready to take the step.

(9) Marriage may ostensibly offer an escape from an unpleasant situation in the home, the school, or elsewhere, and many young people may think it will serve as a means of resolving personal or social problems.

(10) Because of prosperity and the availability of financial assistance from the government, there is less economic risk in early marriage today than there was a generation ago. Affluent parents of teen-agers are often able to support these young married couples.

(11) Getting married is often viewed as a means of obtaining the adult status which society has tended to deny them.

Predicting Early Marriage

Almost no research has been done in the area of predicting or retarding the rates of teen-age marriage and divorce. However, several characteristics stand out among these young people which suggest that they tend to follow certain patterns of behavior. For example, Glick (1957) noted that marital instability in first marriages among adolescents is much more frequent among those dropping out of school. He described this tendency as the "Glick effect," proposing not that one caused the other but that possibly a lack of perseverance might be a contributing factor to both. On the other hand, Bauman (1967) suggested that both marital instability and dropping out of school are related to the age of the youths at the time of marriage, that those marrying at a young age would be more likely to drop out of school than those marrying later. Some high schools still have antiquated policies about married students attending classes, and most school systems still maintain strict regulations forbidding pregnant girls from continuing with their education. In other instances, adolescents may be forced to drop out because of financial pressures. But regardless of one's point of view, research of 1960 census data did reveal that dropouts do experience greater marital instability than those completing school (Bauman, 1967).

Other factors have appeared with considerable frequency among participants in teen-age marriage. Those who marry young are likely to come from lower- or working-class backgrounds of limited education, low incomes, and a need for continued parental support (Burchinal, 1965). The rate of young marriages is also much higher among nonwhites than for whites. Preparation and education for marriage are often inadequate or nonexistent. And those marrying before high school graduation generally have lower intelligence quotient scores and histories of poorer academic achievement than unmarried high school students.

Results of Teen-Age Marriages

Probably most important among all statistics relating to teen-age marriage is the stark fact that the divorce rate is two to four times as high for such couples as for those marrying for the first time in their twenties (Burchinal, 1965; Farber & Wilson, 1967).

Two studies focused attention on a self-evaluation of satisfaction in marriage among young teen-age couples. Undertaken in different localities, this research disclosed that from one third to over one half of the young husbands and wives stated that they regretted marrying when they did (Burchinal, 1959).

Teen-age marriage may also contribute problems to the development of children resulting from such unions. Young couples may not be ready for the responsibilities involved in rearing offspring and may neglect or mishandle these children through ignorance or immaturity.

At the same time, however, it should be noted that not all youthful marriages are doomed to failure or unhappiness. Many such unions result in successful and satisfying relationships. And age per se is not an adequate criterion for predicting the degree of marital competence in two young people (Burchinal, 1965). Many factors relating to marriage readiness, of course, are correlated with age, but these are often open to change or modification. In addition to age at the time of marriage, there are other conditions decreasing the chances for marital success. Many factors interfering with marital competency stem from conditions arising from a lower socioeconomic background, especially among those marrying before the age of 18. And certainly premarital pregnancies or unexpected pregnancies occurring during the first year of marriage, when there are already so many adjustments to be made, can prove especially fatal to teen-age marriages.

Deterrents to Teen-Age Marriage

It is apparent that all high schools should offer realistic, honest programs in marriage, family living, and child care, not only to girls through home economics courses but to boys as well. Such courses would partly answer the demands for relevance in education currently sought by many young people and could prove to be as important in the high school curriculum as basic courses in English and American history. To assure the success of such a program would require the selection of well-qualified, understanding educators with suitable professional training. The emphasis of such courses should be not so much on the risks involved in early marriage as on practical knowledge and the means by which young people might develop their personalities, their interests, and their potentials (Burchinal, 1965).

Parents and other adults should be alerted to the dangers of the self-fulfilling prophecy as it relates to teen-age marriage (Burchinal, 1960). Too often the older generation is punitive in its attitude toward youths who do marry in their teens. School boards often suspend or require the withdrawal of married students, falsely believing that such a policy is a deterrent to marriage. Parents may warn their youngsters that such marriages will never succeed, thereby contributing to the high incidence of failure through their reliance on the use of dire prediction.

SUMMARY AND CONCLUSIONS

Adolescents in our modern society are confronted by many problems—alienation, drug use and abuse, and teen-age marriage—which many people tend to believe are unique to our present rapidly changing world. However, a study of history will reveal that although these disorders may be more prevalent and noticeable today than in the past because of the tremendous numbers of young people in our midst, at least the first two phenomena have existed almost throughout the history of mankind. The third problem, teen-age marriage and divorce, reflects the difficulties created by the present length of the adolescent period and the long period of economic dependence, as well as the changing attitudes toward premarital sex and divorce.

Certain ideas have been introduced as possible means of reversing these trends with particular emphasis on practices by which the schools and society might come to grips with some of the problems. Although these suggestions have not been offered as a final panacea for these difficulties, the authors hope that they may provoke some serious thought and consideration in the minds of the readers.

REFERENCES

Adler, N. The antinomian personality: The hippie character type. *Psychiatry*, 1968, **31**(4), 325–338.

Allen, J. R., & West, L. J. Flight from violence: Hippies and the green rebellion. *American Journal of Psychiatry*, 1968, **125**(3), 364–370.

Bauman, K. E. The relationship between age at first marriage, school dropout, and marital instability: An analysis of the Glick effect. *Journal of Marriage and the Family*, 1967, **29**(4), 672–680.

Berger, B. M. Hippie morality—More old than new. *Trans-Action*, 1967, **5**(3), 19–26.

Blaine, G. B., Jr. *Youth and the hazards of affluence.* New York: Harper & Row, 1966.

Blum, R. H. Life style interviews. In R. H. Blum & Associates (Eds.), *Students and drugs.* San Francisco: Jossey-Bass, 1969. Pp. 209–231.

Blum, R. H., Aron, J., Tutko, T., Feinglass, S., & Fort, J. Drugs and high school students. In R. H. Blum & Associates (Eds.), *Students and drugs*. San Francisco: Jossey-Bass, 1969. Pp. 321–348.

Broderick, C. B. Going steady: The beginning of the end. In S. M. Farber & R. H. L. Wilson (Eds.), *Teenage marriage and divorce*. Berkeley, Calif.: Diablo Press, 1967. Pp. 21–24.

Brown, W. N. Alienated youth. *Mental Hygiene*, 1968, **52**(3), 330–336.

Burchinal, L. G. Comparison of factors related to adjustment in pregnancy-provoked and non-pregnancy-provoked youthful marriages. *Midwest Sociologist*, 1959, **21**, 92–96.

Burchinal, L. G. School policies and school age marriages. *Family Life Coordinator*, 1960, **8**, 45–46.

Burchinal, L. G. Trends and prospects for young marriages in the U.S. *Journal of Marriage and the Family*, 1965, **27**(2), 243–254.

Cadwallader, M. L. In search of adulthood. In S. M. Farber & R. H. L. Wilson (Eds.), *Teenage marriage and divorce*. Berkeley, Calif.: Diablo Press, 1967. Pp. 15–20.

Cohen, M. M., Marinello, M. J., & Back, N. Chromosomal damage in human leukocytes induced by lysergic acid diethylamide. *Science*, 1967, **155**, 1417–1419.

Einstein, S. *The use and misuse of drugs*. Belmont, Calif.: Wadsworth, 1970.

Eisner, V. Alienation of youth. *The Journal of School Health*, 1969, **39**(2), 81–90.

Farber, S. M., & Wilson, R. H. L. (Eds.) *Teenage marriage and divorce*, Berkeley, Calif.: Diablo Press, 1967.

Flacks, R. The liberated generation: An explanation of the roots of student protest. *Journal of Social Issues*, 1967, **23**(3), 52–75.

Forsythe, M. J. Youth and drugs—use and abuse, educational and sociological aspects. *The Ohio State Medical Journal*, 1969, **65**, 17–23.

Freedman, A. M., & Wilson, E. A. Childhood and adolescent addictive disorders. *Pediatrics*, 1964, **34**, 425–430.

Fromm, E. *The sane society*. New York: Holt, Rinehart & Winston, 1955.

Gagnon, J. M., & Simon, W. Sexual deviance in contemporary America. *The Annals of the American Academy of Political and Social Science*, 1968, **376**, 106–122.

Ginott, H. G. *Between parent and teenager*. New York: Macmillan, 1969.

Ginzberg, E. Work and life plans. In S. M. Farber & R. H. L. Wilson (Eds.), *Teenage marriage and divorce*. Berkeley, Calif.: Diablo Press, 1967. Pp. 9–14.

Glick, P. C. *American families*. New York: John Wiley & Sons, 1957.

Gold, L. Reaction of male adolescent addicts to frustration as compared to two adolescent non-addicted groups. *Dissertation Abstracts*, 1960, **20**, 4716.

Gottlieb, D. Poor youth: A study of forced alienation. In H. Gadlin & B. E. Garskof (Eds.), *The uptight society: A book of readings*. Monterey, Calif.: Brooks/Cole, 1970, Pp. 212–229.

Gould, L. S. Conformity and marginality: Two faces of alienation. In H. Gadlin & B. E. Garskof (Eds.), *The uptight society: A book of readings.* Monterey, Calif.: Brooks/Cole, 1970. Pp. 230–244.

Group for the Advancement of Psychiatry, Committee on the Adolescent. *Normal adolescence: Its dynamics and impact.* New York: Group for the Advancement of Psychiatry, February, 1968, **6**(68).

Halleck, S. L. Psychiatric treatment for the alienated college student. *American Journal of Psychiatry,* 1967, **124**(5), 642–650.

Hechinger, F. M. Tradition; security or restriction. In S. M. Farber & R. H. L. Wilson (Eds.), *Teenage marriage and divorce.* Berkeley, Calif.: Diablo Press, 1967. Pp. 1–8.

Hinsie, L. E., & Campbell, R. J. *Psychiatric dictionary* (3rd ed.). New York: Oxford Press, 1960.

Keeler, M. H. Adverse reactions to marijuana. *American Journal of Psychiatry,* 1967, **124**(5), 674–677.

Keniston, K. *The uncommitted: Alienated youth in American society.* New York: Harcourt, Brace, & Jovanovich, 1965.

Keniston, K. The sources of student dissent. *Journal of Social Issues,* 1967, **23**(3), 108–137.

Klee, G. D. Drugs and American youth. A psychiatrist looks at the psychedelic generation. *Medical Times,* 1969, **97**, 165–171.

Kolb, L. *Drug addiction.* Springfield, Illinois: Charles C. Thomas, 1962.

Laskowitz, D. Psychological characteristics of the adolescent addict. In E. Harms (Ed.), *Drug addiction in youth.* New York: Pergamon Press, 1964. Pp. 67–83.

MacKay, J. R. Clinical observations on adolescent problem drinkers. *Quarterly Journal of Studies on Alcohol,* 1961, **22**, 124–130.

MacKay, J. R., Phillips, D. L., & Bryce, F. O. Drinking behavior among teenagers: A comparison of institutionalized and non-institutionalized youth. *Journal of Health and Social Behavior,* 1967, **8**(1), 46–54.

Masland, R. P. Adolescent unrest and the schools—The impact upon health. *The Journal of School Health,* 1969, **39**(9), 603–607.

Matza, D. Subterranean traditions of youth. In D. Rogers (Ed.), *Issues in adolescent psychology.* New York: Meredith, 1969. Pp. 345–364.

Mayor's Committee on Marijuana. *The marijuana problem in the city of New York.* Lancaster, Pennsylvania: Jacques Cattell Press, 1944.

McGlothlin, W. H. & West, L. J. The marijuana problem: An overview. *American Journal of Psychiatry,* 1968, **125**, 370–378.

Modell, W. Mass drug catastrophes and the roles of science and technology. *Science,* 1967, **156**, 346.

Moss, J. J. Teenage marriage: Cross-national trends and sociological factors in the decision of when to marry. *Journal of Marriage and the Family,* 1965, **27**(2), 230–242.

Offord, D. R. The orbiting teenager—A seminar. Problems with smoking, alcohol, and drug abuse. *Medical Times,* 1965, **93**(2), 207–208.

Pollard, J. C. Teenagers and the use of drugs: Reflections on the emotional setting. *Clinical Pediatrics,* 1967, **6**(11), 613–620.

Rogers, D. Alienated youth. In D. Rogers (Ed.), *Issues in adolescent psychology.* New York: Meredith, 1969. Pp. 342–344.

Saint, C. L. Director, Forest Glen Treatment Center, Pineville, Louisiana. Interview held in December, 1969.

Sherwin, R. C. Marijuana at Miami? *The Miami Alumnus,* 1969, **23**(2), 20–21.

Time. Pop drugs: The high as a way of life, September 26, 1969, 68–78.

Time. Why did Walter die? December 26, 1969, 12.

Trump, J. L., & Hunt, J. The nature and extent of student activism. *National Association of Secondary School Principals Bulletin,* 1969, **53**, 150–158.

Ungerleider, J. T., & Bowen, H. L. Drug abuse and the schools. *American Journal of Psychiatry,* 1969, **125**(12), 1691–1696.

United States Census Reports—1960 Census, Washington, D.C.: Government Printing Office.

Weil, A. T., Zinberg, N. E., & Nelson, J. Clinical and psychological effects of marijuana in man. *Science,* 1968, **162**, 1234–1242.

World Health Organization. Expert committee on drugs liable to produce addiction: Second report, World Health Organization Technical Report Series No. 21. Geneva: World Health Organization, 1950.

Zimmering, P., Toolan, J., Safrin, R., & Wortis, S. B. Heroin addiction in adolescent boys. *Journal of Nervous and Mental Disorders,* 1951, **114**, 19–34.

Zinberg, N. E. Facts and fancies about drug addiction. *The Public Interest,* 1967, **6**, 75–90.

V

Problems Unique
to Adolescent
Development

9

Adolescent Learning Problems

The future of any country which is dependent on the will and wisdom of its citizens is damaged, and irreparably damaged, whenever any of its children is not educated to the fullest extent of his capacity, from grade school through graduate school. Today an estimated four out of ten students in the fifth grade will not even finish high school—and that is a waste we cannot afford.

John F. Kennedy
State of the Union Message, January 14, 1963

The adolescent who isn't learning in the classroom has a vital message about himself for those concerned with his development. He may be unconsciously trying to tell us that he has a limited amount of mental ability or a *sensory* or *perceptual motor handicap.* He may be informing us that he lacks readiness for the subject matter because of the inadequacy of his previous education. Or he may be demonstrating an inability to cope with physical, social, or emotional problems through his poor concentration, comprehension, and recall in the classroom (Hewitt, 1964).

Rarely is his message clearly understood, and rarely is the explanation for his learning problem a simple, specific one, for various physical, environmental, and psychological factors often overlap. It is important, however, that the classroom teacher learn to recognize when such learning problems exist, to detect causes suggested by the child's behavior patterns, and to be aware of community resources available to assist in modifying this behavior.

221

ORGANIC LEARNING PROBLEMS

You may recall from your previous courses in psychology that an individual's level of intelligence or mental ability is often closely related to his academic achievement. Intelligence is determined through the use of tests which measure a person's intelligence quotient, or IQ—that is, the ratio of his mental age (MA) to his chronological age (CA). The mental age is computed by comparing his raw score on an intelligence test with the scores of others of the same chronological age. Actually, the concept of intelligence has two rather distinct meanings and may be interpreted in two ways. It can denote an innate or inherited intellectual potential, or it can be defined as representing the average level of performance or comprehension of an individual at a given time (Sanford & Wrightsman, 1970).

Frequently in the seventh and eighth grades a teacher will encounter youngsters of limited mental ability with intelligence quotients, or IQ's, ranging in the *borderline-defective* or *dull-normal* areas of 75 to 90 (Ames, 1968). These students have often lagged behind their peers in elementary school and with junior high reach the upper limits of their intellectual potential. According to Wechsler (1955), close to 20 percent of the general population falls within this range. These young people are above the intellectual level that would usually qualify them for special classes for the retarded but below the level that would assure them of graduating from high school with their peers, especially from a good academic high school. Such students may benefit from some heterogeneous grouping with brighter students but they will also need special tutoring and a special curriculum geared to their particular needs in order to pass.

Sometimes, however, the self-fulfilling prophecy may be in operation. That is, the teacher's expectations of a student's performance may have a strong impact both on the person's level of mental ability and on his academic achievement (Rosenthal, 1969). Or a low socioeconomic background may cause a youngster to appear to be mentally retarded when he actually has average or better-than-average intellectual potential. Many group paper and pencil IQ tests, which is generally the type of measurement administered by the schools, rely heavily on reading vocabulary and reading comprehension, skills often quite deficient among the culturally deprived.

Some young people demonstrate a marked improvement in their mental ability if their major difficulties are resolved or if they are placed in a more stimulating environment (Sanford & Wrightsman, 1970). Far too often, however, we categorize these youths as "dull" and unworthy of our special efforts, a negative approach to a problem meriting considerable positive attention and action.

David is a striking example of such erroneous thinking. He had originally obtained an IQ of 65, which is considered to be in the range of mild retardation. His test scores also indicated that he had a perceptual-motor handicap, but he was classified as too slow for special classes dealing with such defects. Fortunately, a professional worker in the area of perceptual development believed that David would benefit from intensive remedial effort in this field, and she undertook three years of concentrated work with him in this area. As a consequence of their joint efforts, David's level of intelligence rose to 94, which, of course, is in the low-average range of mental ability (McCarthy, 1968).

Through such dramatic improvements, educators, psychologists, and others working with children and adolescents are coming to recognize that an intelligence quotient is frequently responsive to environmental modification and that one IQ score should never be taken as an absolute evaluation of an individual's mental ability.

RECOGNIZING THE STUDENT WITH LEARNING DISABILITIES

Many students who are failing to learn are the victims of learning disabilities. According to Bateman (1964), "the child with learning disabilities is perhaps best described as one who manifests an educationally significant discrepancy between his apparent capacity for language behavior and his actual level of language functioning" (p. 167).

Within this broad framework at least three major subclasses can be distinguished, although overlapping does exist among them. The first category is described as *dyslexia*, or reading disability, which is perhaps the most common of all three classes and yet is often the most difficult to recognize. The second group is *aphasic disorders*, or disorders in verbal communication, denoting children whose comprehension or expressive language difficulties involve the spoken word. Actually, this disorder is very rare among speech-handicapped groups in the public schools (Kirk, 1962). The third subclass is made up of *visual-motor integration* problems, which are often observed in conjunction with reading problems. There are children, however, who demonstrate severe *spatial orientation*, body image, perceptual, coordination, and other similar problems but who are not considered dyslexic (Bateman, 1964).

Although research in dyslexia was done as far back as the end of the nineteenth century, it is only in the past decade that psychologists have started to pull together all of the information and to undertake research in the field, particularly as it relates to education. Dyslexia has been defined as "the failure to develop specific perceptual-motor skills to expected proficiency independent of instruction, motivation, sense organ functioning, intelligence, and central nervous system damage. That it qualifies as specific is indicated by the lack of achievement in certain activities as compared to achievement in other activities. It is not a disease but an arrestation of anticipated development" (Shedd, 1968, p. 484).

A wide range of hypotheses have been suggested to explain the etiology, or causes, of dyslexia. Makita (1968) noted the rarity of learning disabilities in Japanese children, stating that they existed only 10 percent as frequently in Japan as in our Western countries. She proposed that the specificity of our language, as for example the similarities between *d, b,* and *p,* is the most potent contributor to the formation of learning disabilities.

Strauss and Kaphart (1955) have hypothesized that dyslexia is the result of brain injury which may cause the child to test as defective in certain behavioral traits. This kind of brain injury explanation, often referred to as the "Strauss syndrome," has actually become more useful as a diagnostic category than as an etiological explanation.

Other explanations have included the following: neurological disorganization in the absence of a known brain injury; neurological lag, or the developmental hypothesis, which notes that the immature primary grade student often becomes the "late bloomer" in junior high school, high school, or even college; structural deviations in the human brain; *congenital* defect or structural deficit; mild sensory impairment, or *mixed dominance*, wherein the individual may be predominantly right-handed but left-eyed; and electrochemical malfunction of the brain (Frierson & Barbe, 1967). But probably a majority of investigators have come to feel that the cause is basically *genetic*—that is, that dyslexia is an inherited disorder (Shedd, 1969).

For example, Mrs. Brown recalled that she had barely squeezed through art school because of the academic requirements and her difficulty in reading and that her brother had finally been dismissed from college because of academic failure. Two decades later, she states that three of her four children have been diagnosed as dyslexic, and in all probability this is the condition with which she and her brother were both afflicted.

Why should this problem be of such concern to classroom teachers? First, it has been estimated that dyslexia in varying degrees affects from 15 to 20 percent of all students, with the incidence among boys being seven times as high as that among girls (Shedd, 1967). It has also become evident that this condition is frequently unrecognized among many disadvantaged youth, delinquents, and potential dropouts. In addition, emotional disorders are often found to occur as a result of such learning disabilities (Kappelman, Kaplan, & Ganter, 1969; Tarnopol, 1970). And because dyslexic students many times are overlooked by their elementary school teachers, who may have come to regard them as immature, lazy, or lacking in motivation, it is most important that secondary education teachers be alert to such disorders.

Several tests have been devised to assist in the identification of the dyslexic student. There are also numerous symptoms characteristic of the dyslexic. Included are the following typical behavior patterns:

These students appear not to be "trying." On one occasion they seem to understand directions, and a day later they haven't the slightest idea of the procedure to be followed.

They are often described as immature, frequently demonstrating hyperactive behavior on the one hand or resorting to excessive daydreaming or fantasy on the other.

Their handwriting is likely to be angular, scrawled, poorly formed, and difficult for the teacher or parent to decipher. Often they will be observed to cross a *t* or *x* from right to left, rather than from left to right as is usually done.

Their reading is generally most inadequate. As a consequence, they tend to demonstrate a dislike for books and other reading material. They cannot remember right from left, up from down. They reverse letters, such as *b* and *d* or even whole words, such as *was* and *saw*. They fail to perceive the internal detail of words, perhaps seeing two words that appear to be alike and calling one for the other, simply because the outside configuration is the same. This would be illustrated by such words as *defeat* and *defect*.

In the area of spelling, dyslexics demonstrate incredible patterns, often found nowhere else in the English language. They may obtain a perfect score on spelling tests because of memorization and prompt recall; yet a week later they wouldn't recognize the words if they saw or heard them.

Perceptual problems are particularly noticeable among dyslexics. Vision is normal, but somewhere in the central nervous system a *dysfunction* causes the visual message to be perceived erroneously by the brain. Hearing is also normal, but there is often evidence of difficulty in perceiving differences in auditory stimuli, such as *gym* and *gem*. As Stern (1968) succinctly stated the problem, "The child is able to see, but not necessarily able to look; the child is able to hear, but not necessarily able to listen."

Motor coordination is poor, both in the areas of gross or large muscle coordination, such as tennis or baseball, and in fine muscle coordination, such as that used in handwriting. Although such youths may become good swimmers, they often stumble and fall without apparent cause, and their locomotive gait is frequently *dysrhythmic*. This poor muscle coordination is also evident in their speech, which tends to be characterized by slurred articulation or pronunciation, often resulting in mumbled, sloppy speaking.

Dyslexic students recurrently demonstrate difficulty in organizing their material, which is apparent in their written work and in their poor aptitude for spatial relations.

In the area of sequence, dyslexics frequently show confusion on such common sequential material as the days of the week or the months of the year. They also tend to *perseverate*—that is, they have difficulty changing from one activity to another, clinging to the previous activity in which they had been engaged. If they begin by multiplying problems on a page, they will continue to do so, even when the directions have changed (Jones, 1967; Shedd, 1968).

Billy, born three weeks prematurely and hyperactive since infancy, entered school at 6 3/4 years, when he was taught to read phonetically. He liked reading until he reached the fourth or fifth grade, when he gradually showed a loss of interest in it, and his grades also began to slip. In the ninth grade he failed French, although he minimally managed to pass his other subjects. In the tenth grade he was diagnosed as having dyslexia. A case history revealed that his father, who had died when Billy was four, and his uncle, a physician, had probably both had dyslexia, although neither of Billy's two older brothers and one older sister had shown any evidence of it.

At about the same time that he had been tested and diagnosed as being dyslexic, Billy developed a peptic ulcer, frequent headaches, and a sick stomach, about which he complained once or twice a week. After his ulcer had been treated, he spent the summer being tutored in *phonetics*, during which time his reading speed went from 150 words per minute to 500 words per minute. Unfortunately, the community in which he lived had no instructors trained in the skills necessary for teaching dyslexics.

Today, Billy is a college student making a fair adjustment to the curriculum of a southern university. He is still unable to master a foreign language and probably will never be able to do so without specific remedial instruction in overcoming his perceptual difficulties. Meantime, however, he is being treated by *chemotherapy* and being seen by a university guidance counselor each week so that he is able to meet the other academic demands without undue stress.

This case exemplifies many facets of the learning disability problem, including: (1) the close correlation between dyslexia and the occurrence of psychosomatic disorders; (2) the fact that this condition may not always be apparent in the elementary school student, although the most common age of referrals for dyslexics is age nine (Clements, 1968); and (3) that the condition can often be treated at several different levels—educationally, chemotherapeutically, and psychotherapeutically.

When the problem is not recognized until the child has reached junior high school, it is still not too late for training in perceptual development to be started. In Natchez, Mississippi, where a three-year federal grant (1967–1970) made possible the evaluation of all suspected dyslexic children and the special training in perceptual development of those so diagnosed, the results of such training at the junior high school level were most encouraging. During the first year of the program among 23 youngsters, aged 11 to 15, diagnosed as dyslexics with IQ's ranging from 83 to 116 (average IQ 96) and testing at reading levels varying from 2.3 to 6.8 grade level, the average rate of improvement following an eight-month instructional period in specific reading remediation was 2.4 years, with the range of improvement running anywhere from 1 year to 4.7 years.

TRAINING IN PERCEPTUAL DEVELOPMENT

Training in perceptual development varies according to the beliefs of various investigators. Cohn (1964) and Shedd (1969) do not feel that dyslexia should be classified as *minimal brain dysfunction*. Shedd also believes that it should be distinguished from hyperactivity and brain damage. He notes that dyslexic children are not distracted by multiple stimuli, as are hyperactive children—an observation confirmed by one of the author's visits to a junior high school class in perceptual development. Shedd therefore sees no need for cutting down on the stimuli. To the contrary, he emphasizes the necessity for building up *stimulus intensity* in order to reach these students. Also, he points out that teaching machines lack such stimulus intensity and for this reason have not proved to be satisfactory in working with dyslexics.

On the other hand, Clements (1962) regards dyslexia as a manifestation of minimal brain dysfunction and believes dyslexic children cannot work well with other children, that they have a short attention span, are easily distracted, hyperactive, and very impulsive. Thus, he feels that these children require an individualized teaching program, paced at a slower rate than for the average child, with considerable emphasis on oral presentation of material, and with as few distracting stimuli as possible.

Shedd (1969) emphasizes the importance of using as many sense modalities as possible. He suggests a *kinesthetic* approach, in which the young people are required to trace letters on sandpaper with their fingers before writing them on regular paper with a pencil. He also observes that the progress of the dyslexic is very erratic, necessitating frequent review, and the effective teacher is the one who knows how to pace the presentation of the material (see Figures 9-1, 9-2, and 9-3).

FIGURE 9-1. A Perceptual Development Center teacher instructs a junior high student in the alphabetic-phonetic-structural-linguistic approach to literacy, the specific method of teaching dyslexics to read which is used at the PDC.

FIGURE 9-2. A student working with a volunteer. The dyslexic is required to point his finger as he reads to train him to keep his place.

FIGURE 9-3. A dyslexic student using sandpaper—a multisensory method for reinforcement of learning through the tactile and kinesthetic senses, as well as through sight and hearing.

(Photos courtesy of the Perceptual Development Center, Natchez, Mississippi.)

Both Shedd (1969) and Clements (1962) have pointed out that combining training in perceptual development with the use of chemotherapy is sometimes more effective than using either the educational or chemotherapeutic approach alone.

RECOGNIZING OTHER LEARNING DISORDERS

In addition to such organic problems as dyslexia, classroom teachers must also be aware of learning problems that result from physical disabilities, such as impaired and uncorrected vision and hearing. And it is not uncommon for adolescents to develop endocrine disorders, which may also interfere with their performance in school.

For example, John was referred to a center for developmental reading because of his poor academic performance in the seventh grade. His attention span was exceedingly short, and his grades, although not failing, were far below average, particularly in view of his intelligence quotient in the bright-normal range. Following a complete psychological workup, John was referred to his family physician for a physical checkup. The family doctor discovered that this boy was suffering from an underactive thyroid, a condition that often manifests itself in youngsters through hyperactive behavior and an inability to concentrate. After the correction of this physical imbalance through medication and after two months of concentrated tutoring in remedial reading, John's reading level advanced 1.2 grade levels, and his school grades climbed in the same short interval from a D grade average to a B grade average.

An excellent illustration of physiological factors and their impact on behavior and academic performance was cited by Kirk (1962). The subject was a 12-year-old boy who caused extreme difficulties in school. He seemed to behave fairly well early in the morning, but before noon created all sorts of disturbances within the classroom. Upon returning from the lunch period he behaved for an hour or two and then began to pant, run around the classroom, fight with the children, and at times attempt to jump out of the window. One psychiatrist diagnosed him as a psychopathic personality. Another, more psychoanalytically inclined, ascribed his behavior to a traumatic experience which he had had in early childhood.

A third felt that there might have been a brain injury as a result of encephalitis.

As far as the teachers were concerned, they were unable to do anything about his psychopathic personality, his neurotic personality, or the possible brain damage. The boy's behavior continued for several years, until he was finally sent to an institution because the school could no longer handle him within a classroom situation.

In the institution, the same behavior pattern persisted. Teachers would accept him in class for a week or two and then state that they could not manage the class with such a child as a member. Teacher after teacher tried her hand at controlling him, but to no avail.

After a conference it was suggested to the teacher that when the boy began to misbehave in school she should call in the psychiatric social worker. The social worker walked with him around the block, gave him a piece of candy, discussed his problems with him, calmed him down, and returned him to the classroom. This routine usually occurred once in the morning and once in the afternoon.

At a later staff conference, no one seemed able to identify the factor that produced the abnormal behavior nor the factors which diminished it. The staff speculated about many things, including identification with the social worker. A pediatrician at the conference, referring to the series of medical diagnoses made on this boy, discovered that the boy had never had a blood-sugar test. He hypothesized that the piece of candy which the social worker always gave him might have had some relation to decreasing his hyperactive behavior.

A subsequent examination revealed that the boy had hypoglycemia, a condition characterized by a severe deficiency of sugar in the blood. The treatment prescribed was to give him a glass of milk with sugar in it about ten o'clock in the morning, at two o'clock in the afternoon, and again in the evening. From that day on the boy became a model child and learned in school at a much more rapid rate. This boy's behavior deviation was apparently an attempt on his part to reduce the tension or suffocation his body was experiencing when the blood sugar was used up.[1]

[1]Case paraphrased from Kirk, S., *Educating exceptional children*, Houghton Mifflin Company, 1962, pp. 343–344.

THE UNDERACHIEVING ADOLESCENT

In the past, an *underachiever* was quite likely to be described as "lazy." Today, a more informed approach takes a look at the personality and temperament factors in such a student, along with a study of the learning situation with which he is confronted.

The term "underachiever" describes a student "who appears to possess the ability to achieve considerably higher grades than his present record shows" (Wellington & Wellington, 1965, p. 1). Such students can range all the way from those of below-average intelligence to those classified as gifted, and they can be found at all academic levels, ranging from the first grader through the college senior.

But it is the adolescent underachiever with whom we are concerned. He may be a young person with a history of poor academic success throughout his school career, or he may be a student who displays a sudden drop in his grades as he reaches puberty.

Underachievement is probably one of the most sutble and insidious forms of adolescent rebellion (Blaine, 1966). It tends to be subtle because it is rarely recognized as a manifestation of rebellion by either adolescents or adults. It can be regarded as insidious, because it often begins in a quiet, unobtrusive manner and doesn't become recognized or treated as rebellion until a promising academic career is threatened or destroyed.

Kotkov (1965) has described a series of personality traits characteristic of the underachiever. There is the passive receiver, such as Alice's roommate in the following example, who assumes that other students achieve without exerting any effort. She believes that skill and knowledge are inborn in certain people and that struggle and effort for them are painless.

Alice, an honors college student, had a roommate, who had the mistaken notion that Alice had only to "wave a magic wand" in order to achieve her outstanding scholastic record. On the contrary, Alice admitted studying diligently during many long hours both day and night. Unfortunately, she was unable to convince her roommate of the efforts she expended in order to achieve her grades. As a result, the roommate, who had the potential but lacked the necessary motivation to do average college work, remained on scholastic probation during most of her college career and was finally forced to drop out of school.

Such young people are frequently the victims of maternal overprotection. As a result, they are poorly prepared for independent achievement and are likely to overreact to minute frustrations (Kotkov, 1965). They tend to display apathy, a lack of interest, and a certain sense of helplessness.

Another behavior pattern frequently observed in the underachiever, according to Kotkov, is that of the youth with a high level of aspiration and a high degree of perfectionism who faces each new learning task with a fear of failure. He incorporates the patterns of his demanding parents and then becomes acutely aware of his shortcomings. To circumvent what he believes will surely be imperfect performances, he withdraws from scholastic competition in order to avoid embarrassment. Subsequent guilt arises which is transferred into feelings of inadequacy or inferiority, which in turn lead to fears of further failure.

Such persistent feelings of inferiority may be present, despite superior test results and an occasional superior performance to the contrary. As long as he doesn't put forth wholehearted effort, he can regard his academic record as being less than that of his actual capacity, and he has an excuse or an explanation for rationalizing his failures. According to Blaine (1966), this pattern is particularly noticeable among children who arrive late in the ordinal rank in the family and develop expectations of defeat, which prevent them from attempting to compete even when the odds are in their favor. And too often, teachers add to this problem by comparing later arriving students with brothers and sisters who preceded them.

Some adolescents have an underlying fear of success, which exists at an unconscious level. They don't want to attract attention by being above average or superior. Such students are often shy and reticent. For the youth who wants to gain high acceptance from his peers, success may be a very uncomfortable position, one to be avoided at all costs. He fears being teased as an "egghead" or disliked because he's the recipient of praise and academic recognition (Blaine, 1966).

Roth & Meyersburg (1963) describe the existence of a nonachievement syndrome in terms of the following behavior patterns (p. 538):

(1) Poor academic achievement.
(2) General self-depreciation; lack of recognition of pleasure at "being."
(3) No clear system of personal goals or values.

(4) Vulnerability to disparagement by others.
(5) Immature relations with parents.
(6) Frequent depressions.
(7) Lack of insight about self and others.
(8) Free-floating anxiety.

In recent years we have come to recognize the detrimental effects of undue anxiety, which may cripple or interfere with intellectual functioning (Rabinovitch, 1959). Because of conflicts existing outside the classroom, many adolescents are so preoccupied in school that their attention and memory suffer to the extent that their learning becomes impaired. Inner conflicts and emotional stress may prove to be so energy-consuming that they interfere with the student's ability to concentrate. For example, concern about precocious or delayed sexual development in the adolescent can seriously affect his academic performance.

When learning is impeded by emotional stress, the pattern of scholastic behavior is often mystifying. Typical is the student who misses easy problems but solves more difficult ones or solves a given problem one day but cannot understand it the next. Frequently he may demonstrate test panic, in which he reports that his mind goes blank at the sight of an exam, though he had felt well prepared prior to the testing situation. This anxiety may even carry over to his performance on intelligence tests, so that an IQ test score may not be an accurate evaluation of his intellectual potential because of the high anxiety he experiences whenever confronted with an exam or quiz (Wattenberg, 1963). A vicious cycle can result if this test panic persists, the additional scholastic failure producing further emotional problems characterized by even less ability to concentrate (Bakwin & Bakwin, 1960).

The etiology of the nonachievement syndrome described by Roth and Meyersburg (1963) has its roots in a common pattern in the parent-child relationship, wherein the parent ignores the accomplishments and the failures of his offspring. Or he pays attention to the failures but rarely to the successes, which tend to be taken for granted, while the failures are met with punishment.

These early experiences in the parent-child relationship may ultimately lead to serious *pathological* processes (Roth & Meyersburg, 1963). The young person develops a characteristic pattern of self-depreciation. In his attempts to maintain his contacts with his parents, he learns to perceive himself as a failure. He withholds any attempts at productivity and blames himself for his weaknesses and failures. He directs his hostility only against himself, never against others, thereby reinforcing his low self-concept. The opinions of others acquire far greater significance than his own opinion, consequently interfering with the development of his autonomy and self-direction. This, in turn, reinforces his self-depreciating attitudes. And because he has acquired such poor academic skills, the choice of failure becomes inevitably reinforced and the growth of his *phenomenal* world, or environment as he perceives it, is curtailed or limited, and his development is arrested or impeded. His unsatisfied longing for approval makes him especially susceptible to the cultural approval awarded the unscholarly by peer-group acceptance. His personality patterns become reflected in his inability to delineate definite boundaries between himself and others. Whatever he sees or hears, he *introjects* without modification, thereby acquiring no value system of his own. In other words, he is easily led by others, rarely questioning the ideas or standards of those whom he follows.

THE ROLE OF THE TEACHER

A common factor contributing to the inadequate performance of the underachieving adolescent is the teacher's expectations of the student, which may often outweigh other factors in affecting classroom behavior (Chess, 1968). A young person is likely to make a positive adaptation to the requirements of school when the teacher's demands are consistent with the student's temperament and within his intellectual and physical capacities; conversely, learning will be impaired when these demands are inconsistent with his temperamental traits and become a source of stress for him. For example, the hyperactive student may experience difficulty in attending to what his teacher is saying, whereas the less active pupil with an average or less-than-average level of motility will not be affected in such a manner. Perhaps the overactive person may need to have his instructor repeat directions more than one time and in a pleasant, unannoyed manner at that.

It should also be noted that sometimes a teacher may evaluate a student as an underachiever when the young person is in reality achieving at his full level of potential. Such educators may feel that because of a youngster's middle-class background and his adequate command of English he should be capable of doing better. And not only teachers may hold such false assumptions; the college-educated parents of these youths may also harbor misconceptions about the abilities of their offspring.

Educators cannot overlook student temperament and its impact on learning (Chess, 1968). One individual who regards new stimuli, new people, and new learning in a confident manner will very likely respond with a positive attitude. Another may initially tend to withdraw from any new experience and may be able to deal with the novel only after several exposures. Or a particular student may even be selective in his approach to new stimuli, perhaps approaching new people but withdrawing from new surroundings and new academic demands, while his teacher may inaccurately assume that the student lacks readiness to learn what is expected of him.

Sue, a superior student with above-average intelligence, looked forward to her entry into senior high school, where she quickly made many new friends. However, accustomed to a relatively small junior high school, where all of her teachers knew her and where she was regarded as a class leader, she found herself overwhelmed by the size of her new school with its 5,000 students. She became bewildered by the lack of personal attention accorded her by the teachers and by the amount of responsibility she was expected to assume in her class assignments. As a result her academic average slipped, and she soon joined the ranks of the underachievers.

Often, repeated exposure to a new learning task without being made to feel stupid or uncooperative may help a student gradually develop a sense of security; he learns that he tends to respond more slowly to the presentation of new materials and must just allow himself more time (Chess, 1968). Some individuals are naturally more adaptable than others. The student possessing slow adaptability coupled with a negative reaction toward new demands will have a double problem confronting him. His instructors will need to prevent him from becoming disheartened, for his discouragement may actually trigger a vicious cycle, wherein he avoids the subject matter, only to have others assume that he lacks motivation, whereas in reality his low motivation is a secondary reaction to his lack of confidence in his ability to learn.

Students demonstrate wide individual differences in their degree of distractibility (Chess, 1968). One who is highly distractible may actually be more alert to what is going on in the classroom. The teacher must be able to recognize that the highly distractible adolescent isn't always deliberately failing to listen. In fact, high distractibility may be a kind of responsiveness to a learning situation. From the viewpoint of social adjustment, such a student may actually have a greater capacity for empathy and constructive behavior that the less distractible youngster may lack.

Traditionally, educators have regarded a long attention span and marked perseverance in the classroom as assets (Chess, 1968). A long attention span, however, may even prove to be a liability, if the student becomes annoyed at having his attention diverted and responds in a negative manner, for example by sulking or dawdling. On the other hand, it would probably be desirable to lower such distractibility where feasible. Individuals who have sometimes been described as being hyperactive require a well-structured academic environment with a high degree of stimulus intensity within the framework of the subject matter being studied, combined with a minimum of outside distractions.

Sometimes the use of carpeted classrooms, acoustical tile, and the elimination of windows may reduce the distractions for students with a short attention span. Small enrollments and individualized instruction, perhaps with the assistance of teacher aides, may also be helpful to these easily distracted young people. And chemotherapy, when it is administered under the close supervision of a physician, has been observed to be quite effective with hyperactive youngsters having short attention spans (Robbins, 1971).

THE CULTURALLY DEPRIVED ADOLESCENT

A growing problem in our rapidly changing society has been the early identification and education of the culturally deprived youth. By 1970 it was estimated that one out of every two students enrolled in urban schools would be considered a disadvantaged or culturally deprived individual (Riessman, 1962). "In an educational context, 'disadvantaged' refers to children with a particular set of educationally associated problems arising from and residing extensively within the culture of the poor" (Frost & Hawkes, 1966, p. 1). Too frequently, only blacks have been described as being among the culturally deprived. Actually this concept includes individuals from the slums, both black and white, the rural poor, migrant children, Mexican-American children, and Indian children (Frost & Hawkes, 1966).

The consequences of impoverished living have been several. Among these have been (1) a vast number of school dropouts, (2) a high delinquency rate (it has been estimated that 85 percent of all delinquents come from the lower socioeconomic classes), (3) mental retardation often with no organic basis but more likely a reflection of a deprived, unstimulating environment, and (4) educational retardation (Frost & Hawkes, 1966).

From the sociological point of view, the disadvantaged may be defined and described in three ways: according to family traits relating directly to the child, according to personal traits, and according to the social group traits of the families (Havighurst, 1966). The family environment of the culturally deprived is characterized by parents who frequently fail to answer their children's questions or discourage their offspring from asking them. Is it any wonder that these same young people become reluctant to ask questions of their teachers when they don't understand what is going on in the classroom?

In their personal behavior, these disadvantaged adolescents frequently display inferior auditory and visual discrimination along with poor understanding of concepts relating to time, numbers, and other basic ideas. Often they have not been taught to pay attention or to concentrate (Havighurst, 1966). In fact, coming from the noisy environment of a large family crowded into a few rooms, they have learned to "tune out" much of the din surrounding them, and such behavior acquired at home is readily carried over to school.

According to Havighurst (1966), the socially disadvantaged tend to come from social groups characterized by the following traits: (1) a low income, (2) a rural background, (3) experience with wide social and economic discrimination, and (4) wide geographic distribution in the United States, not only in the large urban areas but in many rural areas as well.

Interestingly enough, one may fail to identify these individuals through their clothing, which frequently gives no evidence of their low socioeconomic status. Harrington has said that "America has the best-dressed poverty the world has ever known . . . . It is much easier in the United States to be decently dressed than to be decently housed, fed, and doctored" (1966, p. 9).

Since these young people cannot always be identified in the classroom by their physical appearance, teachers must be alert to other traits that characterize their behavior. Riessman (1962) described the following as being more or less typical of the culturally deprived: (1) They are slow at cognitive tasks, often due to lack of intellectual stimulation at home. (2) They seem to learn more readily through a physical, concrete approach rather than through reading, at which they are often quite deficient. (3) They frequently appear to be anti-intellectual, appreciating knowledge for pragmatic reasons rather than knowledge for its own sake. (4) They tend to be superstitious, traditionally oriented, and somewhat religious, often being rigid and inflexible about their beliefs and practices, reluctant to change their ideas and traditions, and hesitant about accepting new innovations. (5) They come from a male-centered culture, except for a large segment of the black subculture. As a consequence, they place a high premium on masculinity and tend to pursue behavior which they consider to be appropriate to their male role while regarding intellectual activities as being nonmasculine. (6) They tend to feel alienated from society as a whole, with a sense of hopelessness and frustration about both the present and the future. (7) They often place the blame on others for their misfortunes. (8) They desire a higher standard of living but are reluctant to adopt the middle-class way of life. (9) They show deficits in communication skills as well as deficits in auditory attention.

At the same time, these disadvantaged learners disclose many positive traits on which the effective classroom teacher should learn to build (McCreary, 1966). Some of the most provoking behavior of these young people is actually reasonable, useful, and rewarding when viewed within the framework of the kind of lives they lead. And they often possess special skills and practical knowledge which takes the place of much of the book learning that middle-class children receive.

For example, since the death of her grandmother five years ago, Mary, a 16-year-old high school junior, has been entrusted with much of the care and responsibility of her little sister, aged seven, and of her baby brother, aged two. With no father in the home and with a mother employed five days a week, Mary is responsible for the two young children during the summers, after school, and on Saturdays. She also does much of the cooking for the family and most of the laundry.

Through such experiences with life, these adolescents learn something about the realities of our economic and social institutions and can thereby be taught by the teacher to see subject matter in a more relevant, realistic, and authentic manner. For example, by teaching math in terms of family budgeting, the practical experiences of the disadvantaged can be made to work in the classroom in an affirmative way.

On the positive side, these adolescents also demonstrate strong feelings of loyalty to their peer group with an impulse toward mutual aid, a feeling of kinship, and reciprocity (McCreary, 1966). This peer-group cooperation may be partly explained by the fact that such young people are not nearly so competitive and are not under as much strain to establish themselves as individuals as are middle-class children (Riessman, 1962). They also tend to develop early self-reliance, autonomy, and independence, behavior which sometimes results in conflict with the school's attempts to control, supervise, and direct student activities (McCreary, 1966).

John, a high school sophomore of 15, is accustomed to fending for himself. With his mother deceased, his father employed as a taxi driver from 3 P.M. until 11 P.M., and no one else at home, John has learned to depend upon himself. He comes and goes as he pleases, prepares and eats his own meals, and plans his own entertainment. It is not surprising that he often defies the school, whose rigid directives demand that he must eat in the school cafeteria, cannot leave the school during the day, and may not smoke any place in the school building or on the school grounds.

And last, but certainly not least, the culturally deprived do appear to appreciate the value of an education if not the value of the school (McCreary, 1966). Frequently, they dislike the school itself, feeling alienated from it as a consequence of the cumulative effects of a too-demanding curriculum and teachers whom they often view as the source of their frustrations. And their parents often feel that the school regards their children as second-class citizens. But the disadvantaged do recognize that education represents for their young people the one channel for improving their lives in our modern society, although they desire this education more for vocational ends rather than for knowledge for its own sake.

THE EDUCATION OF THE DISADVANTAGED ADOLESCENT

Among the controversies raging today in academic circles is that of the role to be filled by the school in the education of the culturally deprived. One line of thought, while acknowledging the possible superiority of certain nonlanguage skills, rejects the idea that there should be any differences made in school curriculum for the disadvantaged in our urban society, and it argues for the building of readiness for reading and for math during the preschool period and in the primary grades (Havighurst, 1966). Another school of thought regards the socialization of the culturally deprived as being even more important than formal education (Bettelheim, 1966). The assumption is that if these young people have not learned certain essential things in life at home before coming to school, then these must be taught in the classroom: such things as the wrong in stealing something which belongs to another, the error in expressing hostility by hitting another over the head, and the need for learning to endure small frustrations while still going on with the task at hand. And still other educators feel that the school should give these students a practical preparation for life, an education which will prepare them for a trade, as well as teach them how to obtain and hold a job and how to get along with supervisors and fellow employees. Undoubtedly, additional research is needed to determine which goals will most effectively meet the needs of the disadvantaged and of society as a whole.

Regardless of the ultimate aims, however, there are certain practices in the classroom that can enhance the teacher's effectiveness in working with these students. Goldberg (1966) has vividly described a hypothetical model of a successful teacher of the disadvantaged. She points out that foremost of all, a teacher must respect his students. He views their alien culture, not as a judge, but as a student eager to learn as much as possible through study, reading, and visits to their homes. He recognizes and understands the unwillingness of the disadvantaged to strive toward future goals, where such efforts provide little or no visible immediate rewards.

The teacher who will be successful with these adolescents will know that they bear many scars reflecting the effects of inadequate intellectual stimulation from their environment. He is aware of the varied family structures from which his students spring and of the impact of ethnic group cultures on their self-images and on their concept of the world. He recognizes the functional qualities of the languages his students speak at home and on the streets. And he accepts test scores as measures of achievement but not as measures of native intelligence.

With this knowledge, the effective teacher of the disadvantaged accepts their behavior but doesn't necessarily condone it. Instead he attempts to modify that which he regards as important. He establishes clearly defined limits on behavior with a minimum of discussion, and here he remains impersonal, undeviating, consistent, strict but not punitive. He decides which behavior is unimportant and can be ignored and which should be rigidly restricted. For example, he may decide to ignore gum chewing in the classroom while placing very firm, consistent limitations on the use of obscene language.

The successful teacher of the culturally deprived recognizes the dangers in the "self-fulfilling prophecy" of expecting and consequently obtaining a low level of pupil achievement. Therefore, he informs each student of his expectations for him, always expecting just a bit more than the youngster believes he can achieve. At the same time, the instructor doesn't set the standards so high that the youth regards them as too remote to strive toward.

But perhaps most important of all, the hypothetically effective teacher of the disadvantaged needs to adhere to certain idealism, a dedication to a cause, a desire to render help and service to the "have-nots" in our society.

Hopefully possessed with the traits just described, the successful teacher will become aware of the importance of effective motivation among these potential learners. Ausubel (1966) has pointed out that the kindling of a cognitive drive or of *intrinsic motivation* for learning—that is, learning for knowledge's sake, in order to satisfy one's curiosity and to satisfy the need to explore and to manipulate one's environment—is probably the most promising technique for teaching the disadvantaged. Such intrinsic motivation is contrasted with the pragmatic attitude so often manifested toward education by the lower classes. To a student with intrinsic motivation, learning appears to be more potent, relevant, and lasting than to one with *extrinsic motivation,* or one who desires education solely as a means to a job. Actually, a large part of education cannot be shown to be necessary for meeting the demands of day-to-day living. Often, however, intrinsic motivation can be combined with extrinsic motivation including visible rewards, which are important in fostering self-enhancement and encouraging the development of responsibility.

An effective ninth-grade biology teacher in an urban school surrounded by a fair-sized plot of ground decided to try to foster both extrinsic and intrinsic motivation in his students. Dividing his class of thirty into fifteen pairs, he gave each pair a small piece of land on the school grounds and provided each with the necessary means for planting and raising a miniature vegetable garden. The students were encouraged to adequately prepare the ground, fertilize it, water it, and plant the seeds they had been given. They were expected to keep their gardens weeded and watered, and weekly reports of progress in growth were required to be kept in writing. Although it is unlikely that any of these urban-raised children would be likely to go into truck farming, the presence of both extrinsic and intrinsic motivation in this project was quite evident. The satisfaction of youthful curiosity about the growth and development of plants demonstrated the impact of intrinsic motivation, while the ability to make something grow enhanced their feelings of achievement. In addition, the enthusiasm generated from this undertaking may have proved sufficient to result in some of the students later undertaking gardening as a hobby.

THE SCHOOL DROPOUT

Frequently, the consequences of failing to recognize the existence of the learning problems described in this chapter and of neglecting to undertake their modification results in adolescents ultimately dropping out of school. Actually, many dropouts possess the ability to do passing or even superior academic work. Elliott, Voss, and Wendling (1966) have estimated that as high as three fourths of all dropouts have sufficient native intelligence to complete high school.

If this is true, then why has there been a shrinkage rate in recent high school graduating classes of about 36 percent, compared with the number of students originally enrolled in the fifth grade (National Educational Association, 1963)? Actually, the retention record in the public school system has increased during the past three decades. Of 1,000 fifth graders in 1942-43, only 505 completed high school in 1950. A decade later in 1960, 621 graduated from the 1,000 enrolled in the fifth grade during the year 1952-53. By 1975, it is estimated that the retention rate will have risen to 70 percent and by the end of the century to 80 percent, reflecting a decline in the dropout rate in the short span of 60 years from 50 percent to 20 percent (Dentler, 1964).

If these are the facts, then why is the United States so concerned about the present dropout rate? The answer lies in the following: (1) The nation is becoming constantly more urbanized and less agricultural, with greater demands for educated, skilled workers and fewer demands for physical, unskilled labor. (2) Automation is becoming more common, and millions of unskilled and semiskilled jobs have become or will shortly become obsolete. (3) Youth with its vast numbers, a reflection of the high birth rates following World War II, is now experiencing more difficulty in finding employment. (4) The civil rights movement has called attention to the high rate of dropouts among the low socioeconomic groups (Tannenbaum, 1966).

According to Greene (1966), "The dropout is defined . . . as any student who leaves school without graduating" (p. 3). However, Greene goes on to point out that this definition includes both those who leave school voluntarily and those who are expelled from classes by school officials. He notes that this definition also overlooks the fact that some dropouts continue their education in private trade schools, in adult education classes, and through correspondence courses, and many ultimately obtain a high school equivalency diploma through programs offered by the armed services.

How can a classroom teacher learn to identify the potential dropout in order to take preventive action? Unfortunately, the high school teacher is often at a considerable disadvantage, because many potential dropouts who can and should be recognized in the elementary grades (Lambert, 1964) are overlooked at this stage of their academic career. And by the time they reach secondary school, the time for the most effective action has often passed.

The major factors in determining whether an adolescent drops out of school or remains to graduate and receive his diploma are commonly cited as follows (Cervantes, 1965; Greene, 1966):

(1) The potential dropout is frequently older than his classmates, usually as a consequence of his having been retained in a grade at least once during his school career. Because of this age difference, he tends to experience difficulty in relating to his classmates and generally has few friends among them. This lack of peer acceptance, especially at the high school level, becomes more important to the student than his academic achievement or the lack of it. The friends he does have usually have similar problems and have also dropped out of school or intend to do so.

(2) The dropout is generally failing in his school work at the time he decides to leave school, and he presents a history of having consistently failed to achieve in the regular academic program. This has led to a vicious cycle, in that the pattern of failure has tended to result in a self-concept, role expectations, and a level of aspiration that are markedly deficient. These, in turn, have reinforced the expectation of continued failure.

(3) During high school, the potential dropout averages many more absences than he did in elementary school. Almost all research points to a marked attendance regression as the potential dropout moves from elementary to secondary school.

(4) Most dropouts are markedly retarded in reading. Studies indicate that dropouts are usually at least two years behind in reading, and many of them are as much as five to six years behind. Since it is presently estimated that reading is necessary for 90 percent of all subjects taught in school, reading retardation can prove to be a severe handicap.

(5) Although low intelligence is characteristic of the dropout, it is not necessarily responsible for his dropping out.

(6) The dropout usually lacks interest in school and generally is dissatisfied with the curriculum, the faculty, and the school activities. As a matter of fact, Greene (1966) stated that this was the single most important factor given by students for leaving school. At the same time, these dropouts state that their teachers have exerted little influence on their remaining in school or encouraging them to stay and to complete their high school education. Cervantes (1965) emphasized the lack of teacher influence when he said two thirds of the dropouts had testified that they had never really been friends with any teacher, and one third maintained that the teachers

themselves were unfriendly. These are rather startling observations, when one recalls that the teacher has been referred to as the "key to the dropout problem." Apparently the students do not identify with their instructors, who appear to accept them only insofar as they are educable, not on the basis of any personal acceptance characterized by mutual regard and affection.

(7) Potential dropouts do not become involved in school activities. One study of 212 dropouts in Kansas disclosed that 144, or 68 percent, of the dropouts had not participated in a single activity, while nondropouts showed an average of four activities per student in large high schools and six activities per student in small high schools (Bell, 1967).

Eighteen-year-old Sam was a high school senior of limited intelligence and low academic achievement. Under the rules of most public schools, he probably would have been prohibited from participating in varsity athletics because of his low academic average. However, because his school was somewhat progressive in its thinking, Sam was permitted to play fullback on the varsity football team, a role in which he excelled. As a result of his performance with the team, he received much acclamation and recognition from his peers, which certainly enhanced Sam's self-esteem. In another school he probably would have been denied the right to play football with the varsity squad and would in all likelihood have ended up as another dropout. However, because of his success in the school's athletic program and because of the understanding and acceptance of his teachers, Sam managed to stay in school and ultimately graduate.

(8) And finally, regardless of what other factors are present, the family inevitably plays a critical role in determining whether a youth becomes a dropout or remains in school. Because dropouts come primarily from the lower socioeconomic classes (Tesseneer & Tesseneer [1958] have estimated this rate to be anywhere from 72 percent to 84 percent), the educational level of the parents is frequently low. Often they may see little value in education and provide almost no support or encouragement for their children. And rarely is there much interaction between the parents and the school.

In summary, a "dropout syndrome" emerges from the above factors. "The dropout feels that he does not belong. He does not belong because he is retarded in school and thus separated from his age mates; he does not belong because his communication aptitudes— verbal and social—seem truncated [or inadequate]. He does not belong because he is not participating in any of the activities of the school" (Cervantes, 1965, p. 102).

Before leaving this topic, we should take a look at the problem from the student's point of view. Table 9-1 indicates the reasons for leaving as given in the school records and as given by the dropouts themselves.

TABLE 9-1.   Reasons for dropping out of school. (From Wolfbein, S. L. Transition from school to work: A study of the school leaver. *The Personnel and Guidance Journal*, 1959, **38**(2), 98–105. (Copyright 1959 by the American Personnel and Guidance Association.)

Boy Dropouts	Total	Reached Age 16	To Go To Work	Marriage	Military Service	Adverse School Experiences	Other
As given in school records	100%	19%	23%	--	15%	24%	19%
As given by dropouts themselves	100%	6%	25%	--	6%	38%	25%
Girl Dropouts							
As given in school records	100%	16%	13%	22%	--	21%	28%
As given by dropouts themselves	100%	4%	12%	27%	--	31%	26%

One can observe a certain correlation between the factors previously cited and those given by the students, especially those factors pertaining to adverse school experiences. However, one should not overlook the frequency of marriage cited by the girls as an important reason for their dropping out. Nor should one forget that probably a large number drop out to bear illegitimate children, a factor not likely to be reported by them.

Actually, nearly half of all dropouts are girls, girls who are usually capable of doing better school work than many boys. They read better, fail less frequently, repeat grades less often, and even have slightly higher intelligence test scores (Pollack, 1966).

The door should be left open for these young people to return and complete their education. Many of them accurately feel that the schools want nothing further to do with them if they have married or if they have had illegitimate children. In fact, many school systems have rigid rules prohibiting married or pregnant girls from reentering school. As a consequence, they often become the rejects of socie-ty—jobless, bewildered, hopeless fugitives from failure.

THE ROLE OF THE SCHOOLS

A bit earlier, this chapter introduced a number of classroom prac-tices, which have proved to be effective in teaching culturally deprived youngsters. Many of these suggestions would also apply to the teacher who is trying to prevent potential dropouts from leaving school. In addition, attention should be focused on suitable curricula for these likely dropouts, curricula apt to prove effective for the disadvantaged as well.

There is an erroneous belief that all high school graduates must possess the same degree of mastery and skill in the various subjects they have undertaken. Actually, good teaching and a curriculum developed to meet the needs of each individual student will increase the differences between students. It is not possible to establish a curriculum with three or four tracks and expect each student to fit neatly into one of them. What is needed is an individualized program, capable of revision from time to time. It is unrealistic to expect eighth and ninth grade students to plan their curriculum and to adhere to it regardless of the development of new interests, aptitudes, and experiences (Greene, 1966).

Today, the typical school program has evolved from middle-class needs and values and has come to depend upon the ability of students to postpone immediate gratification for long-range goals, something unappealing and unmotivating to the potential dropout with a history of failure and frustration. Therefore, a suitable course of study for the likely dropout must offer specific concrete learning with more emphasis on practical experiences, such as writing letters of applica-tion for jobs, and perhaps less emphasis on theory. Ideally, those going on to college could have their needs for additional theory met in programs patterned after the present special education classes for the gifted. For example, English could be taught to all students in a general program stressing skills necessary for effective com-munication, and in addition, those going on to college might study formal language structure. While the college-bound were studying grammatical construction and the theories behind it, the many potential dropouts with reading deficits might be undertaking additional training in visual and auditory perception. There is also little reason why dropouts and potential dropouts cannot be permitted the flexibility of adult education programs, which are usually individualized, enabling students to proceed at their own rate of speed. Many of these students object strenuously to the rigidity of time schedules presently in operation in most public school systems.

Turning aside from the problem of an effective curriculum for the potential dropout, one should note that the composition of the classroom is important and has an impact on the emotional and social well-being of its students (Drews, 1964). One study of 600 ninth graders, who were described as slow learners, disclosed that these adolescents did better emotionally and socially when placed in homogeneous remedial sections than did a matched group left in its regular heterogeneous classes. The homogeneous groups were given reading material on a level they could absorb, were given encouragement to work on topics of interest to them, and were placed in small groups of 15 to 20 in order to receive individual help. This program resulted in increased teacher acceptance, peer acceptance, and self-acceptance. Among other dividends resulting from this grouping was the development of leadership in those, who, for the first time in their lives, had an opportunity to assume leadership roles both for social events and in the classroom.

Greene (1966) has pointed out that teachers and guidance counselors might find group counseling to be helpful in assisting the potential dropout in finding himself. Such programs could help him improve his perception of himself and of others and develop a sense of trust and a feeling of belonging, qualities usually missing in the dropout syndrome.

SUMMARY AND CONCLUSIONS

Many learning problems are found among adolescents not necessarily within the framework of special education but more likely within the setting of the regular high school classroom. Often these are problems which have existed for some time but have been overlooked by the elementary school teacher. In other instances, these difficulties have been recognized in the lower grades but still demand continued effort and modification.

These learning problems include those arising from organic factors, from genetic causes, and from environmental origins. Identifying these problems is the first step in their modification. Some of them may require the assistance of the medical profession. Others call for an effective, sensitive teacher, one who is well informed about adolescent behavior. And still others may require a special or modified curriculum. Occasionally, individual or group counseling may be indicated. And there are cases in which the resources of education, medicine, and psychology may all be needed.

Failure to identify these learning problems in students can ultimately lead to the adolescent's joining the vast numbers of school dropouts, a waste that our affluent society can ill afford.

REFERENCES

Ames, L. B. A low intelligence quotient often not recognized as the chief cause of many learning difficulties. *Journal of Learning Disabilities,* 1968, **1**, 735–739.

Ausubel, D. P. A teaching strategy for culturally deprived pupils: Cognitive and motivational considerations. In J. L. Frost & G. R. Hawkes (Eds.), *The disadvantaged child.* Boston: Houghton Mifflin, 1966. Pp. 237–243.

Bakwin, H., & Bakwin, R. M. *Clinical management of behavior disorders in children* (2nd ed.). Philadelphia: Saunders, 1960.

Bateman, B. Learning disabilities—Yesterday, today, and tomorrow. *Exceptional Children,* 1964, **31**, 167–177.

Bell, J. W. A comparison of dropouts and nondropouts on participation in school activities. *Journal of Educational Research,* 1967, **60**, 248–251.

Bettelheim, B. Teaching the disadvantaged. In S. W. Webster (Ed.), *The disadvantaged learner: Knowing, understanding, learning.* San Francisco: Chandler Publishing, 1966. Pp. 423–429.

Blaine, G. B., Jr. *Youth and the hazards of affluence.* New York: Harper & Row, 1966.

Boigon, H. W. Problems in learning: "Why do they tell me I can learn when I can't?" *American Journal of Psychoanalysis,* 1968, **28**, 25–34.

Cervantes, L. F. *The dropout.* Ann Arbor: University of Michigan Press, 1965.

Chess, S. Temperament and learning ability of school children. *American Journal of Public Health,* 1968, **58**, 2231–2239.

Clements, S. Minimal brain dysfunctions in the school-age child. *Archives of General Psychiatry,* 1962, **6**, 185–197.

Clements, S. A note of caution on learning disabilities. Paper presented at the third annual state convention of the Louisiana Association for Children with Learning Disabilities, October, 1968.

Cohn, R. The neurological study of children with learning disabilities. *Exceptional Children*, 1964, **31**, 179–185.

Coleman, J. C., & Sandhu, M. A descriptive-relational study of 364 children referred to a university clinic for learning disorders. *Psychological Reports*, 1967, **20**, 1095–1105.

Dentler, R. Dropouts, automation, and the cities. *Teachers College Record*, 1964, **65**(6), 475–483.

Drews, E. M. The schools: Climate affects fallout. In D. Schreiber (Ed.), *Guidance and the school dropout*. Washington, D.C.: Personnel and Guidance Association, 1964. Pp. 24–39.

Elliott, D. S., Voss, H. L., & Wendling, A. Capable dropouts and the social milieu of the high school. *Journal of Educational Research*, 1966, **60**, 180–186.

Frierson, E., & Barbe, W. B. (Eds.), *Educating children with learning disabilities*. New York: Appleton-Century-Crofts, 1967.

Frost, J. L., & Hawkes, G. R. *The disadvantaged child*. Boston: Houghton Mifflin, 1966.

Goldberg, M. L. Adapting teacher style to pupil differences: Teachers for disadvantaged children. In J. L. Frost & G. R. Hawkes (Eds.), *The disadvantaged child*. Boston: Houghton Mifflin, 1966. Pp. 345–362.

Greene, B. I. *Preventing school dropouts*. Englewood Cliffs, N. J.: Prentice-Hall, 1966.

Harrington, M. The invisible land. In S. W. Webster (Ed.), *The disadvantaged learner: Knowing, understanding, learning*. San Francisco: Chandler Publishing, 1966. Pp. 6–19.

Havighurst, R. Who are the socially disadvantaged? In J. L. Frost & G. R. Hawkes (Eds.), *The disadvantaged child*. Boston: Houghton Mifflin, 1966. Pp. 15–23.

Hewitt, F. M. A hierarchy of educational tasks for children with learning disorders. Exceptional Children, 1964, **31**, 209–214.

Jones, H. L. *Information packet*. Perceptual development center for dyslexic children, Natchez, Mississippi, 1967.

Jones, H. L. Project Evaluation, Title 3 ESEA Grant No. 67-04991-0, September 1967-July 1968, Natchez, Mississippi.

Kappelman, M. M., Kaplan, E., & Ganter, R. L. A study of learning disorders among disadvantaged children. *Journal of Learning Disabilities*, 1969, **2**(5), 262–268.

Kirk, S. *Educating exceptional children*. Boston: Houghton Mifflin, 1962.

Kotkov, B. Emotional syndromes associated with learning failures. *Diseases of the Nervous System*, 1965, **26**, 48–55.

Lambert, W. The high school dropout in elementary school. In D. Schreiber (Ed.), *Guidance and the school dropout*. Washington, D.C.: American Personnel and Guidance Association, 1964. Pp. 40–65.

Makita, K. The rarity of reading disability in Japanese children. *American Journal of Orthopsychiatry*, 1968, **38**, 599–614.

McCarthy, J. Direction of learning disability program. Paper presented at the third annual state convention of the Louisiana Association for Children with Learning Disabilities, October, 1968.

McCreary, E. Some positive characteristics of disadvantaged learners and their implications for education. In S. W. Webster (Ed.), *The disadvantaged learner: Knowing, understanding, educating.* San Francisco: Chandler Publishing, 1966. Pp. 47–52.

National Educational Association, *School dropouts,* NEA Research Memo 1963–10. Washington, D.C.: National Education Association, April, 1963.

Pollack, J. H. The astonishing truth about girl dropouts. *Educational Digest,* 1966, **32**(3), 14–16.

Rabinovitch, R. D. In S. Arieti (Ed.), *American handbook of psychiatry,* Vol. 1. New York: Basic Books, 1959. Pp. 860 ff.

Riessman, F. *The culturally deprived child.* New York: Harper & Row, 1962.

Robbins, R. L. Physician, Alexandria, Louisiana. Interview held in January, 1971.

Rosenthal, R. Self-fulfilling prophecy. In *Readings in Psychology Today.* Del Mar, Calif.: CRM Books, 1969. Pp. 464–471.

Roth, R. M., & Meyersburg, H. The non-achievement syndrome. *Personnel and Guidance Journal,* 1963, **41**, 535–540.

Sanford, F. H., & Wrightsman, L. S. *Psychology: A scientific study of man* (3rd ed.). Monterey, Calif.: Brooks/Cole, 1970.

Shedd, C. L. Cited by *Information packet.* Perceptual Development Center for Dyslexic Children, Natchez, Mississippi, 1967.

Shedd, C. L. Ptolemy rides again or dyslexia doesn't exist? *Alabama Journal of Medical Science,* 1968, **5**, 481–503.

Shedd, C. L. Address at workshop for teachers sponsored by the Perceptual Development Center for Dyslexic Children, Natchez, Mississippi, January, 1969.

Stern, A. Learning disabilities. Keynote address presented at the third annual state convention of the Louisiana Association for Children with Learning Disabilities, October, 1968.

Strauss, A. A., & Kaphart, N. C. *Psychopathology and education of the brain injured child.* Vol. 2, *Progress in theory and clinic.* New York: Grune and Stratton, 1955.

Tannenbaum, A. J. *Dropout or diploma.* Urban Problem Series. New York: Teachers College, Columbia University, 1966.

Tarnopol, L. Delinquency and minimal brain dysfunction. *Journal of Learning Disabilities,* 1970, **3**(4), 200–207.

Tesseneer, R. A., & Tesseneer, L. M. Review of the literature on school dropouts. *Bulletin of the National Association of Secondary School Principals,* 1958, **42**, 141–153.

Wattenberg, W. W. In A. Deutsch & H. Fishman (Eds.), *The encyclopedia of mental health*, Vol. 5. New York: The Encyclopedia of Mental Health, A Division of Franklin Watts, Inc., 1963. Pp. 1803 ff.

Wechsler, D. *Wechsler adult intelligence scale manual.* New York: The Psychological Corporation, 1955.

Wellington, C. B., & Wellington, J. *The underachiever: Challenges and guidelines.* Chicago: Rand McNally, 1965.

Wolfbein, S. L. Transition from school to work: A study of the school leaver. *Personnel and Guidance Journal*, 1959, **38**(2), 98-105.

10

Youth Employment and Vocational Choice

Work is the basis for getting acquainted with one's self and one's creativity.

Paul Brodsky
Adolescence

One of the most important developmental tasks of the adolescent period but perhaps one of the most difficult for the young person to fulfill in our modern society is the acquisition of self-esteem and status in the community. All individuals, regardless of age, need to feel some measure of importance to themselves and to the world in which they live. In the first chapter, it was noted that as the adolescent transits from childhood to adulthood, he must mature in four major areas—physical, intellectual, social, and emotional. One aspect of social maturation is the individual's achievement of responsibility in the world of work.

At one time, when the United States and Canada were basically rural, agricultural societies, everyone in the family was involved in helping to maintain the home and the farm. Young people, since they shared in such responsibilities, could feel important and needed, and they developed a sense of personal worth and status (Fredenburgh, 1968). Today, however, the family farm has begun to disappear, and although adolescents (especially girls) from the lower socioeconomic classes and from certain ethnic groups, such as the Chinese-Americans, perform numerous chores around the home and help care for younger siblings, many others from the urban middle

255

or upper classes have little opportunity to contribute to the family's well-being. In addition, many young people are now denied the possibility of participating in a creative work or employment situation because of minimum age requirements for entering numerous fields of industry and business and because of the refusal of some parents to permit their children to become gainfully employed during the early adolescent years.

ADOLESCENT EMPLOYMENT SINCE 1930

The early 1930s witnessed a gradual decline in the exploitation of child labor with its long hours and low pay (up to 80 hours per week at five to ten cents an hour). At the same time, however, the Children's Bureau of the United States Department of Labor (*New Republic*, January, 1933) noted that there were 250,000 homeless and jobless boys roaming the streets and looking in trash cans for food. The explanation for this inconsistency could be found in the fact that numerous states had begun to raise the age at which children could be employed in many industries and factories (*Elementary School Journal*, December, 1932). By 1937, eight state legislatures had established 16 as the minimum age for gainful employment (*Review of Reviews*, May, 1937).

During the thirties approximately 86 percent of the young people between the ages of 10 and 13 who were classified as employed were engaged in agriculture, in most instances on the farms of parents or other relatives (*Monthly Labor Review*, December, 1932). But with the coming of widespread droughts and depressed prices for farm products, some of those in middle adolescence began to move into manufacturing, mechanical, and mercantile occupations; others became messenger and delivery boys; and still others, in fact quite a large number, entered domestic service (*Review of Reviews*, May, 1937). Although legislation against child labor was gradually becoming more stringent, a larger percentage of adolescents were gainfully employed in that decade than today.

By 1940, there were more than 14 million adolescents between the ages of 14 and 19 working compared to only 11 million between the ages of 20 and 25 (*Current History*, June, 1941). Apparently, not all states were yet enforcing minimum-age legislation, although in many areas such laws were becoming quite common. During this period about two million youths left school each year, either as graduates or as dropouts. Many were dropping out of school when they reached 16, which was rapidly becoming the minimum legal age for leaving (*Occupations*, 1945).

In the 1950s, jobs for youths started to disappear. One survey did reveal, however, that 32 percent of the adolescents of that decade were gainfully employed in widely diverse occupations, ranging from office work and supermarket jobs to modeling clothes and working in libraries (*Life*, May 13, 1957). Others were able to find summer employment on farms, where they could drive tractors, work milking machines, and care for poultry, and in offices, where they were employed as temporary typists, file clerks, and switchboard operators (*National Education Association Journal*, April, 1957). Nevertheless, it was becoming more and more difficult for the young person between the ages of 14 and 16 to find afternoon and summer jobs, which are so essential in contributing to youth's initial experience in the world of work and in providing him with the opportunity to acquire the status associated with gainful employment (*Social Service*, March, 1958).

Many of the job openings requiring little or no training, such as certain factory and farm occupations, had largely disappeared by the 1960s. Hamel (1964) noted that many youths seeking employment simply did not meet the requirements established by employers for the jobs that were available. And Krauss (1964) observed that additional education was now demanded for the more desirable jobs in our rapidly expanding technological society.

According to Rosenfeld (1963), unemployment is usually most widespread among youths who have been in the job market for a relatively short span of time, especially among those with the least education, the least training, and the least experience. Therefore, job applicants without a high school diploma began to find it more and more difficult to secure work during the 1960s, for despite the low national average unemployment rate of about 4 percent, the unemployment among those still in their teens stood in excess of 12 percent (U.S. Department of Labor, 1966). And some of these young people were seeking only summer or part-time jobs. Failure to attain such employment usually meant that these adolescents continued to remain entirely dependent upon their parents for finances, often delaying the achievement of self-reliance as well as denying them the opportunities and experiences that accompany employment.

In 1965, Duncan stated that "widespread unemployment of young people could lead to feelings of frustration or worthlessness. It could also contribute to the development of antisocial attitudes, to crime, or even in some circumstances, to the growth of totalitarian political movements" (p. 123). Was this trend in declining employment one of the factors contributing to the unrest and militancy of the past decade?

It is apparent that the past 40 or 50 years have seen numerous changes in the types of jobs and the extent of employment available to the adolescent (see Table 10-1). Nevertheless, despite the many transitions which have occurred in various occupations, the reasons for youth's desire to work have remained basically the same. The adolescent needs to experience some feeling of independence, which can only be achieved through his ability to earn at least some of his own spending money. In addition, such work provides him with the opportunity to acquire status within the community and to enhance his feelings of adequacy and self-esteem. Besides working to satisfy his needs for status and independence, the adolescent often seeks employment to obtain money for secondary and higher education. It is necessary for many students from the disadvantaged socioeconomic levels to purchase school supplies and clothing, and even food, while still in junior high school and high school. Also, many young persons who marry while still in their adolescent years must work to support a wife or husband.

TABLE 10-1.　Percentage of adolescent labor force 1960 and projections for 1970, 1975, 1980. (Based on statistics in Statistical Abstracts of the United States (1969), Superintendent of Documents, Washington, D.C.)

	Male (age 16–17)	Female (age 16–17)	Male (age 18–19)	Female (age 18–19)	Male (age 16–19)	Female (age 16–19)
1960	46%	29%	73%	51%	59%	39%
1965	44%	27%	68%	49%	56%	38%
1970	43%	29%	70%	51%	56%	39%
1975	43%	29%	70%	50%	56%	40%
1980	42%	29%	70%	51%	57%	40%

ADOLESCENT PARTICIPATION IN VOLUNTEER WORK

With the decline in gainful employment available to the adolescent, there has been a compensating increase in the prevalence of volunteer job openings. Many young people may satisfy their needs for acquiring status and feelings of adequacy through such work; some may even discover future careers in this manner.

Volunteer work is often first introduced to the adolescent through the Boy Scouts, the Girl Scouts, and similar organizations. These groups engage in useful community projects, such as anti-pollution clean-up drives, making gifts and decorations for nursing home and hospital patients, visiting the ill, and accompanying senior citizens to church and to other activities. Such volunteer service develops a sense of responsibility in these young people and satisfies some of their demands for feeling needed by the community.

Many adolescents do volunteer work through their participation in extracurricular activities at school. Those who assist with the school newspaper or annual are "working" and learning simultaneously. These activities can lead to interest in future careers such as journalism or advertising. Students who have been selected to serve as office helpers, counselor aides, library assistants, and teacher aides help their schools by lightening the loads of overworked faculty and staff members, as well as learning about the world of work. During the past several years, many adolescents, both male and female, have assisted with the Head Start programs conducted by the public school systems or have tutored disadvantaged youngsters in inner-city tutorial programs. It is quite apparent that the schools offer numerous opportunities for youths to volunteer their services, inculcating in many of these young people a sense of responsibility and a feeling of personal worth and importance.

Candy Stripers, who assist medical staffs in hospitals throughout the country, illustrate one type of volunteer work that is often appealing to young girls. These adolescents aid nurses by delivering mail and flowers, by pushing wheelchairs, and by other unskilled but necessary work around the hospital. Through such services, these young women are exposed to the vast field of medicine, and many become interested in a medical career.

Many adolescents who are interested in science or photography volunteer to work in research laboratories or darkrooms and at exhibit shops in science museums. And both boys and girls have engaged in volunteer work at city zoos and parks, where they help to supervise the younger children visiting these facilities, serve as guides, organize games, and oversee many of the children's activities.

Small communities and towns frequently do not offer many opportunities for paid employment, but enterprising and energetic young men and women can often volunteer their services to various establishments. In Santa Barbara, California, students can become participant observers in offices and businesses, often without pay, as a means of vocational exploration (Freedman, 1963).

Other young people find pleasure and excitement in volunteering as ushers and stage hands for local little theater and opera groups. Several young avid opera fans have served as ushers to the touring Metropolitan Opera Company and without charge have seen many of their favorite operas performed.

Often young people of all ages find employment, money, and enjoyment through the use of their musical talents. These youths form combos or musical groups and play at dances and other gatherings. Some may volunteer their musical abilities, playing instruments or singing at benefits or at meetings of fraternal organizations. Others may perform for churches, sometimes without remuneration; and still others may play for financial gains at restaurants and other establishments. Music in all forms, however, has been a means by which adolescents have volunteered their talents, as well as financed their educational and recreational needs.

Welfare agencies are sometimes able to offer volunteer work to the adolescent. Maisel (1963) states that "unlike commercial employers, the welfare agencies providing these jobs are both willing and able to tailor them to the abilities and needs of their volunteers" (p. 134). He goes on to say that "Frequently the responsibilities they assume on their volunteer jobs carry over into more mature behavior. . . . Many youngsters, for the first time, see life as it is outside their sheltered suburbs" (p. 136).

Older adolescents, especially college students and young working people, often volunteer to help with delinquents and potential delinquents in their communities. In many cities Big Brother and Big Sister programs have been introduced. Under these programs, each volunteer "adopts" a disadvantaged child, whom he or she sees regularly, taking him or her to games and sporting events and tutoring the child in school work where such need is indicated. Many sociology and psychology students have participated in such volunteer services, as well as in programs dealing with mental health and mental retardation. Some of these young people are serving as telephone operators, manning hot lines for adolescents who seek help or advice with their problems. In Baton Rouge, Louisiana, college students are volunteers at Genesis House, which has been described as "a walk-in crisis and prevention center with a centralized referral service" (Miller, 1970, p. B-10), for although it is staffed entirely by youthful volunteers, professional assistance from nine attorneys and six medical doctors is available when it is needed. And in several Kentucky high schools and communities a number of mental-health and mental-retardation clubs have been formed. Over 300 club members in this one state alone publish a mental-health paper, operate county fair information booths on mental health and retardation, conduct drives for toys and equipment to be distributed to mental-health and retardation services, and engage in other related activities (Staton, Tiller, & Weyler, 1969).

From the current trends in volunteer services in which adolescents participate, it is evident that these activities are not just "busy work" and that they actually serve several important functions in the lives of numerous young people. First, those who have elected to volunteer their energies are helping their community and the members in it. Second, they are also helping themselves become more adequate individuals by acquiring a greater sense of responsibility and by developing greater self-esteem. And third, by their continuing to engage in such volunteer services, they are a force that can convince society of the need to recognize the worth and value of adolescents and accord them the status they so desperately seek, frequently by less positive means.

REMUNERATIVE EMPLOYMENT

Part-Time Work for the Adolescent

Some adult leaders have come to view part-time jobs as the answer to encouraging positive attitudes toward the world of work, creating a sense of responsibility among youth, and even as a means of preventing delinquency (Freedman, 1963). Whether it resolves all of these problems is debatable, but it certainly can prove beneficial to many high school and college students by encouraging better work habits, by improving self-esteem, and by creating an awareness of the importance and need for further education.

Unfortunately, many of the part-time jobs available are vocationally irrelevant and rarely introduce the adolescent to skills or training that he can use in the future (Freedman, 1963). Exceptions can be found in the Distributive Education, Diversified Occupations, and Cooperative Education programs offered by many schools throughout the nation. Under such plans, students attend school half a day and work under close supervision in business or industry the other half day.

For example, Richard was enrolled in the Distributive Education program during his junior and senior years of high school. In the mornings he studied English, history, and the Distributive Education course, which dealt with merchandising, salesmanship, and advertising display. In the afternoons he worked in a local supermarket, where he learned, while being paid, about various aspects of the grocery business under the close supervision of the store's manager and of his Distributive Education coordinator, who visited him on the job at least once a week. Upon graduation from high school, Richard continued to work full time at the same store. After a few years of experience, he opened his own neighborhood store, where he has handled a successful business for a number of years.

Another exception can be found in the Junior Achievement Clubs, which introduce many students each year to the workings of free enterprise. This organization finds sponsors for youths who are interested in forming corporations, issuing stock in their companies, and making or assembling articles to be sold to members of the community. In this manner, the young person learns about corporations, stocks, and dividends as well as the various aspects of production. At the end of the fiscal year, the companies are liquidated, and the stockholders are paid for their shares, depending upon the profit or loss of the corporation.

Becky is one of thousands of young people who have been members of Junior Achievement Clubs. Her group formed a corporation for the purpose of manufacturing chopping boards, which they sold during the Christmas season. In addition to covering all of their expenses, the sale of the articles grossed sufficient returns to pay a 7 percent dividend on each $1.00 share that had been sold. As a member of this organization, Becky learned something about the financing of private enterprise and about how to produce and merchandise tangible goods.

The printing and publishing industry, which employs many individuals in jobs such as printer's apprentice, copyboy, proofreader, and classified ad salesman, also provides relevant training in vocational skills. On-the-job training may also be found in many occupations calling for manual dexterity, such as watch repair and electronics. And the student attending a trade school, for example in auto mechanics, will often find a market available to him in various mechanics shops and garages in his community.

During the summers, many cities operate Youth Opportunity programs similar to "Call-A-Teen" sponsored by the Mayor's Action for Youth Opportunity in Oklahoma City. This program locates household chores for 14- and 15-year-old youngsters, who, as noted earlier in this chapter, are at the most difficult age to place in gainful employment. In 1969, during the first three weeks of this program, 727 jobs were provided for nearly 100 boys and girls, who earned more than $5,000 during that short period of time (*Oklahoma City Times*, July 3, 1969).

Government jobs, such as that of postal sorter, are available to many adolescents who desire to work part-time. Through the supervision of public schools and colleges, many jobs under government financing are open to lower-class youths. These include the Neighborhood Youth Corps, the Work Study Program, and the Youth Opportunity Program, all operating from the Office of Economic Opportunity. Tom and Kathy found jobs through their school counselor and the state employment agency in connection with the Youth Opportunity Program. Both are working after school at the Air Base on the outskirts of their community. Kathy is a file clerk in the personnel office, and Tom is working in the maintenance department. They are permitted to work up to 15 hours a week at a pay scale which is above the minimum wage while they continue attending high school. Although many of the jobs under these programs may be less relevant for job training than those cited in this section, they do provide employment for youths who might otherwise be forced to terminate their education.

Before leaving this topic of part-time employment, it should be noted that it can produce certain negative effects (Freedman, 1963). First, it may increase youthful impatience with the rigid demands of many high schools. Second, it may further alienate these part-time students from their peers, with whom they often have only a tenuous relationship at best. Third, it may even enhance their desire to leave school. And last of all, the rewards of such employment may be insufficient to convince alienated youth with few bright prospects for the future of the desirability of adhering to the path of honest hard work.[1]

Full-Time Employment for the Adolescent Dropout

The young person who drops out of school has an even greater need to work than his peers who continue with their education. The dropout especially needs to achieve, because his academic history has frequently been one of failure. Success at work will enable him to gain the self-satisfaction and feelings of accomplishment that he has failed to attain in school. In addition, work will also provide him with the means to support himself, thereby facilitating his emancipation from his parents and giving him the feeling of independence.

Many dropouts have not developed the basic skills of communication and computation that are needed for employment. Others have not acquired the specialized skills or knowledge necessary for specific occupations and jobs. A lack of these skills and knowledge contributes to an unstable employment record for the dropout (Super & Bohn, 1970). His vocational career is typically one of many unrelated jobs, usually semiskilled or unskilled, with little security and small encouragement for the future. Super (1964) has also noted that "at a time when the bulk of opportunities for them seem to be in technological fields and when technology is advancing at a rapid rate, the tendency is for dropouts to move down, rather than up the occupational ladder after they have acquired a few years of experience" (p. 82).

We have noted that the rate of school dropouts is decreasing with each passing decade. At the same time, however, job opportunities for high school dropouts are shrinking even more rapidly than the dropout rate is declining (Bienstock, 1964). Formerly, an individual dropping out of school and desiring to work could usually find an unskilled job opening. Today this is becoming increasingly more unlikely, and unemployment in the United States is rapidly becoming a youth problem, with unemployment rates among adolescents in

[1]See the Appendix at the end of this chapter for more case studies of employed adolescents.

their teens running at 2.5 to 3 times the rate for those over 25 years of age; of course, the dropout is hit hardest of all.

EDUCATIONAL SELECTION

During the past two decades, the growing rate of technological occupations, the need for increased education for the more desirable jobs, and the greater availability of education have encouraged most parents, and society in general, to emphasize to youth practically from the time of birth the importance of an education and the necessity of obtaining a high school diploma. However, as noted in the previous chapter, 25 percent to 30 percent are still not completing high school. And another 30 percent are completing high school in a way that is dissatisfying both to them and to their parents (Stripling, 1967).

What are some of the factors contributing to this dissatisfying attainment of a high school diploma? Perhaps one of the most important lies in the area of curriculum selection. By the ninth grade in most school systems, pressure is exerted upon students to declare the type of study they intend to pursue in order to meet high school graduation requirements. Unfortunately, those who elect a vocational or commercial training program and then two or three years later decide to enter college may discover that they have not completed certain academic courses required for college admission. Conversely, students enrolled in college preparatory curricula are often relegated only to those subjects demanded for college entrance, and therefore they have little opportunity to study elective subjects or to explore their interests in other types of courses.

Another fact contributing to unsuitable curriculum selection is the lack at the junior high or intermediate school level of sufficient numbers of qualified counselors and teachers to guide the young student and help him investigate subjects and occupations of interest to him before his entrance into high school. Ideally, there should be one counselor for every 250 students (Stripling, 1967). However, in most school systems a ratio of one counselor for every 500 to 750 students is more common. As a result, counselors are usually engaged in routine group testing and clerical work and have little time to help individual students explore the educational possibilities available to them.

A third factor contributing to unsatisfactory educational selection is the emphasis by society on the need for a college education. Since World War II a college degree has become a symbol of prestige and has been regarded by many as the only means to upward socio-economic mobility. Therefore, many individuals enroll in a college preparatory curriculum and eventually in college, not because they actually desire a higher education but because their families believe it to be the only door of opportunity open to young people. In fact, Fredenbergh (1968) has suggested that some of the collegiate radical activist behavior may be a reflection of young people's frustration under pressures placed on them by their parents to attend college and to compete intellectually for high-prestige occupations; such goals are often not of the students' own choosing and reflect unfulfilled parental aspirations. Little (1967) has pointed out that only 16 percent of high school graduates enroll in vocational or trade schools, a fact that does not reflect the increasing demand for technicians and subprofessional employees. And since more than one third of those entering college do not graduate, might not many of these young people be happier and better suited to a two-year technical training curriculum, a vocational or trade school program, or an apprenticeship or on-the-job training program?

It is apparent that the adolescent often needs individualized help in choosing the type of education best suited to his needs. Although the ultimate selection of appropriate training and a satisfying occupation should be made by the youth himself, he will frequently need assistance from his parents and from other interested adults. For example, valid career information from adults employed in certain fields and special career days could prove helpful. Pamphlets and brochures describing different training programs can be quite informative.[2] School counselors should also acquaint each student with his results on group achievement tests and discuss the means by which such achievement can be utilized in the world of work. If the young person is not fully aware of his aptitudes and interests, individual vocational testing may be indicated, a service which can often be obtained from the school counselor or from guidance facili-

---

[2]Counselors and school libraries should make such books as the following available for the student's use: *The College Blue Book, A Handbook for Counselors of College Bound Students, The College Finder, Lovejoy's College Guide, Student Financial Aid Manual for Colleges and Universities, An Introduction to Junior Colleges, Vocational and Technical Institute Courses, Vocational Training Directory of the United States, Lovejoy's Vocational School Guide,* and *Directory of Vocational Training Sources.*

ties of nearby colleges. In any case, a careful study and assessment of the type of education he desires should be undertaken, and there should also be an evaluation of the costs of the proposed education in relation to the student's financial assets and the monetary assistance available to him.

One point that is often of considerable importance in the selection of education beyond high school is the proximity of the institution or training facility. Many high school graduates attend colleges and universities within a 50- to 75-mile radius of their homes. Students who commute receive the benefits of attending classes in an academic setting but do not always have the opportunity to participate in the extracurricular activities and cultural events that may be offered on campus. Many adolescents would also prefer to experience the independence gained in living away from home. Nevertheless, for the young person who must economize by residing at home and might not otherwise be able to obtain a higher education, the commuter college is frequently the answer. In addition, such institutions often enable the less mature adolescent to attain a degree of "maturity" before leaving home. Overcrowding in residential colleges and universities is also relieved when students live at home. It is estimated that eventually 75 percent of all college-bound youths will begin their higher education at a junior college or technical school, to which most of them will commute (Stripling, 1967).

According to the United States Department of Health, Education, and Welfare (1961), only four out of every ten persons starting primary school in 1970 will continue their education beyond high school in two-year and four-year colleges and universities, trade and business schools, private technical institutes, and government programs. Since only two of these four will graduate from college, it is essential that individual adolescents be made aware of the numerous avenues through which they can achieve occupational and vocational competence. For example, federal, state, and local governments offer vocational and technical training in many areas—homemaking, commercial occupations, auto mechanics, practical nursing, electronics, agriculture, and various trades and industries. There are also private schools which offer courses in business and in technical and trade areas. Sometimes students can even start their vocational training in high school and continue to pursue such programs following graduation. And many medical schools throughout the nation are now offering training which will prepare an individual for such careers as nursing, laboratory technician, medical technician, medical records librarian, and dental technician.

In numerous occupational fields, on-the-job training or apprenticeship training can provide the necessary background for those desiring to enter areas calling for skilled labor. Certainly, the adolescent who selects an occupation requiring on-the-job training is exposed more quickly to the world of work than the one who continues in formal education. And no matter how extensive his formal education may prove to be, every student will eventually need to participate in some type of preliminary training in the job or profession he chooses to follow. In recent years, more and more professions have been emphasizing practical experience and demanding internships.

THE SELECTION OF A VOCATION

Theories of Vocational Choice

"Having a vocational objective is important in a society in which earning a living is important, in which occupational roles are of major significance, and in which education is, in effect, if not avowedly, occupationally oriented; having a vocational preference, in this context, gives purpose to behavior and makes possible education and vocational decisions" (Super, 1961, p. 35). As an authority in the area of vocational selection, whose ideas have had a profound effect on current theories of occupational choice, Super has come to regard vocational selection as a part of the developmental process that reflects the individual's feelings about himself.

Recently Korman (1969), elaborating on Super's theories, pointed out that, "Basically, the high self-esteem person seems to look at himself and say 'I like what I see and I am going to give it its desires and needs,' whereas the low self-esteem person seems to say when looking at himself 'I do not like what I see and I am not going to give it its desires and needs'" (p. 191). Even when the individual with a low self-concept has his desires fulfilled, he does not necessarily experience emotional satisfaction, although continued fulfillment could conceivably lead to a self-reassessment that could change the determinants of his satisfaction.

There have been numerous theories advanced to explain how one goes about selecting a vocation. In 1951, Ginsberg, Ginsberg, Axelrod, and Herma suggested that an occupational choice is a compromise between fantasy and reality. They saw the individual as moving through three definite stages in the process of making a vocational choice: the "fantasy period," the "tentative period," and the "realistic period." During the fantasy period, which encompasses the first decade of life, a child's thoughts about a future vocation are not related to ability, training, or the availability of job opportunities. This stage of development is marked by frequent changes; one day he expresses a desire to be a cowboy and the next day a policeman, and in neither case does he consider his qualifications and the future offered by the vocation he is considering. During the second period, the tentative period, which covers part of adolescence, he begins to concern himself with the working conditions and requirements he must meet in his selection of a future vocation. About this time he also takes into consideration his interests, and toward the end of the period he considers the aptitudes and education demanded by various occupations along with his personal values and goals. With the third period, the period of reality, which begins around the age of 17, he begins to resolve the problem of vocational choice, recognizing that he must usually compromise with the demands of reality.

In 1956, Roe introduced the idea that vocational choice reflects the adolescent's personality type, which has developed in large measure as a result of early parent-child relationships. She pointed out that each personality type demands the satisfaction of certain psychological needs, such as the need for power and prestige, which the individual seeks to fulfill through various life roles, and that in adolescents these needs are partially expressed through the selection of a vocation. For example, an individual who demonstrates a need for power and prestige might select a career in politics.

Holland (1962) listed six constellations of personality patterns, which he felt influenced the vocational field that an individual would ultimately enter. He suggested that each of these areas represents a different, unique vocational environment with its own life style. Each person must learn to adjust to one of these patterns and must acquire certain skills demanded by his selected area. The six vocational fields are as follows:

> (1) The *realistic* area emphasizes physical skills and masculinity, with little emphasis on interpersonal relationships or verbal ability.

(2) The *intellectual* field revolves around working with ideas rather than with people.
(3) The *social* area places its emphasis on interpersonal relationships and avoids the realistic and intellectual orientations of the first two vocational environments.
(4) The *conventional* area is structured and characterized by rules and regulations that give it a certain inflexibility.
(5) The *enterprising* field is composed of individuals seeking status through domination and manipulation of others.
(6) The *artistic* area stresses the emotional and artistic expression of the inner self and opposes the structure, rigidity, and social orientation of the other vocational environments.

According to Caplow (1954), many vocational choices occur by accident. He notes that certain preliminary choices leading to a vocation must be made as early as the eighth grade, as for example whether to enroll in a college preparatory curriculum or a vocational training program. Because students are frequently badly informed about occupations at this stage in their development and because their training is often irreversible, they tend to stumble into their life's work. He also observes that some careers attract people because of the prestige attached to them. More recently, Tyler (1969) has suggested that choosing an identity is synonymous with choosing an occupation.

Whether the reader believes in one, several, or none of these theories, they do offer a valuable framework for interpreting vocational selection as a developmental process and suggesting that the choosing of an occupation is much more complex than is commonly assumed.

Environmental Factors in Vocational Selection

There are numerous environmental influences affecting vocational choice, and probably none has greater impact than the family. For example, Super (1957) noted that the family inculcates in its young people certain habits and expectations of success that contribute the foundation for later success. The adolescent growing up in a home in which success is recognized and rewarded usually develops a pattern of successful achievement that carries over into other phases of his life: school, social life, and ultimately his job. Conversely, those in whom success is ignored and failure condemned tend to develop, as so often occurs in academic underachievement, patterns of failure that seem to become self-perpetuating.

Some individuals still pursue the careers of their fathers and grandfathers because of interest, economic feasibility, or lack of motivation to follow another type of career. However, this phenomenon is gradually disappearing. Duncan and Hodge (1963), in a study of 1,000 Chicago males, noted that only 10 percent entered their fathers' vocations; it is probable that many of these were examples of "forced inheritance," wherein they found themselves in their fathers' jobs because of restricted opportunity and cultural deprivation that made it difficult to escape from the parents' low-status occupation. Actually, more and more parents are encouraging their offspring to assert their autonomy and make their own vocational decisions, regardless of their fathers' occupational levels.

A second environmental factor, the school, also contributes substantially to vocational selection. Through his experiences at school, the child gradually acquires an awareness of his assets, liabilities, and interests, which provides the basis for his educational and vocational aspirations.

Another factor, the mass media (magazines, newspapers, literature, movies, radio, and television), influences some adolescents' thoughts about different occupations and the possibilities of entering certain fields. Sometimes industries, as well as the armed forces, attempt to advertise the adventure, education, and intellectual stimulation afforded by their companies and by the various branches of the services. Such environmental forces do not always portray a realistic picture of job situations, and these may influence a young adolescent who is quite suggestible. However, as the youth matures, he will tend to become more realistic about his abilities and his social status and will therefore be less amenable to the ideas presented by the media.

Occasionally, community facilities may play a positive role in assisting young people in their selection of a suitable career. The University of Texas Medical Branch at Galveston has helped youth in that city to explore opportunities in vocations related to medicine. This project has been undertaken through the Health Occupation Cooperative Training Program, which introduces high school juniors and seniors to certain occupational fields and helps them decide if they are qualified or interested in any of these areas through an on-the-job training plan (*Galveston Daily News*, June 26, 1969).

Last, but not least, one should recognize the role that the peer group may play in vocational selection. For example, the upper-middle-class youth who prefers to work with his hands in a skilled laborer's job may be dissuaded from doing so for fear that he will be ostracized by his college-bound friends.

Other Factors Influencing Vocational Choice

Often an individual's partiality toward one occupational field over another can be seen as a reflection of particular values that he has acquired during the adolescent period. For example, Osipow (1968) states that "social class membership is an important situational determinant and affects attitudes towards education and work, the amount and kind of education and training acquired, and the economic resources one has to implement his career plans" (p. 216). Also, Powell and Bloom (1962) observed that when senior high school students were asked to name the occupational factors they considered to be the most important in vocational selection, they most frequently stated that "interest in their work" was the primary consideration, with a desire for security being another strong motivating factor.

But regardless of the motives, conscious or unconscious, underlying the selection of a vocation, the more occupational information to which the adolescent has access and the more knowledge he has about himself, the greater the opportunity for him to arrive at a wise choice. Certainly, it is preferable for him to select a career that will utilize his talents and enhance his self-esteem. At the same time, however, it is essential for both the adult and the adolescent to recognize that in addition to the professions, there are many jobs equally as important, which demand responsible, qualified workers who desire to perform a task and to perform it well. And they should be aware of the disparity that often exists between the availability of certain jobs, especially within the professions, and the numbers desiring to enter such fields.

The selection of a vocation by the adolescent is an important step on the pathway to "maturity," but that selection should not be regarded as final or irreversible or as binding him to limited areas. Since it is estimated that within a decade many jobs will become obsolescent and ultimately disappear, while many others, presently nonexistent, will emerge, it is important that youth, whether technically or academically educated, recognize that changing jobs may actually, although not always, be a sign of vocational growth.

SUMMARY AND CONCLUSIONS

The United States and Canada now have an industrial system that no longer requires marginal workers, among whom are many of today's adolescents (Freedman, 1963). This phenomenon has resulted in both opportunities and problems. There is more time for education but a scarcity of employment for youth; this scarcity has increased adolescent difficulties in the transition from school to work.

To help bridge the gap, there has been a compensatory increase in the prevalence of volunteer work. Service groups vary from the Boy Scouts and Girl Scouts to hospital volunteers like the Candy Stripers. The types of work range from assisting with OEO programs and helping in science laboratories or photography darkrooms to working with the performing arts in community little theatres. Such volunteer service has encouraged youth to acquire a sense of responsibility and has enabled them to acquire status in the community and, to some extent, to satisfy their need to belong.

Nevertheless, numerous young people must work part-time to earn some income in order to remain in school. Others need to improve their work habits and increase their awareness of the importance of further education. Unfortunately, many such jobs are irrelevant as vocational preparation and may also present other negative aspects.

For the high school dropout, remunerative employment assumes even greater importance than for the adolescent remaining in school. Too often, however, because of his limited education and work skills, the dropout remains the last one to be hired and the first one to be fired.

Adolescents, as well as the adults working with them, need to realize the importance of appropriate educational and vocational selection. Although several theories have been advanced to explain how an individual reaches his ultimate occupational choice, it remains the responsibility of the school to supply each student with the information necessary to enable him to make a wise and suitable educational and vocational decision.

APPENDIX: EXAMPLES OF ADOLESCENT REMUNERATIVE EMPLOYMENT

James, age 18 and a recent high school graduate, was interviewed while at work on a cable car at Royal Gorge Park. He applied for a position at the end of his freshman year in high school (age 14) and was employed by the City to work in his present position of helping park visitors during their ride from the top of the Gorge to the bottom. He states that the money he has earned has helped him purchase clothing and school supplies during his last three years in high school. He plans to enter a computer school in St. Louis in the fall and will use the money he received this summer for school and personal expenses. He hopes to return to Royal Gorge next summer and earn enough money to finance his second year in the St. Louis computer school.

Toni wants to be a registered nurse. She was employed at a local rest home as a nurse's aide for several months. Now she is working as an aide at one of the city hospitals, where she is learning more medical terminology and has additional responsibilities. Toni is aware that her experiences at the rest home and the hospital and her association with members of the medical profession will help her decide if the career she has chosen really fits her needs and expectations. Also, she is saving money to use for additional education following high school graduation.

Doris, age 16, is working in the city library and learning a little library science while checking books and shelving them. She is spending her after-school hours plus three evenings a week at the library. Doris plans to enter college and pursue a degree in library science. Her present job supplies her with enough money for items she needs at school.

Linda had always been a low-average student in a Montreal high school and had never really enjoyed going to school. Her curriculum consisted mainly of typing, shorthand, and art rather than the program used to prepare students for college. After having failed grade ten twice, she felt embarrassment at having to repeat the year for a third time so she decided to "drop out." Her typing and shorthand were not very advanced, and without a "diploma" she found jobs not only scarce but almost impossible to obtain. Finally, through a relative, Linda was able to find a position as a typist in a general hospital and seemed to enjoy the work and the atmosphere. She is presently 22 years old and has been with the same hospital since its opening five years ago. This 375-bed hospital is large enough to permit advancement for employees, and Linda is presently enjoying the position of executive secretary to the dietitian in chief. She is making an average of $400 a month; she has her own car; she has traveled extensively abroad and to the Caribbean. She has never found it necessary to take additional courses in business but she did take an extensive course with the St. John's Ambulance Corps and is now involved in active duty at major functions in the city of Montreal in the evenings.

Leroy has been a fry cook at a hamburger stand for three months. Previous to his promotion he waited on the counter customers and called out orders. He first started looking for work when he purchased his auto and needed money for payments and gasoline. With his promotion he received a raise, and he is now considering buying a newer model car. Although he is a high school senior and only works after school hours, he is thinking about someday owning a hamburger business of his own. Leroy considered attending college for a while, but he has talked with many of his older friends who are going to college and he believes that he can be both happy and financially successful as an owner of a small business.

Janet and Jim are both high school students who receive financial help through the Neighborhood Youth Corps. They are employed at their high school and receive money for their work through the NYC. Their counselor helped them obtain their jobs; Janet helps in the lunchroom during the lunch period, and Jim works in the student store. These jobs have motivated Janet and Jim to continue their high school studies and have encouraged them to stay in school at least a year longer. There are many Janets and Jims throughout the United States profiting monetarily and educationally by this federally funded program.

Henry arranged with the high school counselor to have the last two periods of his school day free in order to attend barber college in the city in which he lived. He realized that he would have to use his senior year to make up the credits, but he was willing to do this. His parents paid his tuition to barber school, and he attended public school from 8:30 to 1:00 and the trade school from 2 until 8 or 9 P.M. while he was in his junior year. The summer term between his junior and senior years was devoted to the trade school and the hours earned then completed the number required to become a licensed barber. Henry became financially independent during his senior year by working after school and on weekends at his trade. He is now planning to attend college while keeping his license active.

REFERENCES

Bienstock, H. Realities of the job market. In D. Schreiber (Ed.), *Guidance and the school dropout.* Washington, D.C.: American Personnel and Guidance Association, 1964. Pp. 84–108.

Brodsky, P. Problems of adolescence: An Adlerian view. *Adolescence,* 1968, 3(9), 9–22.

Caplow, T. *The sociology of work.* Minneapolis: University of Minnesota Press, 1954.

Current History. Youth in the labor market. 1941, 53, 41.

Duncan, B. Dropouts and the unemployed. *Journal of Political Economy,* April, 1965, 123.

Duncan O. D., & Hodge, R. W. Education and occupational mobility: A regression analysis. *American Journal of Sociology,* 1963, 68, 629–644.

Elementary School Journal. Child labor and school attendance. 1932, 33, 245–247.

Fredenburgh, F. A. An apologia for the hippie generation. *Mental Hygiene,* 1968, 52(3), 341–348.

Freedman, M. K. Part-time work and potential early school leavers. *American Journal of Orthopsychiatry,* 1963, 33, 509–514.

Galveston Daily News, Galveston, Texas, June 26, 1969, C-3.

Ginsberg, E., Ginsberg, S. W., Axelrod, S., & Herma, J. L. *Occupational choice: An approach to a general theory.* New York: Columbia University Press, 1951.

Hamel, H. R. Employment of school age youth, October, 1963. *Monthly Labor Review,* 1964, 87, 767.

Holland, J. L. Some explorations of a theory of vocational choice: One- and two-year longitudinal studies. *Psychological Monographs,* 1962, 76(2), Whole No. 545.

Korman, A. K. Self-esteem as a moderator in vocational choice: Replications and extensions. *Journal of Applied Psychology,* 1969, 53(3), 188–192.

Krauss, I. Sources of educational aspirations among working class youth. *American Sociological Review,* 1964, 29, 867–879.

Life. Getting and spending the teenage allowance. May 13, 1957, 42, 147–152.

Little, J. K. The occupations of non-college youth. *American Educational Research Journal,* 1967, 4, 147–153.

Maisel, A. Q. What will your teenager do this summer? *Reader's Digest,* 1963, 82, 133–138.

Miller, M. The Genesis House; Youths in B. R. prepared to help in any problem. *Alexandria Daily Town Talk,* Nov. 27, 1970, B-10.

Monthly Labor Review. United States summary of departmental statistics, 15th census of the United States, 1930. 1932, **35**, 1334–1336.

National Educational Association Journal. About that summer job. 1957, **46**, 256–257.

New Republic. Child labor comes back. 1933, **73**, 257.

Occupations. Post-war planning for young job seekers. 1945, **24**, 111–114.

Oklahoma City Times, July 3, 1969.

Osipow, S. H. *Theories of career development.* New York: Appleton-Century-Crofts, 1968.

Powell, M., & Bloom, V. Development of and reasons for vocational choices of adolescents through the high school years. *Journal of Educational Research*, 1962, **56**, 126–133.

Review of Reviews. The Brearley Bulletin. 1937, **95**, 44–45.

Roe, A. *The psychology of occupations.* New York: John Wiley & Sons, 1956.

Rosenfeld, C. Employment of school-age youth, October 1962. *Monthly Labor Review*, 1963, **86**, 909.

Social Service. New look: Jobs for children. March, 1958, 32–64.

Staton, E. E., Tiller, C. B., & Weyler, E. H. Teens who care: Potential mental health manpower. *Mental Hygiene*, 1969, **53**(2), 200–204.

Stripling, R. The role of the counselor in educational programs. Address presented at the fourth annual guidance seminar for counselors and educators at Louisiana State University, Alexandria, January, 1967.

Super, D. E. *The psychology of careers.* New York: Harper & Row, 1957.

Super, D. E. Consistency and wisdom of vocational preference as indices of vocational maturity in the ninth grade. *Journal of Educational Psychology*, 1961, **52**, 35–43.

Super, D. E. Vocational development of high school dropout. In D. Schreiber (Ed.), *Guidance and the school dropout.* Washington, D.C.: American Personnel and Guidance Association, 1964. Pp. 66–83.

Super, D. E., & Bohn, M. J. *Occupational psychology.* Belmont, California: Wadsworth, 1970.

Tyler, L. E. The work of the counselor (3rd ed.). New York: Meredith, 1969.

United States Department of Health, Education, and Welfare. *Education in a changing world.* Washington, D.C.: Government Printing Office, 1961.

United States Department of Labor. *Manpower report of the President.* Washington, D.C.: Government Printing Office, 1966.

11

The Adult-Adolescent Communication Gap

Ours is a society where gaps of all kinds exist, but if we dared bridge them, they'd be missed. . . .

A high school senior
Class of '69

During the past two decades, popular magazines have been flooded with articles on the generation gap. All generations have been pondering such questions as whether this problem is unique to our rapidly changing society or whether it is one that has been with us throughout history, and even whether such a gap actually exists at all.

"Our youth now love luxury. They have bad manners, contempt for authority, disrespect for older people. Children nowadays are tyrants. They contradict their parents, chatter before company, gobble their food, and tyrannize their teachers." So said Socrates about 500 B.C.

At the root of this problem of the generation gap, whether it is new today or whether it goes back 2500 years, is the difficulty experienced by both generations in communicating with each other. To communicate means ". . . to share or impart, to signal or tell somebody about some feelings or knowledge" (Dubbé, 1965, p. 57). But the act of communication involves both a sender and a receiver with something of common interest flowing between the two, and until the recipient has received and acknowledged the message of another individual, the act of communication is not really considered to be

279

complete. It should also be noted that although the major form of communication is language, it may also include other forms, such as physical position, signs, facial expressions, drawings, writings, and so on.

Communication is especially important within the family. "It is vital to basic human relationships in the one social living unit which does most to shape individual character. If wholesome, practical, affectionate, and secure relationships are worthy to be generated and sustained, then easy flow of thoughts and feelings is imperative" (Dubbé, 1965, p. 57). Some problems in communication are probably inevitable for most young people. According to a study by Dubbé (discussed in the next section), 95 percent of all young people do experience some difficulty when trying to bridge the generation gap at some times, in regard to certain subjects, and to some degree. When this situation becomes severe, it may have far-reaching consequences on the adolescent's emotional and social adjustment.

THE EXTENT OF THE COMMUNICATION GAP

Probably less research has been done in the area of communication than in almost any other field affecting adolescent behavior and development. Among the investigations which have been undertaken in this field, the research of Dubbé (1965) has perhaps been the most extensive. He devised a questionnaire encompassing 22 reasons for difficulty in communication on 36 different topics, which he placed on individual cards, which were then shuffled in random fashion to minimize factors of boredom and fatigue. When his subjects indicated that they were experiencing difficulty in any of these areas, they were also asked to give a score to show the intensity of the problem.

Dubbé first made a pilot study in 1956 in western Oregon of 50 men and 50 women college freshmen selected at random from 2184 college freshmen. Later, he made a second study of 100 boys and 100 girls, who were high school freshmen also selected at random from eight high schools in western Oregon from a total of 1930 ninth-grade students. In the first study, all but one of the hundred subjects admitted to some degree of difficulty with some of the 36 topics when talking to their parents; the problems varied according to the sex of the student and that of the parent. Boys said that difficulty in communication arose because of fear and conservatism on the part of their parents, while girls stated that a lack of time in talking with their parents was an important factor in their communication breakdown. For the subjects of both studies the topics most difficult for both boys and girls to discuss with either parent were sex and the related subjects of petting and courtship. However, there were a few more issues, such as care of property and use of the car, that proved more troublesome for boys in their relationships with their parents, especially with their mothers, than for girls.

Another study by Eric W. Johnson (1961), head of the junior high, Germantown Friends School, disclosed that when parents were asked to cite the most difficult situation they had encountered with their adolescent children, the communication gap led all of the rest of the problems. He also noted that this gap was felt not only by parents but by their children as well. In a study of nearly 400 boys and girls in grades seven through eleven, 40 percent said that it was "difficult at times" to communicate with their parents, and 11 percent stated that it was "always difficult."

However, this communication gap is not necessarily inevitable nor characteristic of all young people in our society. A recent survey of 1219 high school students[1] disclosed that while 6.5 percent checked on their questionnaires that their communication with their parents was very unsatisfactory and another 11.5 percent stated that their communication with parents was poor, 44 percent said they had established fair or average communication with the older generation, while 24 percent said it was good, and 14 percent described it as excellent (Rothschild, 1969).

Students in this study made such typical statements as:

> "I think parents should realize that this is a new generation, and they can't expect us to conform to all the old standards. Things that were not acceptable years ago are now considered everyday things. . . ."
>
> "I think the generation gap is as it should be, maybe a little to the extreme, though. Many things adults say are right, and many things the kids say are right. But neither would ever admit to being wrong. I think that is the whole problem."
>
> "If you could get adults to talk to us like we're old enough to know something and not treat us like little kids. They act like they're afraid to let down. . . ."

[1]Our thanks go to Mr. W. E. Pate, former Principal of Bolton High School. Alexandria, Louisiana, for his cooperation in making this study possible.

"I think the trouble occurs when the teen-ager doesn't think of his mother and father as his friends as well as his parents, friends that want to help you and know more about you."

"To me, there isn't much of a communication gap between parents and their children. I get along fine with my folks (most of the time)."

"I just think that the gap is part of growing up."

CAUSES OF PROBLEMS IN COMMUNICATION

Johnson (1961) hypothesized that although there will always be some gap, this problem has probably become a more frequent complaint during the past fifty years. With social changes occurring so rapidly, it has perhaps been inevitable that the generations would grow apart more rapidly as well. For example, McLuhan (1964) feels that today's youth are different from those of the past. He believes that this generation, the first to be reared in the electronic age, is different because the medium of television controls their environment. Television confronts an individual both visually and auditorily, instantaneously and enveloping, as contrasted to the mass media of previous generations, that of print, which presents one stimulus at a time, in an orderly sequence from cause to effect. As a consequence, McLuhan thinks that today's young people have developed different ways of perceiving stimuli than those of previous generations. Another investigator, Pacella (1967) has suggested ". . . that television has tended to induce an alienation of family members from each other, since intrafamily communication has been replaced by the one way communication with television" (p. 1977).

The generations also have different attitudes toward sex (Bell, 1966), allegiance to one's country, and obedience to authority. Whereas a few generations ago, parents expected unquestioning obedience from their children, today's parents tend to be more permissive, allowing their children to express their own points of view much more freely, a situation that sometimes backfires since young people's attitudes can seem quite alien and unacceptable to many of the older generation.

There are also many, many more young people today than there were even two decades ago; this large population also accounts for an increasingly impersonal society. In addition, adolescence, which was formerly regarded as a five-year behavioral phenomenon, can now extend up to fifteen years, because of society's increasing demands for more and more education and the resultant lengthening of adolescent economic dependence.

The gulf between the generations may also be due in part to shifts in customs and in part to differences in temperament between the generations, but it is basically typical of human nature. If there were no differences between a 15-year-old and a 35-year-old, it would be a sad commentary on the lack of individual growth and healthy ferment in our society. However, this natural conflict may be more intense today as a result of the speeded-up pace of change; according to Neisser (1967), the amount of social, scientific, and technological innovation that once occurred over an interval of two or three decades now takes place in one.

It is only natural, then, that as younger members of the family emerge into adolescence, there will be some difficulty in communication between the two generations. Young people will tend to withhold information about their personal activities, they will be resentful of parents and other adults who try to pry this information loose from them, and they will become much more critical of adults in general. As a result of this often abrupt withdrawal, parents may respond by more prying or by withdrawing themselves, both responses resulting in a widening of the gap between the adults and youth (Bienvenu, 1967).

Joe, at 17, is the eldest of two children in the Watkins family. He makes superior grades in high school, has a wide circle of friends, loves politics, and wears his hair almost down to his shoulders with shaggy sideburns. His father, a conservatively groomed businessman, is quite disturbed by what he regards as Joe's unkempt appearance. He constantly keeps reminding his son that he needs a haircut. Joe ignores the comments. "Get off my back" is his typical response. Mr. Watkins, whose memory may be somewhat distorted by the years, is likely to reply, "When I was your age, I would not have dared to speak to my father in such a manner." Thus, formerly clear lines of communication become clogged; no real messages are able to penetrate the static.

Perhaps if Mr. Watkins were more familiar with adolescent development, he would be aware of the possible explanations behind Joe's desire to wear his hair long. His behavior may be just one more manifestation of his need to assert his autonomy and independence. Most of Joe's peers are also currently grooming themselves in a similar fashion, and Joe desires, above all, to be accepted by them. His father, on the other hand, may believe that the sloppy hair is representative of sloppy thinking and may even regard the long tresses as being effeminate as well.

Too often, reaching the unresponsive adolescent and establishing some degree of emotional contact with him may be one of the most frustrating undertakings with which parents will be confronted (Pacella, 1963). Mothers and fathers of young people may interpret their offspring's need for privacy as a manifestation of standoffishness and may tend to respond inappropriately themselves, perhaps out of feelings of rejection. Sometimes, parents will even feel a sense of guilt, believing that they have failed.

Unfortunately, too few parents, teachers, and other adults regard adolescent detachment as a right and even a necessity of youth; however, adolescents often need to retreat from the adult world somewhat in order to cope with rapidly occurring physiological and emotional changes.

Parents who were previously placed on a pedestal by their preadolescent children may suddenly discover that they no longer serve as the ideal. Such a discovery can be quite traumatic for the adults, who must begin to accept the rejection of some of the values which they had worked to instill in their children during the preceding years.

For example, Joe at 17 is beginning to realize that there is another political party besides the one his father had always upheld. Mr. Watkins, a third-generation supporter of his party, is quite disturbed to learn that Joe has joined the Young People's Committee of the opposition party and will work at party headquarters during the coming election. Although his decision to work at the headquarters of the opposing political party may have been a means of demonstrating his desire for independence and a questioning of his father's values, it may just as readily have been a reflection of Joe's keen political beliefs.

ACTING-OUT BEHAVIOR AS A FORM OF ADOLESCENT COMMUNICATION

According to Levitt and Rubenstein (1959), a considerable amount of acting-out behavior in the adolescent is an attempt at communication. In interpreting such behavior, one should keep in mind that an adolescent is in reality an actor on the stage of life, often speaking lines whose meanings he himself does not fully comprehend. Further, these lines (words or actions) may offer significant communication to the trained, perceptive observer. And last, adults should take into account the fact that certain factors in the personality structure of the young person are in the process of undergoing change or modification.

Adolescent terminology may frequently convey a great deal of meaning to the perceptive adult. Such phrases as "play it cool" stress the young person's need to remain calm at a time in his life which is likely to be filled with turbulence. It is almost as if the young person were saying to himself, "I'm all shook up inside, but I'll play it cool and no one will know" (Levitt & Rubenstein, 1959, p. 624). Thus, it is the latent rather than the *manifest content* through which the adolescent really attempts to communicate. An adult, in order to understand such adolescent communication, "must learn to disregard the apparent logical word arrangement and to translate the language expression from the secondary elaboration to its real meaning" (Levitt & Rubenstein, 1959, p. 624).

The typical youth cannot always find sufficient outlets for his large amount of vitality. In the distant past, adults encouraged him to release his leftover energy through pioneering, hunting, and fighting wild Indians. More recently they have stressed that he seek outlets for his excess energy through athletics. But the frontiers for pioneering have largely disappeared. And as athletics become more and more competitive, adolescents become passive spectators rather than active participants. As a consequence, young people sometimes resort to more primitive behavior in their problem solving, turning to acting-out behavior, such as illegal drag racing, the unlawful use of drugs, and vandalism.

Actually the adolescent through his verbalizing, as well as through his acting out, may communicate many messages to the alert observer.

As we have mentioned, he may be sending a plea for help or for discipline from those around him. At other times he may be verbalizing or acting out his need for independence and autonomy, perhaps protesting against a *symbiotic relationship*, or too close an association, with his parents (Ekstein & Friedman, 1956). And in still other instances, he may be expressing beliefs and values that are genuinely logical to him.

For example, Mary, a high school junior of 16, was informed by her strict, fundamentally religious, overly conscientious parents that they would not permit her to date until she graduated from high school at the age of 17½. Noting that her peers were already dating quite regularly and feeling that her mother and father were being unjust and unrealistic, Mary pleaded with them to permit her at least to go with dates to various school functions. Her pleadings got her nowhere, and finally Mary decided to run away from home.

The deed itself of running away might be considered by the courts to be a delinquent act, but actually Mary considered her running away to be the only means at her disposal for communicating her emotional reactions against the unjust discipline imposed upon her by her parents. Mary's act was in reality a logical protest against the unreasonable restrictions of her mother and father. By regarding such acting-out behavior as a critical message to her parents rather than as behavior intended to jeopardize adult authority, one can probably best understand the meaning of such acting out.

Many social scientists believe that considerable misunderstanding and disharmony between parent and adolescent actually have their inception in the early parent-child relationship (Pacella, 1963). A parent who regards his young child as a constant source of annoyance and trouble during the youngster's early periods of development may sometimes verbalize his wish that the child "stop acting like a child." Often such a young person is pushed into acting-out behavior because all outlets for his normal impulses and his need for communication have been denied. Thus, the frustrations and resentments that pile up during childhood persist into the adolescent period, meantime becoming far more corrosive and unmanageable. At the same time, parental frustrations accumulate over the years, thereby creating in some families mutual rejection and recrimination between the two generations.

COMMUNICATION PROBLEMS REFLECTING
ADOLESCENT PSYCHOPATHOLOGY

The question arises whether communication or the lack of it may be indicative of the existence of pathology in the adolescent. A study of all adolescents admitted to the Psychosomatic and Psychiatric Institute at Michael Reese Hospital in Chicago between 1958 and 1961 revealed that there was much adolescent complaining about their parents' failure to understand them and in turn their inability to understand their parents (Marcus et al., 1966). This investigation involved a study of 20 families, 10 normal or nondisturbed and 10 disturbed, each intact with both parents in residence in the household and with two adolescent children of the same sex, ranging in ages from 13 to 19. An 80-item inventory was administered to each adolescent patient and to each normal sibling. They were asked to describe themselves and to describe what their mothers would say they ideally expected of them. The mothers' perception of their offspring plus the results of intensive interviews with the patients, their siblings, and the mothers themselves were all used to measure the effectiveness of their communication. Results of these data plus historical data obtained from patient records disclosed that normal family members were in better communication with each other. Normal siblings of disturbed adolescents appeared to have some degree of impaired communication but not to the extent that was visible in the disturbed patients. The disturbed adolescents seemed to understand that they did not meet the expectations of their mothers, thereby indicating some degree of perception, but the more normal adolescents appeared to understand their mothers' expectations more clearly, and their mothers in turn were able to understand their children more effectively.

BRIDGING THE COMMUNICATION GAP

How can adults and adolescents bridge the gap existing between them? According to Johnson (1961), two prerequisites must exist before communication can effectively take place. First, the adult and the adolescent must each be willing to give his attention to the other. Especially important is the parent's willingness to listen to his son or daughter at the moment he or she wants to talk, as illustrated in the following example.

One evening Jerry Ryan, high school senior, came into the family den to discuss with his father whether he should give his girl his senior class ring. My. Ryan, engrossed in reading the newspaper after a busy day at the office, looked up from his reading and asked impatiently, "Well, what do you want?" Jerry muttered something inaudibly and stumbled out of the room, realizing that his parent was more interested in the news at the moment than in his problem.

It is quite likely that a precious moment of communication between the two generations may have been lost forever. Mr. Ryan, in failing to put aside his own interests for a very few minutes, had inadvertently widened the gap between himself and his son. Jerry, in turn, probably felt a certain sense of bewilderment and anger and wondered if there was anyone to whom he could turn besides, perhaps, his peers.

A second prerequisite for communication is the presence of mutually understood assumptions. The parents assume that they are responsible for the adolescent, love him, and believe what they do for him is in his own best interests. The adolescent assumes that he is an individual as important as others, who is about to become an adult with the right to begin having adult experiences. He believes he knows quite a lot and has difficult and important problems. Both generations must be able to understand these assumptions and willingly accept them, or satisfying communication between the two is likely to be rare indeed (see extract below).

THE TRAIN RIDE
By William J. McKean

It happened on a late afternoon commuter train leaving New York's Penn Station. The day had been hot, sweaty and humid. Thick layers of cigarette smoke swirled like heaving storm clouds over a hundred or so travelers taking liquid relief in the overcrowded bar car. But no one seemed to mind too much. It was Friday, the start of another weekend. The beautiful people in the crowd, working on their first martini, dreamed about those walks along isolated beaches and midnight clambakes on the shore. The rest, white- and blue-collar workers, looked forward to family picnics, fishing trips and ball games with their kids.

Just as everyone settled down to make the best of a long ride to freedom, he walked into the bar car. The bell-bottoms were dirty and frayed, the soiled denim jacket much too hot for the day. His hair was long and straggly, and the shaggy beard did little to hide a young, unhappy face. And, oh, did he draw stares. He had strayed into a stronghold of the Establishment—a commuter bar car. Two white-collar men noticed him, too, but concerned themselves more with sucking up cold canned beers. And they were frankly annoyed when the young man elbowed his way between them, hoisted his duffel bag on the rack above and stared idly out of the window.

Now, like it or not, they were a threesome. When the beer ran dry, one of the men asked the boy if he'd like a drink too. The youngster hesitated, then agreed to a Coke. Hostility gone, the talk turned into a three-way conversation. The boy was shy, soft-spoken, but down—not from pills or pot—just down. They talked from both sides of the generation gap about war, politics, government and society in general. It was polite chatter, but the men sensed the boy had other things on his mind. Their curiosity aroused, they pressed him about it, and the youngster dropped the heavy stuff—he was giving up, leaving his country for good. He would stay at a friend's house near the airport that night, then leave for Mexico in the morning. He wasn't a bomb-planting radical. He was a straight, decent kid who gave it his best shot but couldn't change the system he disagreed with.

The men were shaken; Friday's fun was over. They knew their country was losing another son. They reasoned with him, even pleaded—never lectured. They pep-talked him about his voting privileges and how he and others like him could bring changes within the system if they worked together. But it was too late. They had lost him even before they started, and they knew it.

He left the train after a few stops. The men helped him with his bag and shook his hand warmly, wishing him well.

Once back in the bar car, the men soon realized that the stares some of the drinkers had thrown at the boy had turned to menacing glares directed at them. Finally, from a group of men who had watched but never heard the conversation, one man spoke to them.

"What's wrong with you guys?" he asked. "You wear your hair as short as we do, why were you bothering with the likes of him?"

The two men flushed with anger. One of them answered, "You and your friends look about my age, and I'm sure you have teen-age kids like I do. That boy who just left could have been any one of our kids, and do you know he's leaving the country tomorrow? Maybe if some of us cared a little more or listened and showed our love to a kid like this, he might not be leaving. Do you have any more questions?"

The man shook his head weakly and returned to his friends. Perhaps that night some fathers looked at their children a little longer, held them tighter and talked with them a little more about small problems before they became big problems. You can bet at least two of them did.

(William J. McKean, *Look Magazine* ©. Reprinted with permission.)

Specifically, parents, teachers, and other adults will need to ask themselves what they as individuals can do to keep open the communication links and to prevent the channels between the generations from becoming clogged.

It is important for parents to begin as early as possible to talk openly with their children, to answer their questions fully and honestly, admitting when they do not know the answers. Such communication also involves listening with genuine interest and regard to what their young people have to say.

Next, it is important to avoid judging this restless generation solely by its appearance and/or the deeds of many by the misdeeds of a few. Many adolescents do have new ideas, to which adults should at least listen. They have demonstrated the presence of youthful thinking through their work in the civil rights movement, through their demands for more active participation in the formation of more relevant educational curricula, and through such programs as volunteer tutoring of youngsters in deprived areas and volunteer services to the emotionally disturbed and the mentally retarded.

Young people also need more confidence and trust from adults. Unfortunately, many adults have overgeneralized about today's adolescents and regarded them as a generation of troublemakers, who will inevitably become delinquents unless adults get tough with them

(Duvall, 1962). If adults demonstrate a trust and a belief in young people, they are likely to develop a trust and a belief in themselves, thereby moving toward independence and maturity. Parents and other adults who constantly pry into their offspring's activities and behavior are quite likely to stir up resentment and cause static to occur in the communication lines.

Mothers and fathers, in turn, must acquire the trust and confidence of their young people. Parents often make a mistake when they fail to keep the secrets of their children or tell tales about them which they regard as cute or funny, for it is important to the adolescent's growing sense of self that he have his privacy respected.

Further, adolescents should not feel that they are being compared to someone else. For example, teachers should be careful not to assume that Johnny is the same caliber of student with the same interests and the same aptitudes as his older brother, Joe, who preceded him in school. And parents should avoid making comparisons between siblings and should abstain from the temptation of trying to mold them into what they think they should be. Perceptive, understanding adults will assume the role of observant bystanders, ready to come forward when help is needed, demonstrating interest in the younger generation and its problems but being sparing with advice. Even more important, the older generation should be able to withdraw a certain distance when youths indicate that they want to be on their own.

Adolescents want responsibility and the opportunity to prove that they can take it (Dubbé, 1965). For example, a few years ago a sizable group of young people played a large role in preventing the swollen Mississippi River from flooding vast areas of unprotected land. For long weary hours they filled and stacked sandbags to form temporary levees, thereby saving thousands of people from untold disaster. Such opportunities for adolescent assumption of responsibility, however, are still somewhat limited. Sackett (1965) suggests that this may be true because parents of today's young people, most of whom were adolescents during the depression, may be seeking to give the present younger generation what they missed without realizing how their deprivations and responsibilities during the depression contributed to their own growth and development.

It is productive for family members to have an opportunity to express themselves to each other. Family councils or meetings can often promote such communication. By verbalizing their feelings, ideas, and opinions, adolescents may influence the feelings and beliefs of others in the family constellation. And if young people are in turn exposed to their parents' knowledge and experience, they are likely to develop a better perspective on adulthood and its responsibilities and potentials. If parents, educators, and other adults were willing to change some of their own rigid, inflexible policies and traditions toward youthful assertion of independence and individuality, communication problems between the two generations might be eased. As long as the older generation, however, continues to insist that its standards are to remain sacred and unbroken, then many adolescents will continue to violate them (Cross, 1967).

RECENT TRENDS IN COMMUNITY RESOURCES FOR ADOLESCENT COMMUNICATION

It is quite apparent that some parents cannot bridge the communication gap, and that teachers and guidance counselors tend to be ruled out by many young people as figures of authority. In fact, the Bolton High School study (Rothschild, 1969) of 1219 students revealed that only four stated that they most often confided in their guidance counselors, and none said that they had commonly discussed their personal problems with their teachers. Another study of 50 ninth-grade pupils by West and Zingle (1969) disclosed that both boys and girls confided most about themselves to their friends of the same sex, then to their mothers and fathers, next to their friends of the opposite sex, then to the school counselors, and last of all to their teachers. From these studies, it appears that the adolescent often turns to a friend, who may be as painfully ignorant as he, or to a newspaper columnist, whose answer may be inadequate for the individual adolescent's problem.

Many young people need someone totally objective to talk to, someone unswayed by love or hate and unconcerned about punishment or reward. In the Bolton High School study of 1219 students, over 50 percent felt that there was a need for a center where adolescents could phone for help with difficult problems. More than a third of these young people, or a total of 434, said that they would be likely to use such a service if it were available, and 545, or 45 percent, stated that they knew of friends or acquaintances who they believed would avail themselves of such a service if it were to be offered.

To meet such needs, an advice center for youth, The Young People's Consultation Center, supported by the Van Lear Foundation of America, was started in England in 1961 (Wakeman, 1965). This center is open three evenings a week and is staffed by four professionals with experience in social work and training in psychoanalysis or psychotherapy. Psychiatric, medical, and legal aid advisers are also available. There is no fee charged, nor is there a waiting list.

Since its opening in January, 1961, hundreds of young people, as well as some troubled parents, have sought the services of the center. About one third of these have been referrals. The remainder have been attracted by subway posters telling about the center, by reading about it in the newspapers, or by hearing about it from others. Coming from all socioeconomic classes, the ages of these youths have ranged from 15 to 25, with a majority in the years from 17 to 19. Most of these adolescents make from one to six visits to the center, although if it is evident that a serious emotional disorder exists, there is referral for treatment elsewhere. The young people are given absolute guarantees of privacy, and their parents are not consulted unless the adolescent gives his permission.

Another interesting experiment began at the University of Texas in July, 1967, when a continuous telephone counseling and referral service designed to bring immediate aid to university students for a wide range of problems was established (University of Texas, 1968). The service is staffed 24 hours a day, seven days a week, by trained counselors. An individual student can phone for personal counseling, academic counseling, consultation concerning the problems of another person, referral to other agencies or to other professionals, and information about university life and events.

During the first year of operation, 12,827 telephone calls were received, of which 1,361 were calls for counseling (882 calls from women and 479 calls from men). Most of the counseling calls were made late in the evening, from 9:00 P.M. to midnight. An annual report in July, 1968, categorized these counseling calls into six categories, which are shown in Table 11-1. Confidentiality was closely guarded; students were not required to identify themselves unless they wanted to do so.

TABLE 11-1.   Categories of counseling telephone calls received at the University of Texas by the Emergency Counseling and Referral Service, July 1967–July 1968. From the University of Texas Twenty-Four Hour Telephone Counseling and Referral Service Annual Report, July, 1969. Reprinted with the permission of Dr. Ira Iscoe, Director, Counseling-Psychological Services Center.

	Cumulative Total
1. Wish to discuss plans for the future	100
2. Hope to improve school functioning	120
3. Want help because of internal state	227
4. Desire to improve interpersonal relations	197
5. Worried about sexual problem	46
6. Other	290

	Cumulative Total
(a) Referral	50
(b) Consultation	127
(c) Financial or legal	21
(d) Narcotics or alcohol	14
(e) Medical problems	47
(f) Miscellaneous	31
	290

Return Calls for Counseling (not included in the above)   381

Total   1361

This service appears to be spreading to other colleges. Originally, of letters mailed to 67 colleges and universities with enrollments of over 5,000 during the 1967 fall semester to inquire whether similar services were in existence, replies from 47 institutions disclosed that none of them at that time had available a comparable 24-hour center (University of Texas, 1968). However, Louisiana State University now has a 24-hour crisis intervention and information referral service available both to the LSU campus and to the city of Baton Rouge. This service, which is called The Phone, was initially introduced in April of 1970 and now receives financial support from the National Institute of Mental Health. It is manned 24 hours a day by student and community volunteers, who are closely screened and then receive 15 to 20 hours of training to help them develop their ability to relate to others. Tulane University in New Orleans has introduced a similar service (Mohr, 1971).

Communities in other sections of the United States have also begun to offer such services. In Los Angeles troubled young people can now communicate their problems to helpful adults via a 24-hour telephone service, called Hot Line, which connects them immediately to one of thirty professionals skilled in handling adolescent problems. In its first year of operation (it began in April, 1968), 5,000 phone calls were handled by the Hot Line staff of physicians, psychologists, lawyers, social workers, and graduate students. Girl callers outnumbered boys, as they had at the University of Texas telephone counseling center, by a ratio of two to one, perhaps reflecting the tendency of females to be more verbal than males. Most of the adolescent problems involved boy-girl or parental difficulties, although some were concerned with drugs, venereal disease, sexual problems, or the difficulties of social life. Because Hot Line guarantees anonymity for its callers and because of its prompt availability to any young person with a problem, it has been successful. It should also be noted that its primary function is not so much offering cheap advice as to encourage a youth to grapple with his problems and to come up with his own solution (Wright, 1969).

In other cities—such as Philadelphia, Milwaukee, and Minneapolis—similar answering services for adolescents are offered, but they are manned by youthful volunteers, mainly in their late teens and early twenties, with access to volunteer professionals, such as social workers, psychiatrists, attorneys, and medical students, when a need is indicated (Murrell, 1970). It is thought that young people may feel more at ease when talking to their peers, that they believe their contemporaries to be more cognizant of adolescent problems and less likely to pass judgment than their elders. Drugs have been acknowledged to be one of the most frequent problems about which youthful individuals are apt to phone, and knowledge of the different drugs and of typical reactions to them is necessary for volunteers to render effective service.

One other organization should be mentioned in connection with the subject of community resources available to adolescents. In numerous cities a service known as FISH has sprung up. Started in England in 1961, it spread to the United States in 1964, when a branch of FISH was started in Massachusetts. "The early members named themselves FISH after the symbol used by the Christians in the days of Roman persecution. The sign of the fish scratched in the dirt or scrawled on a wall meant that friends were within" (Murphy, 1969).

FISH provides a 24-hour telephone answering service to individuals of all ages, and a number of adolescents have used its services. In contrast to the Los Angeles Hot Line, FISH is manned strictly by volunteers carefully selected by a well-qualified director.

Lois, an 18-year-old college freshman and one of 14 children in a family of limited financial means, became aware of FISH through announcements on a local television station. Having suffered for several years from a severe stuttering problem, for which she recognized there was probably an emotional basis, Lois decided to phone FISH. On duty at the time was a volunteer who happened to be a physician's wife with an aptitude for cutting red tape, and she made prompt arrangements for the girl to be seen at an out-patient center for the treatment of emotional disorders. Within a few days an appointment had been made, and Lois began having regular sessions of psychotherapy with a qualified professional worker. With the treatment begun, Lois' whole outlook on life started to change, and her hopes for the future began to seem much brighter.

It is important for teachers and for others working with adolescents to become aware of the existence of such community facilities and to learn how referrals can be made. Frequently, however, educators are ignorant of the availability of such services. As a consequence, far too many young people in need of counseling and guidance continue to struggle alone with their problems.

SUMMARY AND CONCLUSIONS

Although a communication gap has probably existed between the adolescent and his elders since the beginning of human civilization, it is quite possible that this gap is wider today than it has been at any time in the past. Explanations of this widening breach between the generations may be found in our rapidly changing society with its tremendous technological advances, its shifting customs and values, and its extended period of adolescent economic dependence.

Several suggestions have been offered as pathways to easing the communication gap. However, in order for such approaches to be effective, the two generations must learn to listen to each other and acquire certain mutually understood assumptions about the roles to be played by the other.

Where other means fail, adults should encourage adolescents to consult community mental-health facilities, which are becoming more widespread throughout the nation. Only by providing young people with the opportunity to verbalize their problems and their feelings will adults be able to reduce the increasing rates of delinquency and emotional disorders, which so keenly reflect the world in its present state of turmoil and upheaval.

REFERENCES

Bell, R. R. Parent-child conflict in sexual values. *Journal of Social Issues,* 1966, **22**, 34–44.

Bienvenu, M., Sr. Talking it over at home: Problems in family communication. *Public Affairs Pamphlet,* No. 410, New York: Public Affairs Committee, 1967.

Cross, H. J. Conceptual systems theory-application to some problems of adolescence. *Adolescence,* 1967, **2**(6), 153–165.

Dubbé, M. C. Subjects which one hundred selected college students found difficult to discuss with their parents and reasons for their difficulties. Unpublished Ed.D. Thesis, Corvallis, Oregon: Oregon State College, 1956.

Dubbé, M. C. What parents are not told may hurt: A study of communication between teenagers and parents. *Family Life Coordinator,* 1965, **14**(2), 51–118.

Duvall, E. M. *Family development* (2nd ed.). New York: J. B. Lippincott, 1962.

Ekstein, R., & Friedman, S. A function of acting out, play activity, and play acting in the therapeutic process. Presented at the Spring Meeting of the American Psychoanalytic Association, Chicago, 1956.

Johnson, E. W. Ten pointers on talking to teen-agers. *Parents Magazine,* July, 1961, 38–39ff.

Levitt, M., & Rubenstein, B. O. Acting out in adolescence: A study in communication. *American Journal of Orthopsychiatry,* 1959, **29**, 622–632.

Marcus, D. et al. A clinical approach to the understanding of normal and pathological adolescence. A study of communication patterns in the families of disturbed and nondisturbed adolescents. *Archives of General Psychiatry,* 1966, **15**, 569–576.

McLuhan, M. *Understanding media: The extensions of man.* New York: McGraw-Hill, 1964.

Mohr, M. G. The Phone, Louisiana State University, Baton Rouge, Louisiana, February, 1971.

Murphy, L. *Houston Chronicle,* July 23, 1969.

Murrell, P. J. Help! Telephone volunteers offer emergency aid to troubled youngsters. *The Wall Street Journal*, May 27, 1970, 1, 6.

Neisser, E. G. *Mothers and daughters: A lifelong relationship.* New York: Harper & Row, 1967.

Pacella, M. J. Understanding your teen-ager. *Mental Hygiene*, 1963. **47**, 273–278.

Pacella, B. L. The adolescent crisis today: Morals, ethics, and religion. *New York State Journal of Medicine*, 1967, **67**, 1975–1978.

Rothschild, B. F. Unpublished study. Louisiana State University at Alexandria, 1969.

Sackett, W. W., Jr. Family problems involving the adolescent. *Southern Medical Journal*, 1965, **58**(12), 1558–1561.

University of Texas at Austin, Annual Report of the Twenty-four Hour Telephone Counseling and Referral Service, 1968.

Wakeman, J. Teen-agers need someone to tell their troubles to. *Parents Magazine*, April, 1965, 56–58ff.

West, L. W., & Zingle, H. W. A self-disclosure inventory for adolescents. *Psychological Reports*, 1969, **24**, 439–445.

Wright, F. Medicine today. *Ladies Home Journal*, July, 1969, 42.

Glossary

acting out: transferring a learned pattern of behavior to a new experience that is symbolically representative

acting out neurotic: describing release of tension and conflict by overt, inappropriate behavior; may be aggressive

activism: practice or doctrine that emphasizes vigorous action (such as the use of force for political ends)

affect: emotion or feeling

alienation: diversion of affection, confidence, or attachment that formerly subsisted; in this book, a young person's feeling that he cannot find a meaningful role in today's society, which leads him to adopt nonconforming behaviors

altruism: concern for the welfare of others, as opposed to egoism; idealism

ambivalence: coexistence of opposite feelings toward an individual or situation (such as love and hate, acceptance and denial)

amphetamine: drug used to stimulate the central nervous system, increase blood pressure, reduce appetite, and reduce nasal congestion; used by young people as an "upper"

androgen: male hormone that regulates sexual development and influences maleness

apathy: seeming lack of feeling or emotion; indifference

aphasia: loss or impairment of ability to use language, usually caused by brain damage; may be either a sensory difficulty or a motor difficulty, or both

aptitude: natural potential to learn or acquire skill

asceticism: practice of strict self-denial as a means of religious discipline or service to an ideal *attitude:* an enduring, learned, predisposition to behave in a consistent way toward a given class of objects

authoritarian: demanding unquestioning obedience and subordination from others

autoeroticism: self-arousal or gratification of erotic feelings

autonomy: independence; self-regulation

avoidance: acting so as to protect oneself from pain or conflict

barbiturate: any of various derivatives of barbituric acid used especially as sedatives and hypnotics; used by young people as a "downer"

biochemistry: the chemistry of living organisms and vital processes

biogenetic: referring to the origin of living beings from things already living

bisexuality: having both male and female secondary sex characteristics; also having sexual feeling for both sexes

borderline defective: an individual whose intelligence is slightly below normal (IQ of 70 to 79) but who is usually considered legally competent

chemotherapy: treatment of a disease by administering chemicals which affect the causative organisms unfavorably but do not injure the patient

clique: a small, exclusive group of from two to nine persons with common interests and activities

clitoris: a small organ of erectile tissue that is part of the external female genitals; its stimulation is an important source of sexual pleasure

cognition: process by which one learns about an object; includes perception, reason, recognition

cognitive structure: an individual's way of perceiving the world, both physical and social, including his facts, concepts, beliefs, and expectations

coitus: the act of injecting the penis into another person's body; sexual intercourse

congenital: referring to a condition existing at or before birth; not determined by heredity

cross-sectional study: a study of the relationship between factors in two or more groups investigated at the same time

defense mechanism: behavior of the individual in his defense against anxiety

denial: a primitive, unconscious or preconscious defense mechanism which refuses to admit to some threatening external reality

dependence: reliance on others in making decisions or carrying out actions

depersonalization: a state in which a person loses the feeling of his own reality

depression: emotional dejection, absence of cheerfulness or hope, and decrease of functional activity *developmental age:* age as determined by the degree of development of secondary sex characteristics and by skeletal age; may be younger or older than a given chronological age

developmental tasks: accomplishments or skills that should be mastered at a particular age-stage by each person; these are critical to further achievement and happiness

displacement: a defense mechanism by which one transfers a thought, feeling, or emotion from one person or situation to another less threatening one

dull-normal: describing an individual whose intelligence is slightly below normal (IQ of 80–89)) but who is not considered mentally retarded

dysfunction: impaired or abnormal functioning

dyslexia: a reading disability due to distortion in the development of perceptual motor skills, independent of any speech defect

dysrhythmic: uncoordinated or poorly coordinated

educo-therapy: remediation of academic deficits and modification of maladaptive behavior

ego: generally, concept of self; the part of the personality that is conscious and most in touch with reality; in psychoanalytic terms, the problem-solving portion of the personality

egocentric: concerned primarily with one's self to the exclusion of concern for others

erotic: pertaining to the sensations of sex or the emotions aroused by sex

estrogen: female hormone that regulates sexual development and influences femaleness

etiology: study of causes, origins or reasons; the part of medicine that deals with the causation of disease.

euphoria: an emotional attitude that all is well and nothing can possibly go wrong; in psychiatry, an exaggerated sense of well-being involving sympathetic delusions

expressive role: a role characterized by love and affective responses

extrinsic motivation: desire to do something as a means to an end; for example, a desire to get a good education in order to get a good job or learning in order to obtain good grades

fixation: situation in which an individual remains at one stage of development and is unable to progress to the next stage

genetic: pertaining to reproduction, or to birth or origin; congenital or inherited

genital: pertaining to the reproductive organs

gonadotropin: hormone which stimulates growth and development in the gonads, or sex glands

hallucinogen: a drug that produces hallucination and false perception

heterosexuality: attraction to a person or persons of the opposite sex

hormone: a chemical substance produced by the endocrine glands, which triggers many kinds of bodily activities and behavior

hyperactive behavior: abnormally increased activity; overstimulation

hypothalamus: a portion of the forebrain which helps control visceral functions such as sleep, hunger, thirst, sex drive, and emotion

ideal self: an individual's concept of what he would like to be in terms of values; a structure of values an individual is striving to attain

identification: accepting as one's own the goals and values of another individual

identity crisis: a period during which an individual seeks to define who he is in relationship to society and his environment

ideology: an accepted system of ideas, beliefs, and attitudes

image: a conscious representation of sensory experience in the absence of the relevant sensory stimulation

impunitive: characterizing a reaction to frustration in which one does not blame either self or others but is more concerned with condemning what has occurred; an impunitive person may display embarrassment and shame but not anger

inculcate: to teach or impress by forceful urging or frequent repetition

individuation: in a social group, the process whereby a person emerges as a distinct unit in the group, with a distinct, even unique, role or status

instrumental role: a role held by an individual who imparts values and goals relating to the world outside the family

intellectualization: analysis of a problem strictly in intellectual terms to the exclusion of any emotional or practical considerations

internalization: adopting as one's own the ideas, practices, standards, or values of another person

interpersonal: referring to a relationship between two or more persons

intrapersonal: referring to an individual's relationship with his environment

intrinsic motivation: desire to do something that is not the means to an end; for example, to learn for the sake of knowledge

introjection: internalization of the external world; in psychoanalytic terms, a defense mechanism for warding off threat by symbolic incorporation of an external object as part of one's self

kinesthesis: sense of movement, of knowing where body and limb are and what their movements are

kinesthetic method: process of treating reading disability by having students trace outlines of letters and words

latency: the period of development from about age four or five to about age thirteen during which sexual desires are relatively dormant; in general, emphasis at this time is on recognizing and coping with reality

learning disability: inability to learn certain skills due to organic or functional reasons

longitudinal study: study of the same person or persons over a considerable period of time

LSD (lysergic acid diethylamide): a chemical substance derived from lysergic acid which when taken produces symptoms similar in some respects to those of a schizophrenic reaction

manifest content: any idea, feeling, or impulse considered to be conscious expression of an unreportable or repressed motive (or the latent content); the part of a dream one can recall

marijuana: a habit-forming drug derived from *cannibus induis* which induces feelings of well-being and loss of self-criticism and inhibitions

masturbation: the practice of obtaining satisfaction from stimulation (usually self-induced) of the genitals

matriarchy: a social unit ruled by a female

menarche: the first menstruation

menstruation: the monthly discharge of blood from the uterus of a sexually mature woman

microsocial: referring to the nuclear family, consisting of parents and their children living at home

minimal brain dysfunction: brain damage resulting in mild impairment in functioning, but not involving a major disability such as severe retardation, total blindness, or total deafness

mixed dominance: referring to the theory that speech disorders and some other maladjustments may be due wholly or partly to the fact that one cerebral hemisphere does not consistently lead the other in control of bodily movement; for example, a right-handed person may be left-eyed

modal values: values shared by a majority of a selected or sample population

mores: the generally accepted customs of a social group

nocturnal emissions: loss of semen during sleep

norm: a single value or a range of values, constituting the usual performance of a given group *nurturance:* the tendency that leads one to provide nurture (food, shelter, other care and affection) to the young or to the weak and incapable

oligarche: onset of seminal emission

ordinal position: indicating place in a succession; usually the number series; first, second, third

ovary: one of a pair of glandular organs producing the ovum or egg cell; the primary female organ of reproduction

overcompensation: defense mechanism that overemphasizes one type of behavior in order to cover up felt deficiencies in other areas

ovulation: the production of eggs or the discharge of them from the ovary

ovulatory cycle: menstrual cycle marked by regular ovulation and uterine bleeding

paranoid psychopathic: tendency to grandiose ideas and/or sensitivity to real or apparent criticisms

pathology: a diseased, disordered, or abnormal condition of an organism or its parts

patriarchy: a social unit ruled by a male

peer: a person deemed an equal for the purpose at hand; in this book, another of one's own age or status

penis: male external genital and urinary organ

perception: a process whereby an organism selects, organizes, and interprets the sensory data available to it

perceptual motor handicap: a disability in the combined functioning of sensory and motor nerves in response to various stimuli

perseveration: a tendency to continue in a particular activity to the extent that there is difficulty in beginning a new activity

pharmacology: the science of drugs

phenomenal: referring to the environment which is known through the senses and experience rather than through thought

phonetics: method of teaching reading which relates the vocal sounds to the written language

physiology: a branch of biology dealing with the processes, activities, and phenomena incidental to and characteristic of life or living matter

pituitary: an endocrine gland that secretes hormones, including the gonadotropic hormones; important for growth and development

pragmatic: describing an emphasis on practical results as determining the value of a thing; disinclination toward processes, dogmatism, or elaborate theorizing

prepuberty: the period of transition prior to adolescence which is characterized by hormone-level changes; the period between childhood and adolescence

primogeniture: principle of inheritance by the firstborn, especially the eldest son

projection: the defense mechanism of attributing one's own beliefs and thoughts to others; method one uses to alleviate conflict by seeing in others motives or attributes about which he is anxious

promiscuity: nonselective social or (predominantly) sexual intercourse

psychedelic: pertaining to or generating hallucinations, distortions of perception, and occasionally psychoticlike states

psychogenic: pertaining to the origin of psychic or psychological processes or attributes; (in this book) describing illnesses with no organic basis

psychological moratorium: cessation of activity, such as dropping out of school, for the purpose of establishing one's identity or self-concept

psychomimetic: having the tendency to mimic psychosis

psychoneurosis: a disorder of behavior, without gross disorganization, in which functional or psychogenic factors predominate

psychopath: an individual who is unable to visualize the consequences of his actions or to care and who appears to be incapable of deep emotional feelings; *sociopath* is often used synonymously

psychosexual: describing the development of a masculine or feminine role as the outgrowth of psychobiological drives, awareness, and interest

psychosis: a severe mental disorder, with or without organic damage, involving drastic personality changes, deterioration of intellectual and social functioning, and often partial or complete withdrawal from reality

puberty: a period during which reproductive organs become capable of functioning and secondary sex characteristics are developed

pubescence: early stage of puberty

rationalization: a defense mechanism whereby false, but seemingly logical, reasons are devised to justify (to self and others) one's actions in order to protect his self-concept or self-esteem

reaction formation: defense mechanism of inhibiting, masking, or overcoming threatening impulses by emphasizing opposite ones

reality testing: testing an action to see if it brings the intended results (to see if it will work)

reciprocal role: referring to the explanation for sex-role learning in which children are said to identify with or model certain sex-typed behavior they observe in their parents

reference set: a group of persons, especially peers, who supply individuals with ideas regarding actions, ideas, and so on

regression: psychologically, a return to less mature or earlier forms of behavior as a defense against stress and frustration

repression: a defense mechanism which automatically inhibits threatening stimuli, such as unpleasant thoughts or memories, that produce anxiety

role: the behavior associated with a particular position in a group

schizoid: an enduring and maladjustive pattern of behavior manifesting avoidance of close relations with others and inability to express hostility and aggressive feelings directly

schizophrenia: a psychosis characterized by markedly deviant patterns of feeling, thinking, and acting; a "split-off" from reality, frequently involving hallucinations, delusions, withdrawal, and serious disturbances of emotional life

secondary sex characteristics: genetically transmitted anatomical or behavioral traits, typical for either sex but not for both, and not necessary for reproduction; for example, a greater amount of facial hair and a lower voice in males indicate maleness

secular trend: a directional change in a given variable over a period of time; in this book, the trend for the onset of puberty to occur at increasingly younger ages

sedative: an agent or drug which tends to calm or tranquilize nervousness or excitement

self-actualization: the fulfillment of one's potentialities

self-concept: the way an individual views and feels about himself, as well as his perceptions of himself

self-fulfilling prophecy: principle that one's expectation is a factor in determining outcome; for example, if a particular student is expected to fail, he may do so

self-image: an individual's perception of himself, reflecting the subjective experience of his uniqueness

sensory handicap: a dysfunction in the areas of learning, sight, or other senses

sex role: the pattern of attitudes and behavior that in any society is deemed appropriate to one's sex

sibling: one of two or more offspring of either sex from the same mother or same father

skeletal age: level of bone development based on hand-wrist or knee X rays showing the relative completeness of ossification or calcium deposit on the bones

social isolate: a person who separates himself from relationships with others in society

socialization: learning to behave in a manner prescribed by one's society

socialized delinquent: an individual whose entire mode of behavior is characterized by delinquent acts generally committed in a gang or with others

socioeconomic status: an individual's position in a given society, as determined by wealth, occupation, and social class

somatic: pertaining to the body rather than to the mind (psyche)

spatial orientation: relation of the external world and the physical self

spermatogenesis: formation of spermatozoa

stimulus intensity: strength of a given stimulus

stress: strong, uncomfortable emotional tension

Sturm und Drang: storm and stress (German); in this book, referring to the conflict theory of adolescence

superego: in psychoanalytic terms, the division of the personality structure that is concerned with moral standards; the conscience

surrogate: a person who functions in another's life as a substitute for some third person

symbiosis: a close relationship between two people such that one needs the other to exist; usually neurotic interdependency

synthesis: a combining of elements or forces to create an integrated whole

teenybopper: the pre-adolescent or youngster in early adolescence who attempts to emulate older adolescent behavior

temperament: one's susceptibility to emotive situations and one's tendency to experience mood changes

tranquilizer: drug used to reduce anxiety and tension

trauma: a physical or psychological injury or experience causing serious damage to the individual

underachiever: a person who performs below his ability or capacity to perform

unisexual: pertaining to one sex, as a group of boys or a group of girls

unsocialized delinquent: an individual who has difficulty relating to others and who acts overtly hostile toward those whom he regards as hostile or threatening

vagina: the canal from the uterus to the exterior of the female body

validity: the degree to which a test, rating, or measurement correctly measures the variable it is supposed to measure *visual-motor integration:* coordination of visual and motor systems, including eye-hand relations, eye-foot relations, turning corners in working or in cutting, movement of eyes across a page while reading, and so on

voyeurism: undue visual curiosity especially characteristic of an individual whose sexual desire is concentrated on seeing sex organs; practice of seeking sex gratification by peeping; the practice of a Peeping Tom

Author Index

309

Subject Index